THE COLUMBUS CENTRE SERIES

THE DESTINY OF EUROPE'S GYPSIES

THE COLUMBUS CENTRE SERIES

STUDIES IN THE DYNAMICS OF PERSECUTION AND EXTERMINATION

General Editor: Norman Cohn

ANTHONY STORR
Human Destructiveness

HENRY V. DICKS
Licensed Mass Murder

DONALD KENRICK & GRATTAN PUXON
The Destiny of Europe's Gypsies

Forthcoming

LEON POLIAKOV
The Aryan Myth

The Destiny
of Europe's Gypsies

by

DONALD KENRICK

AND

GRATTAN PUXON

BASIC BOOKS, INC., *Publishers*

NEW YORK

Contents

EDITORIAL FOREWORD

Following a proposal originally advanced by the Hon. David Astor, a research centre was set up in the University of Sussex in 1966 to investigate how persecutions and exterminations come about; how the impulse to persecute or exterminate is generated, how it spreads, and under what conditions it is likely to express itself in action. The Centre was originally called the Centre for Research in Collective Psychopathology, but later adopted the more neutral name of the Columbus Centre, after the Trust which finances it.

The Centre's work has now resulted in a series of books and monographs on subjects ranging from the roots of European nationalism and racism to the fate of the Gypsies as a minority, from the causes of the persecution of 'witches' to the causes of the exterminations carried out under the Third Reich, and from the biological to the psychological roots of the very urge to persecute or to exterminate.

From the beginning, the Centre's work was designed on a multi-disciplinary basis. The disciplines represented in the present series include history, sociology, anthropology, dynamic psychology and ethology. Moreover, while the research was being done and the books written, the various authors constantly exchanged ideas and information with one another. As a result, while each book in the series belongs to a single discipline and is the work of a single author or, in the case of the present volume, two authors, who alone carry responsibility for it, the series as a whole is coloured by the experience of inter-disciplinary discussion and debate.

The enterprise was also designed on an international scale. Although this has been a British project in the sense that it was sponsored by a British university and that 95 per cent of its finance was also British, the people who did the research and wrote the books came from several different countries. Indeed, one of them was a Frenchman who worked in Paris throughout, another a German who worked in Berlin. Everything possible was done to exclude national bias from a study which might all too easily have been distorted by it.

The work was financed throughout by the Columbus Trust (aided, in the case of the present volume, by the Wiener Library). It was originally made possible by massive donations to the Trust from the Hon. David Astor, the late Lord Sieff of Brimpton and Sir Marcus Sieff, and the Wolfson Foundation, promptly followed by further most generous contributions from Mr Raymond Burton, the Rt. Hon. Harold Lever, Mr I. J. Lyons, Mr Hyam Morrison, Mr Jack Morrison, Sir Harold Samuel, the American Jewish Committee, the J. M. Kaplan Fund, Inc., and the William Waldorf Astor Foundation. His Grace the Archbishop of Canterbury, Sir Leon Bagrit, Lord Evans of Hungershall, and Messrs Myers & Company also showed their goodwill to the enterprise by giving it financial assistance.

Since the Centre came into existence many people have devoted a great deal of time and energy to one or other of the various financial and advisory committees associated with it. They include the chairman of the Columbus Trust, the Rt. Hon. the Lord Butler of Saffron Walden; two successive Vice-Chancellors of the University of Sussex, Lord Fulton of Falmer and Professor Asa Briggs; the Hon. David Astor, Professor Max Beloff, Professor Sir Robert Birley, Professor Patrick Corbett, Professor Meyer Fortes, Dr Robert Gosling, Mr Ronald Grierson, Professor Marie Jahoda, Dr Martin James, Professor James Joll, the Rt. Hon. Harold Lever, Professor Barry Supple, Dr John D. Sutherland, Professor Eric Trist, Professor A. T. M. Wilson, Mr Leonard Wolfson, and the Registrar and Secretary of the University, Mr A. E. Shields, who has acted as the secretary of the Centre's Management Committee. It is a pleasure to acknowledge the support and counsel they have so willingly given.

The series also owes a great deal to the devoted service of the late Miss Ursula Boehm, who was the administrative secretary to the Centre from its inception until her death in 1970.

NORMAN COHN

AUTHORS' PREFACE

This book was originally intended to recount only the story of the Nazi persecution of the Gypsies – a story which has not yet been told. It soon became apparent that this chapter in Gypsy history could not be regarded in isolation. It formed part of a chain of persecution and harassment based upon prejudices deep-rooted in European society. We have also tried to show that the Gypsy people now face the subtler pressures of forced assimilation and neglect which likewise threaten them with extinction as a separate people. Their reaction has been the emergence of a national consciousness manifested in the world Romani movement.

D.K.
G.P.

ACKNOWLEDGEMENTS

We wish to thank the Wiener Library for a grant which assisted us in the preparation of the chapters on the Nazi persecution of the Gypsies. We are also grateful to the many institutions and individuals who have supplied information for different parts of the book.

Extracts have been taken from the following copyright works. Adelsberger L., *Auschwitz* (Lettner-Verlag, Berlin); Adler M., *My Life with the Gypsies* (Souvenir Press, London); Ficowski J., *Ciganie na polskich Drogach* (Wydawnictwo Literackie, Cracow); Hilberg R., *The Destruction of the European Jews* (Quadrangle Books, Chicago); Jovanović J., 'La Criminalité des Tsiganes' *Etudes Tsiganes*, Paris; Kogon E., *Theory and Practice of Hell* (Farrar, Straus and Giroux, New York); Kuznetsov A., *Babi Yar* (Mac-Gibbon and Kee, London); Langbein H., *Der Auschwitz Prozess* (Europa-Verlag, Vienna); Steinmetz S., *Österreichs Zigeuner im NS-Staat* (Europa-Verlag, Vienna).

Permission has been obtained where possible and we apologize for instances where we have not been able to contact the copyright holder and also for any other inadvertent breaches of copyright in the following pages.

D.K.
G.P.

PART ONE

CHAPTER ONE

THE GYPSIES COME TO EUROPE

"Siyas amen ekh baro thagar – rom. Ov siyas amaro prins. Ov siyas amaro padishaxos. O Roma beshenas o zuman savre kidende ekh thaneste, ekh lache vilayecheste. Kale vilayechesko alav siyas Sind . . ."

"We used to have a great king, a Gypsy. He was our prince. He was our king. The Gypsies used to live all together at that time in one place, in one beautiful country. The name of that country was Sind. There was much happiness, much joy there. The name of our chief was Mar Amengo Dep. He had two brothers. The name of one was Romano, the name of the other was Singan. That was good, but then there was a big war there. The Moslems caused the war. They made ashes and dust of the Gypsy country. All the Gypsies fled together from their own land. They began to wander as poor men in other countries, in other lands. At that time the three brothers took their followers and moved off, they marched along many roads. Some went to Arabia, some went to Byzantium, some went to Armenia.

"This story was told to me by my old grandfather. He died but he left this tale behind with us."

Thus Ali Chaushev, from Shumen in East Bulgaria relates how the Gypsies left India in three large groups. Today we call these groups the Rom, the Sinti and the Kale.

North India formed the cradle of the Gypsy nation. This much at least is commonly accepted by those who have attempted to reconstruct the ancient history of the Gypsy people. But several conflicting theories have been put forward concerning their way of life and place in Indian society. Probably they existed as a loose federation of nomadic tribes following a pattern similar to other tribal groups. The name by which the Gypsies call themselves, *Rom*, is considered to be cognate with the Hindi *Dom*, used to describe nomads today, and suggests they remained outside the rigid caste system.

The Gypsy scholar, Jan Kochanowski, believes his people were sedentary until rising interference and warfare in the area forced them to migrate.[1] No conclusive proof has been produced for any hypothesis, and speculation must continue.

Likewise there are no contemporary accounts of the first Gypsies to reach the Middle East. The Persian poet Firdausi and the Arab writer Hamza, both writing in the tenth century, place their arrival some five centuries earlier. Firdausi tells of ten thousand Gypsies sent from India to King Bahram (A.D. 430–443) to entertain the Persian population with their music. The legend says that the king gave them oxen, asses and wheat, but:

> "The Gypsies went and ate the wheat and oxen, then after a year came with pale cheeks. The Shah said, 'was it not your task to plough, to sow and reap? Your asses still remain. Load them up, prepare your harps and stretch the silken cords.' So now the Gypsies . . . live by their wits. They have for company the dog and the wolf, and tramp unceasingly."[2]

During the ninth and fourteenth centuries Gypsy communities in the Middle East were massacred[3] and they suffered again during the persecution of the Armenians early this century. Known under a variety of local names, many isolated tribes continue to live in the area as well as in Soviet Asia.[4]

Linguistic and other evidence shows that the Gypsies of Europe belong to groups which left India later, around a thousand years ago.[5] They spent a comparatively short time in the Middle East. Never at any period did they move in a solid mass from East to West 'following the sun' as some writers have thought. The pattern of migration was probably similar to that today, with one family group overtaking another according to local circumstances and opportunity for work. At any given time there would be several different unrelated groups in a particular area. They came to eastern Europe from Asia Minor early in the fourteenth century. Following the pilgrims' route across Crete they entered Greece through the Peloponese. Nomadic Gypsies are recorded 'stopping only thirty days in one place' in Crete during 1322. A recently discovered Bulgarian document[6] reveals that King Ivan Shishman gave over to the Rila Monastery some villages partly inhabited by sedentary Gypsies, showing that such settlements already existed in the Balkans as early as 1378. A hundred years later travellers described a Gypsy settlement outside Modon in Greece where in 1483 three hundred families were living in permanent dwellings. They earned their living by metalwork and shoemaking.[7] Other documents prove that by the end of the fourteenth century a large proportion of the Gypsies throughout eastern Europe had become sedentary. In western Europe the lighter-skinned Sinti were tolerated as migratory workers and the Iberian peninsula had a settled Kale community. Small nomadic groups of Rom however continue to be hounded from place to place in western Europe even today.

Smithing and metalworking of various forms remained a major occupation, though we may presume other trades were followed. Fortune-telling was hardly more than a sideline. But, because of their palmistry and predictions, the Greeks called them by the name of a heretical sect 'atsingani'. From this are derived the words *Zigeuner, cigano* and so on used in numerous languages. The English word *Gypsy*, on the other hand, is a corruption of *Egyptian*, the name by which they became known in several countries during the middle ages because some groups said they they had been expelled from 'Egypt' – though it is doubtful whether they meant the country of Egypt itself.

Eastern Europe has continued to have a largely settled Gypsy population in contrast to western Europe where the word 'Gypsy' is synonymous with 'nomad'. As the Turks pushed into the Balkans some Gypsies began to leave and migrate westwards while others north of the Danube moved on to escape enslavement by feudal landlords.

Small groups had almost certainly reached western Europe before the well-documented bands of the fifteenth century. Scattered references to *Tartars, Ishmaelites* and *Ethiopians*, terms used later on for Gypsies, can be found before this period.[8] A Swedish chronicle dated 1320 mentions black kettle-makers.[9] Possibly some Gypsies had already established themselves in western Europe during the fourteenth century, following their traditional trades without warranting a mention in written records. Their descendants nevertheless suffered when within a hundred years hostility to Gypsies became widespread. Anti-Gypsy legislation eventually affected all groups without distinction.

A striking impression was made by the three groups, each comprising two or three hundred persons, and some smaller parties, who travelled through western Europe from about 1417 onwards. They stopped for a few days in several leading cities and in each case their visit was remarkable enough to be recorded:

> "The men were very black, with curly hair. The women were the ugliest and blackest that have ever been seen. Their faces were all furrowed with wrinkles, their black hair like a horse's tail, their only clothing was a very rough old blanket fixed to their shoulders by a strip of cloth or a string, with only a torn vest underneath. In short, they were the most wretched creatures that had been seen in France in living memory."[10]

In order to cross frontiers easily and to gain some charitable support, these Gypsies claimed that they were on a seven-year pilgrimage. This penance, some said, had started after their expulsion as Christians from Egypt. As a result they were given alms, and mediaeval records show that town councils also donated food. No mention is made of the trades they followed except for one reference to horse-dealing.[11] Because of its novelty fortune-telling is often described but, in accordance with Gypsy custom, several sources of income were no doubt kept open and no total reliance made on alms. When they retraced their steps, or a second party crossed the route of an earlier one, their reception was less cordial. Thus Gypsies who came to Tournai (France) in 1431 received money and free wheat; those who came eleven years later were refused entry to the town.[12]

Gypsies were less demanding than other wandering bands of beggars and ex-soldiers of the time, such as the truands, and they provided entertainment for dull lives.[13] The nomadic Gypsies appeared to have received all the attention. Others who moved westward, however, were already equipped to begin settled life in the west, such as the two hundred families who left Modon during the decade after 1483 because of the Turkish advance.[14] By the beginning of the sixteenth century there were probably several thousand Gypsies in Europe belonging to different groups and practising various trades. Their fate as a small and vulnerable minority is the subject of this study.

CHAPTER TWO

THE ROOTS OF PREJUDICE

Since their first appearance in Europe Gypsies can be compared with modern migrants from Asia. They came in small family groups seeking opportunities to carry on trades and occupations among existing settled populations. There was little space for them and no chance to establish – as earlier migrating peoples had done – their own settlements and homeland. Every territory had already been staked out by other races. The only place left for them was therefore on the fringes of established society where they had to make a living as best they could.

Within a short space of time they found themselves reduced to the status of a second-class people. The process of dehumanization, its origin and outcome will be analysed in this study. Much of the evidence is deduced from folk sayings and contemporary literature, from laws and the preambles to legislation. But its interpretation rests in the last analysis on the personal experiences of the authors over several years of association with the Gypsy people and their detractors today.

From these various sources emerge several stereotypes, carrying a compound of unfavourable characteristics, distortions and mere malicious fabrication. As the theme unfolds the reader should come gradually to understand how reserves of ill-feeling have accumulated, were carried forward from one generation to the next and reached their dreadful yet logical climax in the Nazi holocaust in which a quarter of a million Gypsies perished.

Attitudes right across western and northern Europe varied little and we have for this reason generally ignored political frontiers. We have not attempted to follow national trends in anti-Gypsy thought and action; it is a European phenomenon with which we are dealing in which the different social groups – peasants, clergy and nobility – have played their part.

The Gypsies made a vivid impression on mediaeval society. No

18

one knew of their true origins and when they crossed into Europe they appeared as if from nowhere – an unknown, alien people. Curious townsfolk of every class flocked to stare at the Gypsies, to have their palms read, and they were regarded at first as an amusing diversion.

However the conviction that blackness denotes inferiority and evil was already well-rooted in the western mind.[1] The nearly black skins of many Gypsies marked them out to be victims of this prejudice. Even in Asia there was a preference for fairer complexions, and the tenth-century Persian poet Firdausi wrote:

"No washing ever whitens the black Gypsy."

It took western Christianity to shape from this preference the doctrine of war between light and dark, personified in white angels and black devils.

Early chroniclers wrote with revulsion of the blackness of Gypsies. The monk Cornerius of Lübeck, reporting on Gypsies he had encountered in 1417, refers to their "most ugly faces, black like those of Tartars". Another monk, Rufus, of the same city, drew disapproving attention to their dark skins.[2] An old Yiddish proverb from Russia shows a deep-seated association of blackness with Gypsies when it says:

"The same sun makes the linen white and the Gypsy black."[3]

Both Italian and Dutch use the simile 'black as a Gypsy'. In southeastern Europe their features drew less attention while in Albania it was their red tongues that attracted attention and this characteristic has been absorbed into local folk imagery.[4] It is interesting that Europeans often associate red tongues with black people.

Most absurd of the racialist arguments about blackness was the accusation that, despite the disadvantages of being black in a white society, Gypsies deliberately darkened themselves, using walnut and other vegetable substances. Evidently there is no one more debased than a person who pretends to be coloured. Archbishop Cajanus, convinced of this practice, issued an order saying Gypsies must not be permitted to blacken their children in future.[5] Here the morality of black and white is clearly at work in the clerical mind. The final twist may be left to the Englishman who, while petitioning against a Gypsy family being given a vacant house in 1969, remarked:

"Gypsies only look black because they don't wash."[6]

There are in fact several references in mediaeval law cases to persons disguising themselves as Gypsies. It was an offence at certain periods in many countries to associate with Gypsies and this would be part of the proof of guilt. At the same time the nobility could dress up as Gypsies for balls while their wives played at fortune-telling.

The process of vilification soon gathered momentum and other accusations were found or invented. When people heard Gypsies speaking their mother tongue they were ready to believe, as some still do today, that it was no more than a kind of gibberish used to deceive others. The remarks of a Spaniard reveal this feeling:

"When I go to the market there in the corner stand the accursed Gypsies jabbering to each other in a speech which I cannot understand."[7]

Resentment against those speaking a foreign tongue is not of course confined to Gypsies but in their case it came to be associated with the idea of a criminal jargon. The genuine mystery and widespread ignorance concerning the origins of the Gypsy language provided sufficient grounds for immediate suspicion and dislike. Until recently Romani was the only Indian language spoken in Europe and seemed to an English parliamentarian in the late eighteenth century an 'obscure and mystical language'.[8] A few scholars recognized Romani as a separate language but not until the end of the eighteenth century did linguistic studies firmly link it to the Indo-Aryan group.[9]

The Gypsies' apparent lack of roots or attachment to any known land was another factor in their demotion. From this arose disbelief in their existence as a separate ethnic group, despite the claim by some of them to be Egyptians. One writer called them "A race of Jews who later became mixed with Christian vagabonds".[10]

Another strong factor in the unfavourable attitude was the suspicion attached to anyone who crossed from the Turkish-occupied lands at the time of their first arrival. From that direction came infidels, enemies of the secular states and the church, lacking an organized religion of their own, the Gypsy people were from the beginning open to attack by Christian clergy and Moslem priests. A widespread and sometimes fatal intolerance developed because they failed to practise with any conviction one or other of the prevalent religions. In south-eastern Europe Gypsies have been regarded as essentially an irreligious people. Scorn and contempt have been heaped on them for this reason and come through in stories woven around this theme.

A Romanian tale recounts how Gypsies built a stone church and the Romanians one of bacon and ham. The Gypsies haggled until the latter agreed to exchange buildings – then promptly ate their church. Hence today they have no religion and little regard for that of others, the story says.[11] Another, recorded in Bulgaria and Turkey, said that when God was giving out the different religions, the Gypsies wrote theirs on cabbage leaves. A donkey came along and ate the holy book with the same result.[12] A Turkish proverb says there are seventy-two and a half religions in the world and the half belongs to the Gypsies.[13]

In the Basque country Gypsies had to listen to services through the window from outside the churches[14] and in Albania they were relegated to seats at the back of the mosque.[15] Even when classed as Moslems by the authorities in Turkey they had to pay the same taxes as Christians and other non-Moslems.[16] Priests and hodjas alike placed Gypsies outside normal society. One Islamic preacher exhorted his congregation during Ramadan not to give alms to begging Gypsies, warning that such charity would bring upon their shoulders part of the curse which the outcasts carried.[17] Orthodox clergy in Bulgaria during the nineteenth century declared it a sin greater than theft to give anything to Gypsies.[18]

The church in western Europe generally rejected the Gypsy people even when they professed to be converts to Christianity. Their claim to be Christians expelled from Egypt by the Moslems carried little weight. In Holland the label *Heidens* – heathens –

adhered to them for centuries. Archbishop Petri of Sweden decreed in 1560:

> "The priest shall not concern himself with the Gypsies. He shall neither bury their corpses nor christen their children."[19]

Priests in Magdeburg were ordered not to baptize Gypsy children without obtaining higher authorization.[20] This reflected a widespread doubt in ecclesiastical circles concerning both the basis of the Gypsies' desire to be baptized and the inconvenience of receiving such unorthodox people into the church. These doubts were justified. The main motive for the Gypsies as a group at this time was to conform to the religion of the country they had come to inhabit, thereby removing at least one reason for their persecution. They sought conversion as an expedient and it was certainly one of the rare instances when the church hesitated to accept this kind of nominal conversion. On their side, some Gypsy parents increased clerical opposition by contriving to have their children christened several times over for the sole purpose of gaining gifts from Gaje (non-Gypsy) god-parents.

Refusal of admission to the church had another reason. From their first arrival Gypsies had begun to exercise a strong influence over people of various classes. Predictions and magic held a strong attraction and came at times into almost open competition with the claims in the sphere of the supernatural made by the priests. Priests and palmists competed for the superstitious minds of both common folk and gentry throughout the middle ages.

After the first recorded visit of Gypsies to the French capital the Bishop of Paris excommunicated those who had had their palms read. To expiate the sins of his congregation he ordered a procession to be held. The French ecclesiastical court at Troyes in 1456 condemned a number of people for a similar offence and they were ordered to offer candles as a penance. A chaplain at Rouen was criticized by his superiors in 1509 for having his palm read.[21]

While their reputation for fortune-telling brought trouble and resentment from the clergy, it came to enhance their popular image, giving Gypsies a magical aura. They added colour to the mediaeval scene. Undoubtedly many showed a special talent for

22

reading the faces if not the palms, of their clients. They often practised the art with intelligence and wit.

By the second half of the fifteenth century references to fortune-telling can already be found in contemporary literature, showing the importance of its role. The first appears in a play written in Lucerne about 1475.[22] The Portuguese playwright Gil Vicente in *Farça das Ciganas* (1521) portrays four Gypsy women who read palms, and the Serbian writer Čubranović (1525) and Molière in *Le Mariage Forcé* (1664) also introduce them.

False predictions are always forgotten, while those that seem to come true are retold and exaggerated everywhere. Today the belief in fortune-telling and more sophisticated astrology is kept alive by popular papers and remains strongly in vogue. Reports and anecdotes about predictions continue to take up space and feed popular belief.

A letter to a national British newspaper is typical of many:

"At Yarmouth last summer a Gypsy stopped me and said, 'You look cheerful now – but what a mess you'll be in soon. September 14th is the date you'll never forget.' On September 14th we had the worst floods I've ever seen and we lost everything that we had on the ground floor of our home. How did that Gypsy know?"[23]

A few weeks later a hundred Manchester University students vacated their hall of residence because a Gypsy had predicted years earlier that there would be a serious accident on March 17th, 1969, and as the date approached a student had dreamt he saw a plane collide with the tower.[24] The disaster did not occur, though a light plane crashed three days later killing the pilot.

Suspicion and dislike of newly arrived Gypsies by the three pillars of power in mediaeval Europe – the church, the state and the trade guilds – soon hardened into entrenched opposition. Gypsies found themselves ever more frequently rejected. The most menacing threat was the growing accumulation of anti-Gypsy laws which we shall examine in the next chapter. Curtailment of normal Gypsy occupations by the jealous craft guilds added to their difficulties. As far back as we can trace, an important part of the Gypsies' stock-in-trade had been metalworking and other small crafts. They not only carried out blacksmithing, shoeing and repair work, but manufactured vessels and tools. On occasion groups of Gypsy metalsmiths were employed as armourers in different parts of Europe[25] and in Serbia at least they largely replaced local smiths because their handiwork proved superior. Others produced baskets, combs and jewellery, selling them in the market in direct competition with guild members. The guild masters would not tolerate this threat posed by wandering vagrants, as they saw them, to even a part of their monopoly.

These pressures resulted in the Gypsies' resorting to petty crime and trickery. Their position on the fringes of society had been precarious at the best of times. Henceforward many of them were compelled to live on their wits, pilfering and stealing where they could. In this they were no better and no worse than the hordes of vagrants and 'sturdy beggars' who crowded the road and towns during certain periods as a result of the scourge of war and plague, land enclosures and other evils which befell the lower classes.

An unfavourable image of Gypsies developed in the popular mind. The authorities, less than fifty years after the first Gypsy groups reached western Europe, began to receive a growing number of complaints. Small-scale thefts became common while landowners found that Gypsies distracted peasants from their work, as was expressed somewhat later – and no doubt with some romantic exaggeration – by the fictitious Sir Roger de Coverley:[26]

> "The Gypsies set the heads of our serving maids so agog for husbands that we do not expect to have any business done as it should be whilst they are in the county."

A host of folk sayings across Europe began to allude to Gypsy cunning and downright dishonesty. In Hungary the quip 'you can see the Gypsy in him' means his trickery is obvious. A Lithuanian folk-tale[27] explains why it is not a sin for a Gypsy to steal. Two Yiddish proverbs from Russia confirm this association with petty crime:

> "A Gypsy doesn't steal from near his camp"
> "One Gypsy doesn't rob another".

24

The quick wit of a Gypsy is awarded admiration in the following Hungarian story. Todor, a Gypsy horse-dealer, sold a mare to a peasant farmer with the remark that if any defect was revealed in the horse he would take back the animal. Three days later the farmer led the horse into Todor's camp saying:

> "Here is your horse, Todor. I don't want it after all because it's got a defect – she's blind in one eye."
> "How can you *dare* call that a defect," exclaimed Todor. "That's not a defect, it's a misfortune."

The same accusations appear more formally set out in laws, for example that issued by King Henry VIII of England in 1530:

> "Diverse and many outlandish people calling themselves Egyptians, using no craft or feat of merchandise . . . have gone from shire to shire and place to place in great company and used great and subtle means to deceive the people, bearing them in hand that they by palmistry could tell men's and women's fortunes and so many times by craft and subtlety have deceived the people of their money and have also committed many heinous felonies and robberies to the great hurt and deceit of the people they have come among."

Similarly the Venetian government in 1558 spoke of the "bad qualities of the Gypsies and the trouble, damage and many disturbances" which they had caused.[28] In Scandinavia they were accused of "moving round and deceiving people with their swindling, lies, thefts and magic"[29] while a Portuguese law, early in the same century, refers to the "many crimes which the Gypsies commit and the sorcery they claim to know".[30]

A French lawyer writing at the same period thus justified the expulsion of Gypsies:

> "It was very necessary to remove these terrible persons from the simple common people on whom they had played a thousand tricks and subtle swindles, claiming that they had knowledge of good and bad fortune, that they foretell life and death, conspired to give young people love potions and drugs . . . and never left a place without having evilly stolen something."[31]

Those against whom the legislation was aimed were perhaps only a few thousand who had succumbed and been turned into outlaws. Their depredations were so numerous and their movement necessarily swift so that they appeared to the authorities to be everywhere. Others kept a foothold in legitimate society and began from an early date to form settled quarters, particularly in south-eastern Europe and the Iberian peninsula. In Turkish-occupied Balkan countries whole streets of copper-workers and other Gypsy artisans came together in quarters of the larger towns. Although evidence is scanty, it is reasonable to suppose that the majority of Gypsies, in eastern Europe at least, fell within this category, either employing themselves in small workshops or plying their business as itinerant craftsmen.

To combat the so-called *Gypsy menace*, however, legislation was copied from one country to another without regard for the consequences. As today, nobody asked where the Gypsies could legitimately find a living and attempt a normal family life. As we shall see, banishment or death were the only alternatives offered.

Distrust was further nurtured through the dissemination of stories purporting to illustrate not only the wrong-doing of Gypsies but the supposed guilt attached to being a Gypsy. This guilt-ridden label *being a Gypsy* has a continuity in legislation over many centuries and is contained today in the 1959 Highways Act in Britain and the special pass-books for Gypsy nomads in France and elsewhere.

It was said for example that Gypsies had been cursed by God because they had refused shelter in their tents to Joseph and Mary on their flight from Egypt. Some Gypsies even attempted to mitigate rather than deny this charge by claiming that they were on a long pilgrimage of penance for this crime – probably only adding credibility to this tale.

In a Spanish carol Gypsies steal Jesus' swaddling clothes:

"Into the porch at Bethlehem
have come the evil Gypsies.
From the newly born babe
they have robbed the coverings.

26

Rascally Gypsies with faces
like black olives.
The poor child they've left
of clothes bereft."[32]

Another from Provence portrays the Three Wise Men as Gypsies:

"We are three Gypsies who tell good fortunes
We are three Gypsies who steal wherever we may be.
Kind child, so sweet, cross our palms with silver
And each will tell you all that is to happen to you."[33]

Gypsies have been repeatedly associated with the crucifixion and forced to share with the Jews some of the blame for Christ's death. A Greek Easter carol tells the story:

"And by a Gypsy smith they passed,
a smith who nails was making.
'Thou dog, thou Gypsy dog' – said she,
'What is it thou art making?'
'They're going to crucify a man
And I the nails am making.
They only ordered three of me
but five I mean to make them.
The fifth the sharpest of the five,
within his heart shall enter'."[34]

Variations of this legend – in which a Gypsy is haunted by a red-hot nail that never cools, and must ever wander – are current in Ireland.

The church in general either promoted such legends or at least failed to suppress them. At the same time the ecclesiastical authorities supported anti-Gypsy laws. The Presbytery of Aberdeen in 1608 fined two men for selling meat and drink to Gypsies. They had to repent publicly on their knees before the pulpit the following Sunday.[35] The Bishop of Lincoln a decade later cited the Bible in an exhortation to the Earl of Salisbury urging strong anti-Gypsy measures:

"Considering that almighty God . . . did enact that law in the fifteenth chapter of Deuteronomy:

'Let there not be a beggar among you' against begging and laziness and that the common and statute laws of this kingdom (being both of them excerpts from the law of God) . . . do utterly condemn and extirpate . . . Egyptians . . . His Majesty is justly offended at you who . . . do suffer your country notwithstanding to swarm with whole troops of rogues, beggars, Egyptians and idle persons."[36]

The clergy lent their weight wherever they exercised temporal power. Thus Pope Pius V as head of the Papal States ordered male Gypsies to be sent to the galleys to serve at the battle of Lepanto and expelled from Rome a humanitarian monk who dared to oppose this order.[37]

That some Protestant clergy shared the antagonism of the Catholics towards Gypsies is shown by the words of a Lithuanian minister in 1787:

"Gypsies in a well-ordered state are like vermin on an animal's body."[38]

Only in one important respect did Gypsies escape the wrath of the church. The Inquisition considered them unworthy of attention.[39] The tribunals did not bother to condemn Gypsies for card-reading and other semi-magical practices. For once, Gypsies benefited from the low opinion held of them and only one trial has been recorded, in Portugal. A Gypsy woman brought before the Inquisition there in 1582 for making a model of a dead man for magical purposes was released unpunished.[40]

It was not until the nineteenth century with its new humanism that the churches began to show a benevolent, if patronizing, interest in Gypsies. The Quakers in England organized the first mission in 1815 and other Protestant bodies followed including a mission in Germany commencing in 1828. A Catholic priest, Father Farkas, founded a school at Neuhauser in Hungary during 1850, and other small Catholic missions and schools followed in Belgium, Italy and Spain. Only a small number of Gypsies came into contact with these early efforts but they do represent a positive approach by the non-Gypsy world. A contrast indeed to the malevolence shown by the clerical authorities previously. The prejudices of the church were unfortunately not entirely buried as will be seen later in this book. The worst outrages, over which the Catholic Church must share the blame, were those committed during the terror in Fascist Croatia, ending in 1944.

Gypsies in New England had to bury their dead in deserted Indian graveyards because they were refused Christian burial.[41] As late as 1868 the Vicar of Baldock in Hertfordshire refused to bury a Gypsy woman even in the unconsecrated part of the cemetery.[42]

More sinister than the tales heaping guilt upon the Gypsies for their alleged past and present actions was the effort to show that the Gypsies were a bastard people with unnatural origins.

These aspersions began soon after the arrival of the first Gypsy groups in Europe. Alongside the objections we have already examined, concerning their blackness, foreign tongue, alleged spying and so on, these deeper inroads on their character had begun. Thus Agrippa wrote in 1530:

> "These people coming from a region lying between Egypt and Ethiopia, descendants of Chus, son of Ham, son of Noah, still bear the mark of the curse of their progenitor."[43]

The obscene idea was put about that Gypsies were the offspring of an unnatural mating. According to one version Eve lay with Adam after his death and produced the first Gypsy.[44] A variation in the Turkish-occupied Balkans said the first Gypsy was born as a result of an incestuous union between Chen and his sister Guin.[45] Another story said they were the descendants of a prehistoric race of dwarfs.[46]

Common to these stories is the belief that the Gypsy people inherited collectively the guilt for some ancient offence and carried a dreadful curse. Since their origins were obscure up until the revealing linguistic studies of the eighteenth century, it was certain that such myths would be believed and take root. Where belief in the immemorial wickedness of Gypsies faded there were always ready to hand supplementary stories of more recent invention. In Montenegro, for example, people thought that local Gypsies were the descendants of a Serbian traitor named Vuk Branković.[47]

Related to the charge concerning their unnatural origins is the recurring theme that Gypsies are suspect because they are racially impure. It is not that they have simply intermarried with the populations in the numerous countries through which they have passed. All but the most fanatical racialists would have to admit that almost everyone today is a mixture of various racial elements. What the Gypsies have done, so the theory goes, is to intermarry with the lowest criminal orders between Calcutta and Stockholm. This, it is said, has produced degenerate hordes who live in and on every refuse dump in Europe and infest the dirtiest shanty dwellings outside our cities.

It is allowed that there exist somewhere – though in minute and rapidly dwindling numbers – the true Romanies. These precious few are extolled as racially pure, clean in habits, noble in spirit. But they are never found; they are of course a phantom people. Those who indulge in such fantasies would recoil in horror if shown the Kalderash Gypsies in the slums of Montreal or the Kale Gitanos in poor tents near Barcelona. Their Gypsies are ghosts whose wagons and horses pass silently in the night, disturbing the stillness of country lanes only with the jingle of a harness and faint strains of a violin. Parliamentary debates, in Britain and elsewhere, contain many references to these imaginary beings.

Of course there has been intermarriage during the migrations across the world. But as a matter of fact, taking partners among the Gaje (non-Gypsies) has never been fully approved by the Gypsies and has therefore been limited. Mixed marriages in the Middle East and the Balkans, North Africa and Spain produced children of still generally dark appearance – varying little in their swarthiness to west and north European eyes. Only when Gypsies took blond and blue-eyed partners did today's fair-haired Gypsy children appear. It is a pitiful twist in racialist thinking that Gypsy haters should display even more contempt and venom against those who are now clearly partly of their own precious Anglo-Saxon, Nordic or whatever blood they happen to be.

Unfortunately merely dismantling these arguments by logic is not enough. They are rooted in the emotions and the subconscious. There is always another layer to uncover. Thus when the racial theories are swept aside we find that the detractors have once more changed ground. Once again they assert that the majority of the people who call themselves Gypsies are not Gypsies at all. They are social misfits, the drop-outs of society who have taken up a pseudo-Gypsy way of life to avoid social responsibilities, taxes and other inconveniences of contemporary life.

Clearly it is not fact and reason we are up against. When Gypsies first arrived they were disliked because they were considered 'black and ugly'. Now it is because many of their children are fair and blue-eyed. Notoriously, once branded, a scapegoat group can do nothing right. Exclusiveness causes hostility and suspicion; assimilation brings denigration.

Another source of deeper fear and false accusation has been Gypsy magical practices. These survive commonly in the various forms of fortune-telling. Sympathetic magic was commonly employed alongside herbal cures for illness in animals and people. Magic on its own was used to help the love-sick. Most often it was harmless and used to good purpose.

On the medical side, Swedish country people used to buy arsenic and other remedies from Gypsies to treat their animals. But belief in their powers went further than this:

> "There was a Gypsy woman who came to a place where a woman lay about to give birth. 'Perhaps you would like me to give the pains to your old man,' said the Gypsy woman, 'Yes,' thought the woman. 'That's a good idea.' In a few moments the husband began to have strong pains in his stomach. Meanwhile the mother gave birth without any pain."[48]

Belief that Gypsies had special power over fire has been widespread. People in Prussia thought they could stop fire spreading simply by drawing a line around it.[49] A Swabian folk verse refers to the same miraculous ability to control fire:

> "Gypsies are no fools.
> When they travel around the world
> they cook wild birds in a hat
> and the hat doesn't burn."[50]

A village where Gypsies had lodged would never be burnt down it was said in Schleswig.[51] On the other hand in other countries Gypsies were often blamed for starting moorland fires.

In literature there are to be found numerous instances of the positive effects of Gypsy magic, especially in love affairs. Giancarli's *La Zingana* (Mantua 1545) includes in the story an old woman who falls in love with a young man and goes to the Gypsy Agata to learn spells to make him return her love.

The magical aura surrounding the Gypsy people is still prevalent today. The fear of their powers has not disappeared. Throughout Britain and France, certainly in Germany and Hungary, Gypsies are said to have 'the power of the evil eye'. There are plenty of people who make a point of giving to Gypsies while they might not bother with ordinary beggars at their door, simply as a precaution against the unknown. This fear of the Gypsies' curse has frequently caused a menacing backlash. Once it brought about the death of supposed Gypsy witches[52] and in some parts of Europe is still a potent source of ill-will.

This ill-will has been fed, as with the belief in prediction, by stories like the following which apparently bear witness to Gypsy powers:

> "She took some strands of hair from the housewife's head and then she went away and poured out oaths. The woman was never healthy afterwards. She faded away."[53]

Sometimes magical antidotes were employed to counteract the power of a curse. It is recorded that a woman took a lump of burning coal and threw it in the direction a Gypsy woman had gone.[54] A general precaution in Sweden was to spit three times on anything bought from a Gypsy.[55]

Somewhere in the myths concerning original sin, impure blood and magic was born the least founded accusation of all: cannibalism. In Turkey and Albania it was thought that Gypsies commonly dug up graves and ate corpses.[56] Part of the explanation may lie in the fact that Gypsies in these countries often buried their dead in unmarked graves and local people may never have seen a Gypsy tomb.

A story from Spain tells of a shepherd from Cadiz who lost his

way and met a Gypsy band. They invited him to sit near the fire
and have a meal with them. But he heard them say among themselves "There's a nice fat friend", upon which he pretended to be
tired and slipped quietly away.[57] A Welsh poem written at the
end of the seventeenth century reflects the same belief:[58]

"I feared that they would kill me for supper and swallow me without salt."

One of the most infamous trials for cannibalism occurred in
Hungary in 1782. Almost two hundred Gypsies were arrested and
charged with this crime and systematically tortured until they
confessed. As a result the following sentences were carried out at
the town of Frauenmark, Kamesa and Esabrag: 18 women were
beheaded, 15 men hanged, 6 men broken on the wheel and 2 men
quartered. A further 150 Gypsies were in prison still waiting their
turn to die when the Emperor sent a commission to investigate the
case and discovered that the confessions were false. The persons
they had allegedly eaten were still alive.

A group of Gypsies in Slovakia stood trial for cannibalism as
late as 1927. The trial revealed only that a Gypsy wanted to elope
with a non-Gypsy girl and killed her father in a fight. The youth
and his friends were accused of murdering him and later of killing
and eating several other persons though their deaths had occurred
while the Gypsies were under arrest. The additional charges were
eventually dismissed but for the original killing the young man
was sentenced to life imprisonment.[59]

Much more widespread is the conviction that Gypsies steal
children. In literature and on the opera stage it is a regular feature
of Gypsy life and it is securely fixed in the popular mind everywhere.

The first writer to use this theme was Cervantes in *La Gitanilla*
(1612) in which Preciosa is stolen by Gypsies while a child and is
brought up by them. They teach her to dance and sing but in her
thought she remains a Spaniard. At the end of the novel she is
restored to her family and married to her Spanish lover. This novel
attracted many imitators and stage adaptations were made with a
variety of different endings.

The fear of child kidnapping by Gypsies is kept alive more by scolding parents and child-minders than by actual instances of theft. An English nursery rhyme says:

"My mother said, I never should
play with the Gypsies in the wood."

and similar tales are current in other countries.

Reports of even alleged cases are hard to find. A farmer who had lost his boy around 1762 claimed to have recognized him among a group of Gypsies by a mark on his thigh. But the *Gentleman's Magazine* reporting the story doubted the truth of it. At Bow Street Court in 1802 several Gypsies were accused together of kidnapping a girl called Mary Kellen. The girl had complained to the police that she had been taken away by force by the Gypsies near Plymouth. It was later found that she had escaped from a workhouse at Rotherhithe and had asked to join the Gypsies. As a result the latter were released and a collection taken on their behalf. Typical of the falsification that occurs is the fact that despite the dismissal of the case the story was reprinted as true in the United States in 1824 and again in 1911.[60] Wide publicity was also given to the case of two girls who went to see the Bristol illuminations in 1832 and alleged they were captured by Gypsies, locked up in carts, had their faces blackened and were given ragged clothes to wear.[61]

A rumour went around Montego Bay, Jamaica, during 1923 that two dark men with long beards, said to be Gypsies, were seeking little children to cut their hearts out. On the following day the premises of one local school were invaded by worried parents who demanded to take their children out of class in order to protect them from the Gypsies, and attendance dropped to a quarter.[62]

More recently the *Corriere della Sera* in Italy, dated August 14th, 1968, carried the headline:

FOUND: THE BABY KIDNAPPED BY GYPSIES

The text of the story did not in fact mention Gypsies but referred simply to a five-year-old mentally deficient child who had disappeared. It was later found alone in a half-built house. The same month other Italian newspapers published the picture of a three-year-old French child who had been lost in the Pyrenees 'presumably stolen by Gypsies'. Someone thought they saw the child in a camp near Milan and telephoned the police. Evidently Italian police as well as journalists believe that Gypsies kidnap children. They rushed motorized police to the camp, only to find that the lost child was not there.[63] French periodicals have been just as offensive and on several occasions have omitted to publish retractions when the sensational stories have proved unfounded.[64]

Likewise in 1968 rumour spread in Manchester, and was given national coverage by the *Daily Mirror*,[65] that Gypsies were planning to kidnap a local child because one of theirs had been run over and killed by a car. The parents at a school near the camp kept their children at home after helping to spread the rumour.

The only plausible reason for these tales is that Gypsies have large numbers of children and people notice among them the occasional one with a light skin or blond hair. These they assume to have been stolen, whereas in fact on occasion Gypsy families have adopted the illegitimate or abandoned children of settled girls and one Romanian group considers it lucky to have a light-skinned child.

Fortunately the Gypsies arrived too late in Europe to be blamed for spreading the Black Death plague. Yet they have over the centuries been continually accused of bringing dirt and disease. The belief that Gypsies are unclean is, of course, tied to the bundle of assumptions discussed in this chapter. It is the most common and yet least often challenged myth. The fear of sickness from encampments persists. Alleged to be bringing cholera to certain districts in Italy during 1910, the Gypsies were driven away by local residents who armed themselves as vigilantes. Then a medical inspection showed the Gypsies had no trace of the disease.[66]

A local newspaper at Wigan (England) recently noted that Gypsies were blamed for bringing rats to one street[67] while an outbreak of salmonella in Staffordshire was put down to the presence of Gypsies at Stoke-on-Trent.[68] Numerous legal proceedings for trespass have included for good measure allusions to insanitary conditions, though medical opinion has usually minimized the danger.

The starting point for the accusation is usually a fouled and untidy roadside camp lacking sanitation and refuse disposal. On the face of it these encampments are a disgrace to any local authority which has the power if not the legal obligation to provide minimum services. However the initial spate of objections and complaints appear justified and reasonable. The situation cannot be whitewashed. But there is an air of panic about the public outcry. Someone is outraged because they saw a child defecating. What exposes the motives of the blandest protesters is that concern is never shown for the health of the Gypsy families compelled to live in such appalling conditions. When the health hazard is mentioned it is always in relation to the surrounding householders. Indeed the situation is frequently made worse by an official warning to settled people not to encourage Gypsies by giving them water. The nearest public pump, if one exists, is turned off. The Gypsy families are served with notices alleging that they are committing a *nuisance*.

The purpose is clearly to drive the Gypsies from the locality. But there is an element of fear and a panic-ridden desire to exorcise the very spirit of the Gypsies from the place. It is believed that from their camp emanate not just untidiness and disease but corruption and anarchy which if not stamped out will creep through the suburban gardens into the very being of the community.

Within Gypsy life, however, considerable importance is given to cleanliness. For the very reason that families are often forced to take up temporary residence on waste ground, where rubbish from householders tends to collect, rules on hygiene have to be strict. Previously numerous regulations were codified in a body of traditions and taboos, called by some groups the *Romania* and upheld by the *Kris* or council of elders. Until the present century and even now among certain groups, the Kris ensures moral and physical cleanliness. But for this emphasis on hygiene and the authority in every camp to maintain standards the Gypsies would hardly have survived.

In many small but important details the rules continue in force even among groups whose adherence to tradition is not considered strong. Most Gypsies in Britain would not rinse dishes in the same vessel used for washing clothes. Some consider it unclean to wash men's and women's garments together.

Table surfaces are kept spotless and the debris of a previous meal never permitted to remain. Shoes and underwear are never placed on a table. The pride and care maintained to uphold the highest standards inside caravans – despite lack of water and fouled and littered ground around the home – are common knowledge. Less is known about the careful taboos followed when calling and collecting from Gaje houses. One can only write from personal experience and there must be many variations in different parts of the world and at other periods. But at a stranger's house Gypsies will be careful to refuse, without offending, any drink offered them if they hear anyone cough or suspect illness in the home. One precaution is to take the offered cup in the left hand and drink from the opposite side. For the same reason much of the food and cast-off garments given to begging Gypsies end in the ditch. The clothes are sold rather than worn because they are considered *mokadi* or *marime* (unclean).

Much more could be said about the *Romania* and the *Kris* and the severe punishments previously inflicted for contravention of the rules. Vessels rendered unclean because of misuse were broken and clothes regularly burned. Perhaps the strength and importance of the communal laws can best be judged from the fact that the early Gypsy groups in Scotland, Lithuania and elsewhere were permitted a large degree of self-government. Such autonomy was in fact the subject of a formal treaty between Gypsy leader Johnny Faa and James IV of Scotland.[69] Even later, Gypsies brought to trial had the right to be tried by a jury composed half of their own people.

Let it be said too that Gypsies often express contempt for the low standards they see kept by householders. Remember that in western Europe at least Gypsies engaged in scavenging occupations come into everyday contact with the littered backyards and grubby kitchens of the same Gaje who condemn them for uncleanliness. Gypsies have a healthy abhorrence of city slums, lodging houses and cheap snack bars.

They regard the indoor lavatory with suspicion as a source of infection, and its use by both men and women as most undesirable if not immoral. They will not use the chemical closets provided in their modern caravans for these reasons. The instinctive rejection of communal lavatories provided in blocks on caravan sites has distressed ignorant officials. It is interpreted as more evidence of Gypsy dirtiness. In fact it is their insistence on ritual cleanliness which leads to the misuse of the communal arrangements and sometimes to their deliberate destruction. This is not vandalism but a protest against the imposition – without prior consultation – of a system which cuts across Gypsy belief and social rules. In brief, hedges are considered far cleaner than block toilets, though properly sited individual closets are acceptable. A Gypsy arrested in Canada and placed on remand in prison almost died of thirst recently because the drinking fountain in his cell was located next to the urinal and he could not bring himself to use it.

From supposed unclean habits to dirty sex life is no step at all. A German author at the beginning of the century wrote that every *brothel-queen* in England was a Gypsy,[70] and ordinary people in Albania considered Gypsy girls no better than prostitutes.[71] The fact that London prostitutes during the nineteenth century dressed up as Gypsy women to attract clients at Epsom during Derby week brought them into disrepute but hardly accounts for the widespread low opinion of Gypsy girls in this respect.

Coupled with the conviction about the low morals of Gypsy women is the belief that Gypsy men have designs on Gaje women. The French sociologist Maucorps found from a survey of present-day attitudes in France that Gypsies are commonly supposed to molest non-Gypsy women.[72] This is shown too in an Albanian tale:

"An Albanian girl took her brother's horse to a Gypsy smith Sulyo. But he said he would not shoe the horse unless she let him kiss her. She refused and later the brother came, struck the Gypsy with his sword, cleaving him in two and then said, 'Will you kiss my sister now, Sulyo?'"[73]

It is widely believed of course that Gypsies enjoy a better and fuller sex life than the average house-dweller. The Gajo mind alternates between the conviction that the Gypsies are just loose in their morals and therefore below contempt and the suspicion that Gypsies enjoy a natural and spontaneous love-life, enhanced by their handsome looks and romantic attraction.

The fact is that there is within the tight social organization of most Gypsy groups far less sexual freedom than among non-Gypsies. The least suggestion of promiscuous behaviour, the slightest flirtation, is immediately noticed. Young people of both sexes among the Gypsy communities today have little opportunity to enjoy each other's company away from chaperoning relations. Even in Britain, for a Gypsy boy to ask a girl to accompany him to a cinema or dance hall is to begin a serious courtship which is expected to lead to marriage within a year. Marriages are indeed family affairs largely guided by long-standing alliances between certain family groups giving a narrow choice for approval.[74]

In view of the strict moral code of the Gypsy people generally it is surprising indeed that they have gained such an undeserved reputation for immoral living. One can only conclude that ignorance and envy, employing liberal imagination, are capable of bringing into being totally false assumptions. Prostitution has always been forbidden by Gypsy law, and although Gypsy dancers may be most alluring they are always respectably clothed and protected by relatives among men musicians. A Gypsy man or woman committing adultery could have part of their ear or nose cut off in punishment[75] and be banished from the community. Within living memory an English Gypsy was branded for adultery.

Perhaps it is their very unobtainability that has caused people to sully the Gypsy's reputation with gossip. The beautiful Gypsy girl is a well-known figure in paintings and literature and the handsome Gypsy lad is a feature of British and German folk ballads particularly. In the *Gypsy Laddie* the Gypsies come and sing by a castle wall and the lady falls in love with Johnny Faa, leaving her husband to follow him.[76] Something of the duality, the split feelings concerning Gypsies, can be gathered from Victor

Hugo's *Notre Dame de Paris* in which an archdeacon first perse-
cutes a Gypsy dancer and later tries to seduce her himself.

Their attractiveness is vouched for in Bulgaria where 'Gypsy
Love' is the name given to an old-fashioned hot-to-the-touch
house-stove and 'Gypsy woman' (Tsiganka) is a powerful drink,
half aniseed – and half plum-brandy.

In literature this image is common and Shakespeare can be
quoted:

> "This captain's heart is become the bellows and the fan to cool a
> Gypsy's lust."[77]

By contrast with the general antipathy the Gypsies have often
been held in esteem by the nobility. They provided a lively diversion and neither competed with, or menaced, the world of the
aristocrats. It early became the habit of rich gentry to invite
Gypsy entertainers with their music and dancing into their homes.
Titled people even protected the Gypsies from the harsh laws.
After the French authorities had passed the anti-Gypsy law of
1606, Louis XIII himself invited a party of Gypsies to his palace in
the following year to dance in his presence.[78] Many others
remained in refuge on nobles' estates. A special decree was issued
in 1682 by which any aristocrat sheltering Gypsies would forfeit
his lands to the crown. Several lords in Scotland during the same
period assisted Gypsies with gifts of land and one, Sir William
Sinclair, rescued a Gypsy from the gibbet. For many years after a
group came annually to play music at his residence as an expression of gratitude.[79]

From the earliest times amid the anti-Gypsy writings one could
find a nobler view of the people and their way of life. Thus in
Cervantes' *La Gitanilla* a Gypsy woman says:

> "We are the lords of the plain, of the crops, of the woods, of the
> forests, of the wells and of the streams. The forests supply us wood
> free of charge, the trees fruit, the vine grapes, the garden vegetables,
> the fountains water, the streams fish and the preserves game,
> the rock shade, the hills fresh air and the caves houses. We sleep as
> easily on the ground as in the softest bed . . . We are insensible to
> pain."

Bright clothing, their carefree manner and lively musical abilities have all been portrayed frequently by writers and composers, one of the most famous being Bizet in his *Carmen*, first produced in 1855. The nineteenth century indeed saw an upsurge in romantic writing and feeling about the Gypsy people[80] and went a long way towards transforming the popular image. From then onwards alongside the stereotype dirty, dishonest, child-stealing villain we have the dark, handsome violin-playing lover Gypsy, a 'noble savage' camping in the woodlands and living off the earth. Both are far from the truth and neither in the long run have much assisted the Gypsy people to obtain recognition and minimum respect.

CHAPTER THREE

EXPULSION AND REPRESSION

Leave or be hounded to death: this became the choice constantly forced upon Gypsies in most of Europe. Relegated to the position of an outcast minority, they faced banishment from one country after another.

Warning placards went up in Germany and Holland to illustrate the fate of any Gypsies apprehended. One shows a Gypsy hanging on the gallows while another man and a half-stripped Gypsy woman are being flogged. The inscription reads:

Punishment for Gypsies and beggars entering this district.[1]

Such a stream of legislation flowed out from governments and parliaments that it is not practicable even to outline the decrees. The historical ground has been well covered in precious studies[2] and we shall devote attention to a survey of the various policies pursued. Suffice to say that historian Scott-Macfie lists a hundred and forty-eight laws promulgated in the German states alone between 1416 and 1774.[3]

English law imposed death for being a Gypsy in 1554 and Elizabeth I included in the decree:

"those who are or shall become of the fellowship or company of Egyptians".[4]

Swedish legislators made hanging the penalty for any male Gypsy caught.[5] Christian V of Denmark in 1589 ordered capital punishment for the leaders of Gypsy *bands*.[6]

The first anti-Gypsy laws issued in each state indicate the rapid spread of this kind of legislation.

1471	Lucerne
1482	Brandenburg
1484	Spain
1498	Germany (Freiburg Diet)

1524   Holland
1526   Portugal
1530   England
1536   Denmark
1539   France
1540   Flanders
1541   Scotland
1549   Bohemia
1557   Poland and Lithuania
1637   Sweden.

Far from diminishing, the volume and severity of the legislation increased as time went on. During the seventeenth century France under Louis XIV added to previous measures the shaving of the heads of women and children and their confinement in workhouses. An incident recorded in 1685 describes how local police attacked a group of Gypsies killing a man and a woman. Two men taken prisoner were forcibly enlisted in the army.[7]

The district of Ober-Rhein in 1709 ordered any Gypsies taken by the authorities to be deported or sent to the galleys, even if no charges had been made against them. Five years later Mainz decreed the execution of all Gypsy men captured, and the flogging and branding of women and children.[8] Infants could be taken from their families and placed in institutions under a law passed at Frankfurt-am-Main in 1722. The parents were to be branded and expelled.[9] Both men and women over the age of eighteen faced death as Gypsies under Friedrich Wilhelm of Prussia.

The rising crescendo of decrees against Gypsies was linked in part with the consolidation of national states and a lowered tolerance towards minorities. Some Gypsies deemed undesirable were expelled from France in 1510 and shortly afterwards all Gypsies ordered to leave Languedoc province. Within a few decades laws had been passed which on paper banished them from the whole of France. Gypsies ignoring these regulations – if caught – could be flogged and deported by force. Reasons put foward for this intolerant policy refer only to the "alleged religion and penance of the Gypsies and their frauds".

43

When Emperor Maximilian I reaffirmed Germany's laws in 1500, Gypsies got notice to quit the land by Easter of the following year. The Emperor's legislators in this instance accused the Gypsy community of being spies for a foreign power.

True the threat from the Turkish-occupied side of Europe was at this time real and menacing. Yet on examination little or no evidence can be found to justify the accusation. To regard as malefactors and spies Gypsy families who in general carried not offensive weapons but the tools of their various trades was absurd. Besides they took no interest in state politics. Yet the charge, first uttered during a debate in the Diet of the Empire in 1497, has persisted into modern times.

Early travellers and geographers who assumed the Gypsies they saw in eastern Europe to be the same persons noticed previously in the west added some credibility to the spy belief. However fanciful, it became a recurring theme in the preambles of mediaeval legislation. No proof was ever produced to show that Gypsies in fact crossed and recrossed frontiers carrying any specific information valuable to an enemy. One contemporary historian and theologian who examined and rejected the notion as unfounded was Gijsbert Voet of the Dutch Reform Church.

However unjustified, the cumulative effect of the widespread anti-Gypsy laws was to make Gypsies non-citizens. No longer protected by the rule of law, those who avoided arrest and expulsion by the official agents of order could be abused and mistreated by anyone with impunity and their belongings stolen. Two cases show that Germans who slew Gypsies stood to be acquitted in accordance with Maximilian's law. In one case the judge ruled that "by taking the life of a Gypsy the defendant did not act against the policy of the state".[10]

Even migration to northern Europe, where the climate made nomadic life raw and wretched, did not place Gypsies out of reach of relentless law-makers. Early families of Gypsies entering Finland from Sweden and Estonia in the sixteenth century were driven back. Danish and Norwegian law in the following century ordered the confiscation of any vessel used to ferry Gypsies into either country.[11] Legal bars against Gypsy migrants have remained in force in Scandinavia throughout the nineteenth century and up to the present time.

Deportation laws were not revoked in Denmark until 1849 when it became possible for Gypsies already residing in the state to be naturalized. Foreign Gypsies, even those related to Danish citizens, could still not enter Denmark legally. Some that attempted to join their families during 1878 and again in 1897 were summarily deported.[12] Sweden in 1909 sent a family group back to Denmark where they were already having trouble, and the process continued.

In the same self-defeating way, France and England pushed Gypsies back and forth across the Channel. Deported the short distance to Boulogne and Calais, they moved away from the port towns only to be hounded by the French authorities.[13] Others arrested in France had moved from Germany, though conditions for normal survival were hardly better in one or other of these countries.

In Aylesbury in England seven men and a woman were sentenced to be hanged in 1577 after being found guilty of 'keeping company with Egyptians'.[14] The position remained similar in Scotland through to the eighteenth century. For the crimes of fire-raising and being a Gypsy Janet Stewart in 1714 was sentenced to be scourged through the streets of Jedburgh. After twelve lashes she was held in the town prison for three days and then nailed by her ear to a post for nearly an hour. Some of her companions were transported to America, a fate shared by many in England. Much of Scottish anti-Gypsy legislation remained on the statute-book until 1906.

Expulsion proved a no more successful policy in Portugal. Beatings and deportation decreed in 1538, forced labour in the galleys and a prohibition against Portuguese citizens selling them houses still left Gypsies roaming about the country.

To encourage active participation in driving out Gypsies, bounties were widely offered. Public posters in the German states offered a reward for anyone who brought in a Gypsy dead or alive.[15] Money could be claimed for discovering and denouncing Gypsies to the authorities under a law enacted in Ober-Rhein in

1711. The French government from 1765 began to give money for the capture of Gypsies, setting a price of twenty-four francs for a male and nine francs for a female. This system reduced Gypsies to the status of vermin.

As late as the nineteenth century in Denmark 'people hunted Gypsies as they hunt foxes' according to one writer.[16] A great Gypsy hunt covering four districts of Jutland took place on November 11th, 1835. The day brought in a *bag* of over 260 men, women and children.[17]

A Rheinland landowning aristocrat is said to have entered in his list of game killed during a day's hunting:

Item: A Gypsy woman with her sucking babe.

At a conference held in the Swabian Parliament on the subject of the *Gypsy Filth*,[18] plans were outlined for rounding up Gypsies. If they approached a village, bells would be rung and the militia sent out to intercept and arrest them.[19]

The Dutch government in the eighteenth century organized nation-wide *Gypsy Hunts* in a concerted effort to expel them all from Holland. With the help of local constables, empowered to pursue the chase into other police districts, the policy for once succeeded. No Gypsies were counted in the country until new migrants crossed the frontiers in the following century when efforts had of course lapsed. Switzerland had tried the same tactics as early as 1514, ordering their departure from Swiss towns. They were driven out of Geneva and officers on one occasion posted outside the gates to prevent a party returning. After a skirmish, the Gypsies fled and sought asylum in a monastery to avoid punishment.[20] In the Italian states, Papal and other local police kept up continual pressure.[21]

The catalogue of repression becomes tedious and varies only in detail. In Moravia they cut off the left ear of Gypsy women; in Bohemia it was the right. The Archduchy of Austria favoured branding, and so on.

These activities, widespread and prolonged for centuries in central, western and northern Europe, amounted to a slow policy of outright genocide. Thousands suffered death, mutilation or banishment. The majority of Gypsies continued a precarious existence thanks only to slow communications, the inaccessibility of certain regions and at times the shelter and patronage of well-placed aristocrats.

As many do in Europe today, Gypsies were compelled to follow a constant circuit from one country and one district to another. The provinces they entered intensified measures against them while in those they vacated, laws lapsed. Viewed in retrospect, killings could only have been selective whatever the letter of the law. The machinery for efficient extermination did not exist until a later date.

A common precaution taken by Gypsies was to encamp on the borders of two states, or districts, to facilitate escape. When the rigorous campaign in the Netherlands drove them out, their numbers grew in Germany and France. But a point came on occasion when retreat was impossible; Gypsies then prepared themselves for armed resistance. After the Netherlands proclaimed independence Gypsies faced long prison sentences, a fate considered by them almost worse than quick death and this fact drove them to revolt.

In Germany where arrest meant death anyhow, some Gypsies formed themselves into combat groups for self-preservation. One of the biggest confrontations occurred in 1722 when a thousand armed Gypsies, bringing with them a light artillery, fought a battle against regular soldiers.[22]

Some years later troopers were sent to surround and attack a large encampment and a serious skirmish ensued. During the siege a woman and her two children were burnt alive in a hut. Another woman and a seven-year-old child died on their way to prison.[23]

Nineteen Gypsies taken at Käswasser in 1722 were tortured to make them confess to crimes. Four were then condemned and broken on the wheel. A day later a man and two women went to their death. After beheading, the man's body was bound to the wheel and the heads of the women stuck on poles. Execution of the remainder was delayed only a few weeks.[24]

Many other instances could be quoted and it is hardly surprising that some Gypsies in desperation became bandits. Even so, among the numerous outlaw bands labelled as Gypsy the majority of members were in fact Gaje.[25]

An exception among the better-known of the larger bands who lived by robbery was the notorious group led by a man called Hannikel. His portrait and evidence of his knowledge of Romani show that he was undoubtedly a Gypsy himself. His men specialized in robbing from another pariah minority – the Jews – because neighbours often neglected to come to the latter's assistance. Hannikel's men more than once openly entered villages carrying torches and claimed to be soldiers dispatched to arrest Jews for illegal trading. His career ended on the scaffold in 1787.[26]

Resistance and banditry became the last resort of a desperate people. More common was retreat into remote areas. When central government, monopolizing the enactment of new laws, could employ no speedier agent than a horseman, outlying regions sometimes offered relative shelter to fugitives. Thus the Basque provinces in France proved safe for many years. But in 1802 the republican Prefect of the Basses-Pyrenees ordered the combing-out of Gypsies in his territory. A massive operation, in which the military of France and Spain co-ordinated efforts to seal off both sides of the border to prevent escape, resulted in the round-up of five hundred Gypsies.

They were concentrated together at the prison of St. Jean Pied de Port. The original intention of the French government had been to send the men to Louisiana, a plan which provided part of the motive for the operation. The women were to have been held in prison indefinitely and their children distributed among villagers. Eventually, under threats, thirty-eight men enlisted in the colonial army. But the mass transportation suddenly ceased to have any value because Louisiana passed as a purchase to the United States. Napoleon subsequently signed an order for them to be settled in the farming colonies somewhere in the barren district of Landes. This scheme likewise aborted and the remaining Gypsies, including the women in prison, were eventually released. Several had already died under the wretched conditions and because of poor food.[27]

The Louisiana plan – transportation to the sparsely populated

New World – represented a convenient way for states to rid them-selves of Gypsies and gain hardy colonists. Portugal had already sent hundreds to Brazil in the sixteenth century[28] and Spain sent many to her South American lands.[29] When laws imposing the death penalty for merely being a Gypsy became outmoded, the authorities relied on netting the Gypsies under petty criminal law. It was then practical and economic to ship them to overseas terri-tories where there was a manpower shortage.

The idea that it would be possible to expel all Gypsies as a final solution has never been completely buried. The Toulouse paper *L'Express du Midi* carried a leading article in the early nineteen-hundreds proposing again their banishment from France.[30] On a smaller scale the town council of Llanelly in Wales in 1912 took it upon themselves to evict sixty Gypsies by force from the borough, a practice again common in western Europe since the Second World War.

If they cannot be driven out, they must be forcibly settled and assimilated. Logic alone counselled the adoption of this policy by one state after another, once expulsion proved a failure. With extermination ruled out as impracticable, a second-best approach would be to strip the Gypsy people of their self-dependence, their distinguishing culture and language. Nomadism would be pro-hibited, a host of regulations designed to hem in and curtail their wanton activities and they would thus be compelled to merge themselves into the anonymous masses of settled society.

When one surveys the desolation that assimilation has brought to Gypsies and numerous other minorities, it is hard to grasp that much effort was cloaked by apparent benevolence. Those respon-sible often believed themselves motivated by Christianity. The process has since been recognized by the world as a form of geno-cide.

Stretching from the fifteenth century to the present day, and often co-existing with more bloody measures, assimilation reveals itself as a long-drawn-out conspiracy to sever the roots of Gypsy life. Politicians did little to co-ordinate their policies, but across the whole of Europe they copied legislation as one method after another rose in vogue.

Almost every European country has at one time or another out-lawed nomadism. Spain curtailed the right back in 1492. Today Gypsies are forbidden to travel in caravans and tents in most parts of communist eastern Europe, and it is practically illegal in the west.

Portugal for a period deliberately stopped the growth of per-manent Gypsy settlements by breaking up the established *Gitan-eria* (Gypsy ghetto) in Lisbon and other towns. Even marriage between Gypsies was officially barred in Spain in 1633. The German authorities tried in 1830 to take away by force all the children of Gypsy families in the area of Nordhausen and place them in an institution.[31] A similar action took place early this century in Norway on the grounds that it was unhealthy for the children to live in tents and wagons.[32]

In one of the earliest decrees against the Romani language, Spain outlawed the speaking of their mother-tongue in 1633 and the law was reaffirmed in 1783. Women caught wearing their Gypsy dresses could be whipped in Provence,[33] and similar laws against this clothing existed in Portugal.[34]

Late fifteenth-century laws in Spain directed Gypsies to find employment with masters and to settle permanently – or be hounded from the country. A few decades later any Gypsy found wandering could be placed in serfdom. Two hundred years on, Spanish officialdom was still attempting to stop nomadism and decreed severe corporal punishment and even the death penalty for Gypsies who left their place of residence.[35]

On the other side of Europe, Sultan Murad (1633–40) tried to prevent the Gypsies from moving around in Serbia, and Serbian national rule proved as hostile – and often as futile. The bureau-cracy even insisted on issuing certificates for cattle owned by Gypsies, without which they could not be moved, though evi-dently this idea did not succeed. In a sweeping threat the govern-ment announced in 1891 that all Gypsies caught travelling on the road at the commencement of the new year would be arrested and imprisoned.[36]

For the first scheme for mass assimilation we must return to the eighteenth century and examine the policies of Maria Theresa of

Hungary. From 1761 onwards she issued a series of decrees intended to turn Gypsies into *New Hungarians*. Like the Persian Shah a thousand years earlier, the Empress handed out seed and cattle and expected them in return to become good farmers. Under her plans, government-built huts replaced tents, and travel and horse-dealing were forbidden.

Gypsy children were taken away to be fostered by Christian people. There exist descriptions of how this was carried out at Fahlendorf and at other Gypsy colonies. Even normal marriage became difficult. Unless he could satisfy the civic authorities that his income sufficed to support a family, a man was denied the right to take a wife.

These extreme curtailments on Gypsy life commended themselves to her successor Joseph II. He adopted the same policy in forcing settlement on the large Gypsy communities in Transylvania, ordering the children to attend schools and regular church services. Those wilful enough to try and avoid these observances found themselves in some cases led to schooling and prayer on the end of a rope. Young Gypsies were separated from their families and sent to learn a trade. The Gypsy language, style of dress and even music – except on holidays – were outlawed. Curiously, Joseph II forbade intermarriage with non-Gypsies, a measure which surely slowed the process of assimilation. In several localities Gypsies bitterly opposed his policies and there was bloodshed. Open revolt caused Joseph within a year to bring in a more tolerable programme, but with the same aim.[37]

Throughout eastern and central Europe migratory Gypsies often fitted better into the social and economic structure. They provided a cheap labour pool which could be exploited by large estate owners; and could be relied upon to perform menial tasks regarded with distaste by the host population. Roadsweeping became an exclusively Gypsy occupation in Bulgaria. Often in the Balkans a Gypsy was found to fill the post of hangman.

Extreme exploitation occurred in the Romanian principalities. From the end of the fourteenth century, within a few years of their earliest arrival in Europe, they became the bonded serfs of local rulers. The first recorded instance of a transference of Gypsy serfs is in Wallachian documents dated 1385. By 1482 there were groups of Gypsy serfs working on estates in Moldavia. The exact circumstances in which they became serfs is not known. It is possible, as some writers believe, that under duress of famine they sold themselves into serfdom in order to survive. Others may simply have fallen into debt and redeemed themselves from prison by this method.

Their freedom extinguished for ever, Gypsy serfs could be sold as chattels by their owners, who were most often nobles and church dignitaries. Their status was similar in every respect to that of Negro slaves on the plantations in the southern United States. In time, the government itself came to own numerous serfs. State-owned serfs were permitted to travel within Romania carrying out allotted tasks and occupations.[38]

Restrictions in the Civil Codes applied to all Gypsy serfs:

Moldavian Civil Code.
Chapter 2, section 154.
Serfs cannot legally marry freemen.

Section 162.
Serfs can marry only with the permission of their masters.

Wallachian Civil Code.
Article 2.
Gypsies are automatically serfs from birth.
Gypsies without a master are classed as serfs of the Prince.

The church found Gypsy serfs useful and used its influence to maintain serfdom. The ecclesiastical powers in Moldavia protested in 1766 against intermarriage between Gypsies and Romanians which was increasing:

"In some parts Gypsies have married Moldavian women and Moldavian men have taken as brides Gypsy girls *which is entirely contrary to the Christian faith* for not only have these bound themselves to spend all their lives with the Gypsies but also their children remain for ever in unchanged serfdom."

As a result of this unqualified opposition by the church, the ruling prince of Moldavia ordered all existing marriages between Gypsies and Romanians to be immediately dissolved. Priests were ordered to refuse any requests to perform such marriages in future and had to sign a paper affirming that they knew of this decree.[39]

The Austro-Hungarian empire also held Gypsies in near enslavement throughout numerous provinces where they were reduced to the status of serfs without any rights. Their position can be judged from the fate of one who escaped from his master in Siebenbürgen in 1736. After recapture the master is said to have recorded in his diary:

> "In the case of one, Peter Chitschdy, it was the second offence. At my dear wife's request I had him beaten with rods on the soles of his feet until the blood ran and then made him bathe his feet in strong caustic. Afterwards for unbecoming language I had his upper lip cut off and roasted and forced him to eat it."[40]

The low social position of Gypsies in this part of Europe resulted in the formation of quite a different popular stereotype. Instead of the quick-witted, if rascally figure pictured in west European stories, anecdotes still current in Hungary and Romania, and in Poland, portray the Gypsy as dull-minded. One story relates:

> "A landowner bought a fine horse for himself. The Gypsy Todor longed for this horse very much every time he saw it and began to beg his landlord to give it to him. The landowner got bored with this eternal begging and said:
> 'Listen, I'll give you the horse, Todor, if you can stand thirty blows with the stick.'
> Todor admired the horse so much that he decided such a handsome creature was worth a beating. He lay on the punishment bench and gritted his teeth. The landowner began to beat him without mercy. Then after the tenth blow he said with a sardonic grin:
> 'Todor, I've thought about the matter and changed my mind. I don't want to give you the horse.'"[41]

A Polish tale tells about a foolish Gypsy who wanted to see

what it was like to be hanged. He told his companions to put a rope around his neck and pull until he whistled to them to stop – with predictable consequences.[42]

Gypsy author Mateo Maximoff has described in one of his novels[43] how conditions in Romania remained inhuman right until the nineteenth century. The leading politician in the struggle for the eventual emancipation of the Gypsies, Kogalniceanu, wrote:

> "In my youth I used to see in the streets of Jassy human beings with chains on their hands and feet, some of them even with iron rings about their heads and necks. Cruel floggings, starvation and exposure to smoke, being cast naked into the snow or frozen river; this was the treatment meted out to Gypsies. The sanctity of their marriages and family ties were not respected. The wife was taken from her husband, the daughter separated by force from her mother, children torn from their parents' embrace, separated from each other and sold to the four corners of Romania. Neither humanity nor religion, nor the law had any mercy for these hapless human beings."[44]

Opinion was gradually influenced against serfdom. The Netutsi Gypsies and others organized a desperate insurrection and fighting groups took to the mountains. Constitutional political agitation helped, but not until after the Romanian national revolution in 1848 was freedom gained. In 1853 it became illegal to sell more than three Gypsy families together or to separate members of one household. Final abolition came in 1856 when 200,000 Gypsies were released from bondage.

Failure to assimilate often brought expulsion as a punishment. This caused antagonisms between different states because the progress of integration could be upset by the influx of Gypsies from another country. Bulgaria combated this danger by pairing a law in 1886 prohibiting nomadism with a second forbidding entry of Gypsies from abroad. Implementation brought hardship and separation to families whose members were scattered throughout the Balkans and depended on freedom of movement for their occupations. But as everywhere such regulations could not be totally enforced.

In Norway the state parliament at the same period voted expenditure on a three-year scheme to induce the nomadic *Fanter* people to settle permanently. Between the wars numerous families in the New Forest area of England were herded into forest compounds and forced to live in debased conditions.[45]

Exceptionally Portugal forbade Gypsies to acquire houses for a brief period after 1648 and the Turks in the Balkans sometimes 'assisted the spring migration of the Gypsies' by burning the roofs off their winter dwellings.[46]

In general the authorities had to come to terms with the continued presence of Gypsies and those that did not press at once for direct assimilation, sought to contain the Gypsy population. Numerous special laws were enacted for this purpose. For example, the Czarist government in Russia ruled it an offence in 1759 for Gypsies to enter St. Petersburg. In Spain, until 1783, Gypsies could establish legal residence only in the designated *Gitanerias* in certain towns. Barriers to normal business were sometimes formidable. Serbian coppersmiths held a protected monopoly in the Banat during the seventeenth century, Gypsies being barred by law from manufacturing copper utensils.[47] The Guild of Locksmiths at Miskolc in Hungary canvassed successfully in 1740 for an order stopping Gypsies doing any metalwork *outside* their tents. As can be imagined this restricted them to small operations. Frequently the extra taxes levied on Gypsies effectively limited the trades they followed. This was a handicap in mid-eighteenth-century Russia.

The musical profession alone flourished because Gypsy music in various styles has been widely appreciated in Europe. Gypsy dancers, however, have not escaped restriction. Around 1920 an Albanian law stopped Gypsies from dancing in public for money. From 1934 onwards – the first restriction having lapsed – dancers had to pay a special fee to licence their performance.[48]

To control Gypsies in France legislation was enacted in 1912 obliging them to carry special identification papers. These notorious 'anthropometric certificates' contained the following details:

Name, first name, nicknames, country of origin, place and date of birth, height, chest measurements, size of head, length of right ear, middle and little finger, length from left elbow to left middle finger, length of left foot.

As if this was not sufficient for identification, the bearer was also required to produce two photographs and a set of fingerprints. The regulation applied to all Gypsies without fixed address and lacking French citizenship.

The German state of Baden introduced a similar certificate in 1922. Five years later Prussia fingerprinted eight thousand Gypsies and Bavaria passed measures to combat 'Gypsies, tramps and the work-shy'. The regulations forbade Gypsies from travelling and camping in their family groups, or *bands*[49] as the German law insisted on calling them. No sporting guns or other firearms could be held by Gypsies and any Gypsy over sixteen without regular employment could be sent to a work-house. For those not born in Bavaria immediate deportation was decreed.

During the same period the Soviet Union was attempting large-scale settlement. As we shall learn in Part Three, this campaign, carried forward with early revolutionary fervour, was first experienced as a revival of Gypsy national feeling. But the ultimate aim was probably assimilation. The higher circles of the Communist Party wanted the Gypsies to become sedentary and to accept state employment in factories and on the land – in a word, to be proletarianized. Everywhere indeed the rise of a more bureaucratically directed society brought demands for control. A conference in Hungary back in 1909 proposed that Gypsies should have their horses and wagons confiscated, together with any weapons they possessed. One speaker went so far as to urge that every Gypsy should be branded so as to assist identification.[50] A writer in Oslo put forward in a series of articles during 1930[51] the demand that Gypsies throughout Norway should be sterilized. Here and elsewhere these seeds of anti-Gypsy feeling fell on fertile ground and prepared the way for later events.

PART TWO
The Nazi Period 1933-1945

CHAPTER FOUR

THE NON-ARYAN ARYANS

When the Nazi party came to power in 1933 they inherited anti-Gypsy laws already in operation. The attitude of the general public had long been one of mistrust and dislike, and the Nazis certainly had no romantic feelings towards the Gypsies. That same year an SS[1] study group suggested sending them all out to sea and sinking the ships. This was no flight of imagination as later events showed.

The Nazis quickly established a racial hierarchy with the 'Aryan' Germans at the top. They never recognized the Gypsies as Aryans although Romani is an Aryan language. Dr. R. Körber in his article 'Volk und Staat' (Nation and State) (1936) wrote:

"The Jew and the Gypsy are today far removed from us because their Asiatic ancestors were totally different from our Nordic forefathers."[2]

A similar line of reasoning is followed by Professor H. Günther in *Rassenkunde Europas* (Anthropology of Europe) which P. Friedman calls 'the Bible of Nazi anthropology':[3]

"The Gypsies have indeed retained some elements from their Nordic home, but they are descended from the lowest classes of the population in that region. In the course of their migration they have absorbed the blood of the surrounding peoples and have thus become an Oriental, Western Asiatic racial mixture, with an addition of Indian, Mid-Asiatic and European strains . . . Their nomadic mode of living is a result of this mixture. The Gypsies will generally affect Europe as aliens."[4]

When two laws passed in 1935[5] made non-Europeans second-class citizens, legal commentaries on them considered the Gypsies to be in this category. Thus Stuckart-Globke:

"In Europe generally only Jews and Gypsies are of foreign blood."[6]

Dr. Brandis wrote in a similar vein:

"Apart from the Jews, only the Gypsies come into consideration in Europe as members of an alien people."[7]

In pursuance of the idea that the Gypsies were not Aryans, as this term was understood by the Naxis, experiments were carried out in later years to show they had different blood and skull structure.[8] We have not accepted the suggestion of some writers that the Nazis, in order to get round the problem of their being Aryans, classified the Gypsies as 'asocials'.[9] It is true that generally in the concentration camps they wore black triangles as did the asocials, but they formed a separate group among these. In at least one camp they wore distinctive *brown* triangles[10] and in many cases the sign 'Z'.[11] We think that the quotations cited above show that the Gypsies were considered as non-Aryans from the beginning of the Nazi period. Although the 'scientific' study of the Gypsies was to be concerned to show their anti-social nature, this was true too of the study of the Jews.

The origins of German research into the Gypsies goes back to Alfred Dillmann, a government official, who in 1899 founded a Gypsy Information Service in Munich, later called the Central Office for Fighting the Gypsy Nuisance.[12] Nazi interest in the Gypsies as a race began in the year they gained power. The Gypsy scholar Dr. Sigmund Wolf was regularly sent long lists of persons whose genealogy he was asked to trace back to their eight great-grandparents. These requests came from the Party Information Service[13] or direct from the Central Office in Munich. In that year Dr. Achim Gercke, an expert on genealogy working in the Ministry of the Interior, asked Dr. Wolf to sell him all his Gypsy family trees and to work for him. However the scholar refused. At about the same time Dr. Gercke set up a National Centre for Genealogical Research[14] in Berlin and continued to send requests for information. Finally in 1936 Dr. Wolf's home in Magdeburg was raided and all his material was taken away by the Gestapo Centre in Magdeburg. He was later informed that his material was being used by a Dr. Ritter[15] and that he would be put in a concentration camp if he continued to protest about the affair.[16]

The main Nazi institution concerned with research into the Gypsies was founded in 1936 by Dr. Robert Ritter which one year later became the Racial Hygiene and Population Biology Research Unit of the Ministry of Health at Berlin-Dahlem. The Ministry of the Interior was the prime instigator of the setting up of this unit and gave it help and support.[17] Ritter and his staff published numerous writings on the Gypsy question and suggested possible solutions. They were also engaged in drawing up genealogical tables of German Gypsies and classifying them as being pure or of mixed race.

The already existing office in Munich possessed 19,000 files on Gypsies when Ritter started work. Some of the persons concerned were not however Gypsies, and others had left Germany.[18] He intended to have every Gypsy in Germany interviewed in order to build lists of other members of their families and thus to draw up complete genealogical tables.[19] His aim was to track down every pure and part Gypsy in the country.

Systematic genealogical investigations did not start until December 1938,[20] after the issuing of the Decree on the Fight against the Gypsy Menace.[21] By February 1941 Ritter had classified 20,000 persons as pure or part-Gypsy.[22] By Spring 1942 he had 30,000 files,[23] a figure approximately equal to the total Gypsy population of Greater Germany.

Announcements concerned with the calling up of young persons show also the progress of the classification and tend to bear out Ritter's claims on the numbers covered. In 1940 on the occasion of the recruitment of women to the Work Service, Gypsy and part-Gypsy women were to be excluded. The criminal police were asked to help the recruiting officers in doubtful cases on the basis of information they had to hand. If no official classification documents existed then they were to judge on appearance, manner of life, social position, literacy and so on. Only especially doubtful cases had to be referred to the office in Munich.[24] Thus classification was by no means complete at this date.

By 1941, in reference to the call-up of young men for military service, it was stated that all Gypsies should have been classified and the classifications be available in local police stations. Where the experts' decisions were not to hand, the police were asked to inform the Central Police H.Q. (RKPA). The classification must then have been almost complete and the researchers not so busy as in the previous year.[25] Why a decree of March 1942[26] gives the much lower figure of only 13,000 classifications is not clear.

By 1944 official circles assumed that all Gypsies would have their classification documents. More important, it is noted that no future reference to Gypsies will be made in decrees concerned with the call-up.[27] The unstated reason for this was, as we shall see later, that the majority of the German Gypsies were by then in concentration camps.

Ritter claimed after the war that he stopped working on the subject of Gypsies in 1941, well before the massacre of the German Gypsies.[28] He was never tried and is now dead. A document recently discovered shows that his statement was untrue. It is dated 1943 and signed by Ritter himself.[29] We shall return again to the subject of his guilt.

In the following pages are outlined the ideas expounded by other researchers, ideas upon which future policy was to be based. The 'racial scientists' show a considerable consensus of opinion on the subject of the Gypsies. All agree that they are of Indian origin but have become mixed on their journey:

> "The Gypsies originate from India and have taken into themselves the most varied mixture (Beimischungen) of other races during their journey through Persia, etc."
> "They are mainly of Oriental blood with far and near East traces and a little European addition."[30]

They represent a foreign element in the nation:

> "The Gypsies are completely different in nature (wesensfremd) from us and obey other rules of life. They are a foreign element in every nation."[31]

So too H. Schubert who says that "only the Jews and Gypsies

regularly count as foreign (artfremd) in Europe". He divides the population of Europe into four groups:

German and similar races (stammesgleich)
Foreign races (stammesfremd)
Jewish and Gypsy
Coloured[32]

The researchers claimed that the Gypsies were immoral, criminal work-shy and ineducable.

"They are . . . a criminal element in their whole make-up . . . The desire to travel is avoidance of all physical work turned into a custom through generations . . . For 500 years the Gypsies have been living in German territory without it having been possible to educate them to be useful people, either by state help or compulsory education."[33]

Dr. Küppers wrote that venereal disease was rife among Gypsies.[34] They could not be integrated into normal society:

"The history of the Gypsies shows plainly that drawing them into the cultural life of our people is completely ruled out."[35]

If they intermarry they marry the worst elements of Germans:

"An especial source of danger are the Gypsies of mixed races as they are the result of marriage between Gypsies and less worthy members of the host population. Thus the number of asocial elements, hereditarily tainted persons, criminals and prostitutes is increased."[36]

Römer too regrets the intermarriage of Gypsy and German:

"Since the arrival of the Gypsies some of them have unfortunately entered into a relationship with Germans."[37]

Two writers at least did not feel so strongly about the danger of intermarriage:

"The Gypsies are less of a racial danger (than a social menace) as mixing with the sedentary population is confined to exceptional cases."[38]

Knorr also thought that intermarriage was not a danger. The

number of Gypsies was small and the Nazi marriage laws sufficient to stop future intermarriage.[39]

Statistics quoted by various writers set out to show Gypsies to be a burden on the social services. Thus the journal *Volk und Rasse*[40] pointed out that some parishes in the Burgenland (Austria) had to pay large sums out for the confinement costs of Gypsy mothers.

Gypsies represented a further danger because of their high birth rate.

"Their fertility is above that of the host nation. Ten to fourteen children is no rarity."[41]

Another news item quoted claimed that in Oberwart (Austria) the Gypsy population had increased by 400 per cent between 1890 and 1933 while the local peasant population only increased by 20 per cent.[42]

We may note that in none of the above is any distinction made between asocial and non-asocial Gypsies, nor on the whole between sedentary and nomad. Küppers however did admit that the nomads often had good qualities. Nevertheless in his opinion measures had to be taken against them also.[43] Apart from this the researchers treated the Gypsies as a homogeneous group, except that the suggestion was often made that part-Gypsies were worse than pure Gypsies. This was to affect future legislation.

We now turn to the conclusions of the racial scientists – the solutions they proposed. Rohne in 1937 suggested setting up special Gypsy quarters in towns.[44] Römer proposed their deportation to 'lands where they can live easily as nomads' to avoid the danger of their mixing with Germans.[45] The newspaper *NS Landpost* of March 19th, 1937, mentions, presumably with approval, the idea of the Polish Gypsy King Janusz I Kwiek to set up a settlement in Abyssinia. Four years previously District Commissioner Mayerhoffer had urged at a meeting in Oberwart (Austria) that the Gypsies should be deported to Polynesia.[46]

Römer said novelists should stop idealizing the Gypsies.[47] Justin advised that attempts to educate them should be abandoned.[48] Rüdiger recommended their elimination but made no specific proposals.[49]

Apart from deportation, the other radical solution was sterilization. The first recorded mention we have found in Germany dates back to 1937, but there were probably earlier references. In that year the journal *Reichsverwaltungsblatt* (no. 10) said that 99 per cent of the Gypsy children in Berleburg were ripe for sterilization.[50]

Discussions that year in Hungary of plans to sterilize the Gypsies there received publicity in the Nazi press[51] and both Ritter and Justin later recommended the sterilization of part-Gypsies. A concise summary of existing thought in 1939 is provided by Dr. Behrendt writing in *NSK*, in an article entitled 'The Truth about the Gypsies':

> He says they come from India originally and are now a mixed race. There are two million in Europe and North America. In Germany itself 6,000 pure Gypsies live together with 12,000 part-Gypsy or non-Gypsy travellers. The laws of the Gypsies do not permit them to practice birth control. They are criminal and asocial (according to Behrendt) and it is impossible to educate them. All Gypsies should be treated as hereditarily sick. 'The only solution is elimination.' The aim should therefore be "*elimination without hesitation* of this characteristically defective element in the population". This should be done by locking them all up and sterilizing them.[52]

Dr. Hecht in a speech in 1941 said there existed only three possible approaches to Gypsies and other foreign elements in German territory:

Biological separation
Assimilation
Deportation

No decision had been taken on which of the three should be adopted.[53] It was in fact to be a fourth unmentioned solution.

We should mention briefly a Swedish sociologist, B. Lundman, who contributed to German racist literature. In 1938 he wrote that he had found persons of mixed blood in many parts of Sweden. 'Unfortunately' in some parts he found even more Gypsy blood than expected, more than a third of the population of some villages had some Gypsy blood. He claimed that the villages with a higher proportion of Gypsy blood had a looser sex life and were poorer. He also noted the unsatisfactory progress of those of his students who had part-Gypsy blood. In his opinion it was too late to do anything about the problem as there were so many people of mixed race, and suggested that a firm government would sterilize at any rate the groups at the bottom of the social scale and that this would encourage the *purer* people not to marry into the mixed groups.[54] We may contrast this attitude with that of the Danish sociologists Bartels and Brun who even under German occupation opposed the sterilization of persons of mixed Danish and Gypsy blood.

Ritter's views on the Gypsies, part-Gypsies and non-Gypsy travellers (the Jenisch) are contained in a number of articles.[55] 'Ein Menschenschlag' (A human type) (1937) was virtually the death warrant of the Jenisch. It stated that they were not Aryans but earlier inhabitants of Germany. Ritter claimed after the war in his defence that he had saved some travellers from the camps when he declared them to be non-Gypsies. This was not true. They were merely put into the concentration camps under a different classification, as asocials. Ritter himself had visited the camps and knew what the situation was. In 1940 in 'Primitivität u. Kriminalität' he wrote:

> "The primitive person does not change and does not allow himself to be changed ... The further birth of primitive asocials and members of criminal families should be stopped by the separation of the sexes or sterilization."

In 1938 in the state health journal he said that Gypsies could not be changed and he returned to this theme again in 1939:[56]

> "What is the way to cause this travelling people to disappear? There is no point in making primitive nomads settle and their children go to school."

In the same article he says any sexual contact between Gypsies and Germans must be legally forbidden and that the Gypsies of mixed blood should be put in closed work colonies. The pure Gypsies should be given limited areas in which to wander, and winter quarters separate from those of the non-Gypsy travellers.

Ritter again condemned the part-Gypsies in 1941. They were:

"In the majority unbalanced, characterless, unreliable, untrustworthy and idle, or unsteady and hot-tempered. In short, work-shy and asocial."[57]

In his report[58] he stated that:

"The Gypsy question can only be considered as solved when the majority of the asocial and useless part-Gypsies have been collected in large camps and set to work, and when the continued procreation of this mixed population is finally prevented. Only then will future generations of the German people be freed from this burden."

His definition of part-Gypsy was stricter than that of a part-Jew.

"A part-Gypsy is a person who has one or two Gypsies among his grandparents.
"Further, a person is classed as a part-Gypsy if two or more of his grandparents are part-Gypsies as defined above."[59]

This meant that if two of a person's sixteen great-great-grand-parents were Gypsies he was classed as part-Gypsy and later, in 1943, could be sent to Auschwitz.[60] Without going into details we may mention that a person with one Jewish grandparent (*four* great-great-grandparents) was not generally affected by Nazi anti-Jewish legislation.[61]

Ritter was anxious to hunt out Gypsies who had merged into society. According to him, many denied they were Gypsies and produced documents such as membership of the Music Academy or the baptismal certificates of their parents showing that these had a profession. Others had joined the Nazi party, taken up jobs as salesmen or lived in towns. However, with the aid of the genea-logical tables he would be able to hunt them out.[62] Later we find that German citizens were encouraged to denounce Gypsies to the police.[63]

Although Ritter did recommend that pure nomadic Gypsies should be allowed to continue travelling under their own laws, none of his other proposals resound to his credit. In our opinion he was personally responsible for the large number of Gypsies killed in Germany. He set up the principle under which a person with one-eighth Gypsy blood counted as a part-Gypsy and insisted that these part-Gypsies represented a danger to established society. Some 18,000 of the German Gypsies were classed as part-Gypsies and would not have been killed had the same rules been applied to them as to part-Jews. In addition Ritter worked with the police authorities to register all the Gypsies, used threats to obtain information about Gypsies' relations, and visited the concentration camps where he was treated as if he was a high-ranking SS officer.[64]

Next to Ritter, Eva Justin was the most well-known of the racial scientists who concerned themselves with the Gypsies. She apparently first visited Gypsy settlements in 1933, posing as a missionary[65] and was given the Romani nickname 'Loli Tschai' (red-haired girl) as they thought she resembled an earlier missionary who had that nickname. Later they were surprised to find her behind the interrogation table in the police headquarters when Gypsies were called in to be questioned about their families.

In the foreword to her book[66] she wrote that she hoped it would be a basis for future racial hygienic laws which would prevent any further flow of 'unworthy primitive elements' into the German people.[67] She studied the history of 148 Gypsy children of mixed race who had been brought up in orphanages or by non-Gypsy foster-parents. She found that the morals of this group were worse than that of a control group of children brought up in a nomadic tribe – by their own parents! She concluded that Gypsies could not be integrated because of their primitive way of thinking.[68] If a Gypsy is educated and remains in the German community, he usually becomes asocial, so all attempts to educate Gypsies and part-Gypsies should stop. The children being brought up in the German community should be sent back to their tribes and socially assimilated adults should be sterilized. "The German people do not need the multiplying weed of these immature primitives."[69] So, she concludes her study:

> "All educated Gypsies and part-Gypsies of predominantly Gypsy blood, whether socially assimilated or asocial and criminal, should as a general rule be sterilized. Socially integrated part-Gypsies with less than half Gypsy blood can be considered as Germans."

"Asocial part-Gypsies with less than half-Gypsy blood should be sterilized."[70]

She does not make any recommendation concerning the nomadic Gypsies.

After the war, in February 1964, the Frankfurt magistrate decided that there was insufficient evidence to justify a prosecution against Eva Justin. She had taken the theme of her book from Ritter and did not believe in it any more. They accepted that she had not known Gypsies would be sent to concentration camps because of her ideas. Nor could the Gypsy witnesses be sure – after twenty years – that it was Eva Justin who had hit them in a concentration camp.[71]

Many Gypsies have stated that Ritter's staff threatened them with sterilization or the concentration camp if they withheld information about their genealogy.[72] Some women in Marzahn camp had their hair shaved off because they could not tell the police the names of their great-grandparents.[73] Ritter himself stated that his unit worked in the closest co-operation with the Central Police Headquarters and the Munich Gypsy Police Unit. The racial scientists have escaped unpunished for their role in the escalation from discrimination to massacre to which we will now turn.

The following material on the Nazi period has been gathered mainly from captured documents and files. These represent only a fraction compared to the papers destroyed by the Germans when they realized defeat was near. We have used the personal accounts of survivors both to supplement this written evidence and also so that the reader should not forget that the figures and statistics quoted refer to individual human beings. Since the majority of Gypsies were illiterate those that survived the camps did not write of their experiences and there is no literature comparable to that on the destruction of the Jews. Reparations claims and interviews made many years after the end of the war can but give a small picture of the suffering of the Gypsies under Nazi persecution.

It was evident from the first that there could be no place for nomadic and semi-nomadic Gypsies in the efficient state planned by the Nazis. New laws were enacted and existing legislation strengthened, and many actions against the Gypsies taken without any legal basis – even within the perverted system set up by the Nazis.

During the first year of Nazi rule a law for 'the prevention of hereditarily diseased offspring'[74] allowed the sterilization of some non-Gypsy travellers, and other edicts later in the year[75] affected 'asocial' persons. In the following year the expulsion of 'undesirable' foreigners was ordered. Under this law Agnes Goman, born in Düben (Bitterfeld District), was sentenced in 1935 to five days' imprisonment for not having an alien's passport, and then recommended for expulsion.[76] In the same year Barbara Steinbach, born in Potsdam, and her husband Christian, born in Hanover, were arrested and accused of using a false name. It was said that their real name was Batschuri and they were deported to Hungary.[77]

Bader, the Chief of German Police, made no secret of his ideas. Before an International Police Commission meeting in Copenhagen in 1935 he declared:

> "The Gypsies, as a foreign element, will never become full members of a host population. Anyone who as a Gypsy disturbs public order and breaks laws should expect no mercy. The solution of this problem lies in the direction of giving an opportunity to all Gypsies and half-Gypsies who wish to conform and work to do so. All others must however be pursued with remorseless rigour and imprisoned or expelled. It might be worth considering including such Gypsies under those persons affected by the Sterilization Law."[78]

In fact the German government was far from 'giving an opportunity to the Gypsies to conform and work'. As non-Aryans they were excluded from the Civil Service and later from the Armed Forces.

Possibly under German pressure, the International Criminal Police Commission (later called Interpol) founded in 1936 in Vienna an International Centre for the Fight against the Gypsy Nuisance.[79] The German police had instructions to give this Centre every support.[80] The archives of this Centre were apparently destroyed in 1945[81] and it has not been possible to follow its activities. When Himmler became police chief shortly afterwards he initiated further measures against the Gypsies. In July 1936 four hundred Gypsies were sent from Bavaria to Dachau concentration camp, a presage of the transports to follow. Even in 1936 Dachau was far worse than a labour camp, and attempts to escape were punishable by death.[82]

In some places Gypsies were forced to live in special settlements. In 1933 those in the Dusseldorf district were collected in a settlement (between Eller and Oberlik in Vennhausen),[83] and before the Berlin Olympic Games the Gypsies were removed from the capital to a camp set up near Marzahn. The camp was later surrounded by police and dogs and no one allowed to travel farther than Berlin.[84] More residential camps were established in the period 1937–8.[85]

"That winter caravans were stopped on the road and the Gypsies divided into two classes. The semi-wandering Gypsies were given permanent accommodation and told that they must not move in caravans again. The travelling Gypsies had to help build camps for themselves and their families. Every Gypsy man who was able-bodied was given work."[86]

Gypsies had to sign a declaration that they understood that if they left their place of residence they would be put in a concentration camp.[87] They had to have permanent addresses and stop using the poste-restante service. Further they were forbidden to keep cats and dogs,[88] restrictions imposed by the Laws against Crime of December 1937. In September 1937 a Gypsy camp was opened in the Dieselstrasse in Frankfurt am Main. The police sent there nomadic Gypsies and also some house-dwelling Gypsies whose neighbours had complained about their conduct.[89] Two years later all Gypsies from the Frankfurt area were sent to the camp but they were not restricted in their movements until 1942.[90]

Meanwhile both sedentary and nomad Gypsies were being excluded from the German community. The Law for the Protection of German Blood (1935) stated that:

"A marriage cannot take place if offspring dangerous to the preservation of the purity of German blood can be expected from it."

Dr. E. Brandis in his commentary on this law pointed out that it prevented marriages between Germans and either Jews or

Gypsies.[91] A part-Gypsy was sent to Sachsenhausen for relations with an Aryan girl.[92] Another Gypsy, Franz Klibisch, was sent to a concentration camp for relations with a 'German fighting woman'.[93] A similar interpretation was given to the Nationality Law of the same year.[94] This distinguished between first-class 'citizens'[95] and second-class 'nationals'.[96] Gypsies with German nationality were classed as 'nationals' under this law but lost even this status in April 1943.[97]

The Laws against Crime (1937) bore particularly upon 'asocials', a class including "those who by anti-social behaviour *even if they have committed no crime* have shown that they do not wish to fit into society, for example, beggars, tramps (Gypsies), prostitutes, persons with infectious diseases who do not follow treatment, etc."[98] It is interesting to compare the groups with whom the Gypsies are classed in this early law with the 'Jews, Gypsies and Poles' of later legislation.

After this law was passed an express letter was sent to every district (Bezirk) ordering the police during the week June 13th to 18th to arrest at least 200 males of working age and send them to Buchenwald concentration camp. The classes to be arrested included Gypsies and non-Gypsy travellers. Gypsies in permanent employment should in theory have been excluded, though in fact in some districts they were taken to make up the numbers. Persons with previous convictions had been already re-arrested on June 5th. Döring thinks that although these measures were taken under the Laws against Crime, the real aim was to get labour to build concentration camps. Some persons were sent to camps other than Buchenwald.[99]

Following this law, all the males, including youths, were taken from the Gypsy camp in Dieselstrasse, Frankfurt, to concentration camps. Some later returned, possibly among those released to celebrate Hitler's birthday (20–iv–1939) only to be arrested again later.[100] Other Gypsies imprisoned included a sixty-five-year-old [sic] man accused of being 'work-shy', Adam Böhmer of the Gypsy camp Am Holzweg, Magdeburg.[101]

Joseph Franz arrested about the same time, also as 'work-shy' spent one and a half years in Magdeburg prison before being sent to Mauthausen (January 1st, 1940) then to Dachau and Sachsenhausen, after which no more is known of his fate.[102] A.S. was sent to Sachsenhausen in June 1938 for the same reason and kept there until 1940 when he was released with other Gypsies to work on unexploded bombs.[103] The men from Marzahn camp (Berlin) were taken to Sachsenhausen.[104]

In May 1938, on Himmler's orders, the Central Office for Fighting the Gypsy Nuisance[105] was linked with the office in Berlin. From then on it would make use of the combined experience of the police and the knowledge gained by the racial scientists, in particular Ritter's research centre. On May 16th it became part of the Central Police Headquarters. These moves were linked directly with legislation drafted later in the same year.[106]

In July the Gypsies from the western border of Germany were deported to Berlin. In August they were however sent back.[107] This move seems only to confirm the element of confusion in the general train of events. The Berlin authorities were trying to dispose of their own Gypsies and did not want any more.

At the end of 1938 the combined efforts of the racial scientists and police experts produced the first law directed specifically against Gypsies. The racial nature of the law will be clear from the extracts printed below:

Fight against the Gypsy Menace

A.1.1(1) Experience gained in the fight against the Gypsy menace and the knowledge derived from race-biological research have shown that the proper method of attacking the Gypsy problem seems to be to treat it as *a matter of race* . . . It is necessary to treat pure Gypsies and part-Gypsies separately.

(2) To this end it is necessary to establish the racial affinity of every Gypsy living in Germany and also of every vagrant living a Gypsy-like existence.

(3) I therefore order that all settled and non-settled Gypsies, also all vagrants leading a Gypsy-like existence are to be registered with the Central Office for the Fight against the Gypsy Nuisance.

(4) The Police authorities will report all persons who by their looks and appearance, by their customs or habits are to be regarded as Gypsies or part-Gypsies . . .

2(1) . . . An official census is to be taken of all Gypsies, part-Gypsies and vagrants leading a Gypsy-like existence who have passed the age of six.

(2) The nationality has to be entered on the index card. In cases where German or foreign nationality cannot be proved the persons concerned are to be classed as stateless.

3(1) The final decision about the classification of a person as a Gypsy, part-Gypsy or Gypsy-like vagrant will be made by the Criminal Police on the advice of experts.

Instructions for carrying out this order, issued in March 1939, further tightened the racial control. Racially pure Gypsies received new brown passes, part-Gypsies light blue passes, and non-Gypsy travellers grey passes. Under the law nomadic Gypsies were not allowed to stay more than two nights in any one place, the police would tell them where to camp and separate Gypsy and non-Gypsy travellers.

No more foreign Gypsies were to be allowed to enter Germany and those already there expelled (though this latter provision was obviously not effective as later laws made provision for foreign Gypsies). Every police headquarters (Kripoleitstelle) was to set up a unit for Gypsy problems and one or more persons were to be specifically responsible for Gypsies.

The March 1939 instructions contain this significant paragraph which indicates the racial nature of the law:

"The aim of the measures taken by the state must be the racial separation once and for all of the Gypsy race (Zigeunertum) from the German nation (Volkstum), then the prevention of racial mixing and finally the regulation of the conditions of life of the racially pure Gypsies and the part-Gypsy."

An important thing in the law from the authorities' point of view was the registration of the Gypsies. When this had been done it would be possible to see the real numbers involved.

This is the last law concerning Gypsies which mentions the non-Gypsy travellers. The main action against them was based on the Law for the Prevention of Unhealthy Offspring (14–vii–1933) and the Laws for Security and Improvement (24–xi–1933) and they were also included in some of the laws directed against Gypsies up to December 1938. Some were sterilized under the 1933 laws. By 1938 their numbers had been decimated and the remainder of no importance to the Reich. Such action as was necessary could be taken under existing laws and little mention is made of them in subsequent legislation.[108] In 1941 (7–viii) it was suggested that travellers who had been found to be non-Gypsies could best be dealt with by being put in prison as asocials.[109]

We can assume a minority of families settled down in houses while for the majority, the adults ended up in camps as asocials and their children in orphanages. They were wiped out. According to Wolf the post-war Jenisch are not the offspring of the pre-war Jenisch but families that took to the road after 1945.[110]

Much legal argument has taken place on the question of when racial persecution against the Gypsies began,[111] and we shall not attempt to cover the same ground. Many German courts have been concerned to place the date as late as possible in order to cut down on compensation claims.[112] One milestone in the legal viewpoint was the Settlement Law of October 1939 which prevented the Gypsies from travelling but made no such provision for non-Gypsy travellers. On the other hand a German court ruled that all the measures taken against the Gypsies up to March 1943 (when they were sent to Auschwitz) were merely 'security measures'[113] and not racial persecution. We shall leave the reader to form his own judgement. Döring and Arnold[114] have suggested various stages in the Nazi treatment of the Gypsies. In this study we shall take as a turning point the beginning of the policy of deportation from Germany, later abandoned and replaced by a policy of extermination.

CHAPTER FIVE

THE ROAD TO GENOCIDE

The mere imposition of restrictions on Gypsies did not satisfy the Nazis. To make Germany free of Gypsies followed logically from the policy applied to Jews. Heydrich[1] organized a meeting on September 21st, 1939, at which it was decided that Gypsies should be sent to Poland. The plan covered all the Gypsies in Greater Germany (including recently annexed Danzig, West Prussia and the Warthe region) altogether 30,000 in number. A few categories were in theory to be exempted, those five years in regular employment and families in which the mother or father was a non-Gypsy.[2]

It was Heydrich who, on Himmler's orders, issued the Settlement Edict,[3] dated October 17th, under which Gypsies were prohibited from leaving their houses or camping places. A count was made in the period October 25th–27th and the Gypsies were then collected in special camps until they could be sent to Poland.

Meanwhile the order prevented a Gypsy travelling from place to place even without luggage. To visit relatives at Christmas 1939 they had to obtain special passes.[4]

The Berlin city authorities, without waiting for the Settlement Law to be issued, arranged for the deportation of Gypsies in the area. On October 13th, SS Captain Walter Braune sent a telegram to Lieut. Wagner in recently annexed Moravska-Ostrava.[5] The telegram was for Eichmann, then arranging the deportation of Jews:

"Colonel Nebe[6] called on October 12th and asked for information as to where he can send the Berlin Gypsies. If the transport is to take much longer the city will have to build a special camp at great cost and still greater difficulties."[7]

Eichmann replied to Nebe in Berlin three days later:

"With regard to the deportation of Gypsies, the first transport (of Jews) from Vienna is announced for Friday October 30th. Three to four trucks of Gypsies can be attached to this transport. Transports now leave regularly from Vienna, Moravska-Ostrava and Katowice (Poland). With regard to the onward transport of the Gypsies I intend to put the specialists of the Police H.Q. in Vienna in touch with SS Lieutenant Günther in Vienna and SS Captain Günther in Moravska-Ostrava, so that detailed arrangements for carrying this out can be arranged. The easiest method is, as suggested above, to attach some trucks of Gypsies to each transport (of Jews) . . . With regard to a start in Germany itself, you are informed that this will start in 3–4 weeks time."

Two days later, Captain Günther in Brno (Moravska-Ostrava) had a teleprinter conversation with Captain Braune back in Berlin, part of which concerned Gypsies:

"Günther: The next transport from Moravska-Ostrava probably leaves on October 25th. Perhaps Gypsies can be attached to this transport.

Braune: All right. I will inform Nebe or Major Werner accordingly."[8]

Meanwhile the Security Central Office (RSHA) decided to stop temporarily the transport of Jews, but Eichmann arranged that the transport due to leave Moravska-Ostrava for Nisko on October 25th should still go, probably on the 27th. It seems unlikely however that any Gypsies were in fact included in this transport since Nisko was a Jewish 'settlement area'.

The deportations planned for the end of 1939 were postponed, presumably because of a lack of transport, but not for long. At a meeting in Berlin on January 30th, 1940, the deportation programme was confirmed.

"Heydrich: After the two mass movements (of Jews and Poles) the last mass movement will be the removal of 30,000 Gypsies from Greater Germany to the General Government of Poland."

Seyss-Inquart, Deputy Governor of the General Government, repeated the figure:

"30,000 Gypsies from Germany itself and the eastern area."[9]

A special department was created in the Security Central Office, Department IV D 4 (later called IV B 4) to deal with this deportation of Jews, Gypsies and Poles.[10] Eichmann was the head of this department. The following exchange took place during Eichmann's pre-trial interrogation:

"Interrogator: The deportation of Gypsies to concentration camps, was this also done by your department IV B 4?

Eichmann: Yes of course . . . not to concentration camps but to ghettos."[11]

Responsibility for Gypsies was also shared by Nebe's department (V) which included the Police Criminal Biology Section.

The first moves in the deportation were initiated by express letter on April 27th, 1940. In the middle of May, 2,500 Gypsies faced transfer to Poland from the following towns:

"Hamburg and Bremen 1,000
Cologne, Dusseldorf and Hanover 1,000
Stuttgart and Frankfurt am Main 500."

Certain groups were again to be excluded: Gypsies married to Germans or with a father or son in the forces, those who owned land, and anyone with foreign nationality. Persons not able to walk were to be sent to relatives or taken into care. These exemptions compare with similar arrangements for Jews. Collected together at one point for each area (Hamburg, Cologne and Stuttgart), the Gypsies were then taken on by train. The deportation was carried out more or less according to plan and it was intended to carry out further transports. An official statement speaks of 2,800 Gypsies 'evacuated' to Poland from western Germany during 1940.[12] The extra 300 were either a small transport from south Germany[13] or a transport to the Gypsy ghetto at Lodz.[14]

The Gypsies from Hamburg were deported to Belzec, a primitive camp consisting of some huts and tents put up by the Gypsies themselves. They had to work on digging trenches and other tasks. Three months later they went on to Krychow. This camp had stone buildings including an old factory. Here the Gypsies laboured on drains. Apart from the first fortnight the camp was guarded. Then, twelve weeks later, they were given back their documents and allowed to travel, some being placed in near-by villages[15] as related below:

> "Elizabeth Taikoni was sent to Belzec in 1940. There she had to sell her belongings to get food. She was taken to Krychow and then released and allotted to a village to which she was taken by lorry. In her village nine Gypsies were settled and the villagers and the mayor were ordered to feed them. Later she went to Warsaw and lived in an empty house. The police ordered her to leave the house and she went to Siedlce and then to Chelm. In Chelm she begged because she was unable to seek work as she had to look after her sick father. In 1942 she was arrested and sent to Maidenek (Lublin) with her father. He died there. Three months later she was freed and went to Tschenstochau. Here she looked for work but could find none, so again she had to beg. She was arrested once more for begging and sent to a camp near Tschenstochau, then to another at Tomaczow and finally to a third camp where she stayed until the Russians liberated the camp."[16]

Another Gypsy from Hamburg passed through Belzec and Krychow and then through a series of camps in Warsaw, Siedlce, Breslau and Liegnits.[17]

Some Gypsies from Cologne went first to Lochitzen and then to the ghetto at Kielce. One man from this transport escaped in Poland and remained free until 1942. He was recaptured but escaped again. Detained once more he was sent to a work-camp at Rabka-Zaryte, a comparatively fortunate fate. Others who escaped and tried to hide among Polish Gypsies were shot on capture.[18] Katherina Weiss, arrested in Koblenz, was sent with her husband via Cologne to the camp at Warsaw-Marimont. Later she went to other camps, including Konepol (Kornispol b. Tschenstochau).[19]

The transport from Stuttgart also included Gypsies from Mainz, Worms and Ingelheim. About 100 went from Mainz leaving only sixteen behind in the town. These sixteen arrived at the Dieselstrasse camp in Frankfurt on June 24th.[20] Gypsies from Stuttgart were sent to the Jewish town of Czenzidjow and then to the ghetto at Radom. Apparently a fourth transport, from south Germany, was unloaded in open country in Poland and the Gypsies left to fend for themselves.[21]

Gypsies deported to Poland were told that if they came back they would be sterilized and sent to concentration camps. They had to sign a document to show they understood this.[22]

Apart from the problem of Gypsies returning, others wanted to join deported relatives in the East. As a general rule it was decided that this would not be permitted. Christian Winterstein of Worms was however given permission to go if he paid his own transport.[23] The General Government authorities wrote to Berlin in November 1940 saying they did not want relatives to come at least for the present as the situation was already chaotic. They thought after April of the following year it might be possible to admit them. Late in 1941 however an order signed by Otto forbade Gypsies to travel to the General Government:

"A further settlement of relatives of the Gypsies resettled in the General Government in May 1940 cannot take place for the moment because of the war in the East. Further information will be given about this in due course. I may mention now that such reunion of relatives will be at their own expense. For the moment I am keeping all requests to join deportees in this office."[24]

This was reaffirmed in December 1942:

"In May 1940 and November 1941 a number of Gypsies were sent to the General Government and the Warthe region. Since then their relatives have followed them and made inquiries about them, causing difficulties. Any such persons should be arrested and no permits to travel to the General Government and the Warthe should be given."[25]

The last edict was designed to prevent Gypsies moving out of Germany in the period just before their removal to Auschwitz. Some 3,000 persons had been deported, leaving 27,000 Gypsies remaining in Germany when it was decided in October 1940 to stop further deportations to Poland.[26] Various reasons have been put forward to explain the halt. Transport was needed for war purposes; Governor Frank of Poland objected as he was trying to organize the country efficiently; the classification of

Gypsies was not yet complete. Also priority was being given to the expulsion of the Jews as their flats were needed for Germans returning from the Russian-occupied Baltic states. A combination of these reasons probably led to the decision.

Deportation was however still the solution envisaged. A small transport left in November 1941.[27] At a meeting in Prague the same month it was agreed to deport the German Gypsies to Riga.[28] But this plan too was abandoned as the Nazis fell upon a simpler 'solution' to the Gypsy problem.

A mass murder of Jews had taken place at Treblinka in December 1940. An experimental gassing station was established at Auschwitz in September 1941 and the first permanent gassing camp was set up at Chelmno in December. Some sources suggest that the decision to annihilate the Jews had already been made in June 1941. Certainly a conference at Wannsee on January 20th, 1942, marked its definite acceptance. Later the same year the policy was extended to Gypsies.

Meanwhile those still in Germany had been progressively restricted. All Gypsy fortune-tellers faced arrest after November 1939, probably because some had predicted that Germany would lose the war. A story current among the Gypsies said that Hitler hated them because one had forecast his downfall.

"Shortly before he came to power Hitler had sought out a Gypsy fortune-teller named Adler and asked her to predict his future. She came to Munich, saw Hitler and predicted great power for him. But she had also predicted a sudden fall, more rapid than his rise. He got very angry and thought he could break the evil powers of the Gypsy people by exterminating them."[29]

One wonders whether there might have been a wild idea of using the fortune-tellers to foresee the plans of Hitler's enemies.[30] Lina Steinbach of the Marzahn camp near Berlin was among those put in prison under this law and later sent to Ravensbrück.[31]

Gypsies were deported from Border zones in 1941.[32] In other areas they continued to be forced into holding camps. In 1939 all the Gypsies from the Frankfurt area had been moved into the camp in Dieselstrasse. From 1941 they were not allowed to travel and sell, being allocated instead to regular jobs. In 1942 the camp was moved to Kruppstrasse and surrounded by a high wire fence with two policemen on guard. The Gypsies had to be inside by dusk and the gate shut until 5 a.m.[33] Others were put into a camp behind barbed wire at Dusseldorf-Lierenfeld, were badly treated by the police and compelled to work in columns under SS guards.[34]

Although Gypsies had officially been excluded from the army by law as early as November 1937, many classified as pure and part-Gypsy were still serving. Some had even received medals. Early in 1941 the army authorities reaffirmed that *on the grounds of racial policy* no more Gypsies and part-Gypsies should be called up. Those in the army were to be placed in reserve units and no further decorations were to be awarded to Gypsies. The police sent lists of the persons concerned to the army.[35] In the same month a secret order went out that Gypsies should not be employed in army factories and other top security workshops.[36]

Gypsies were released from the air force by a law dated January 7th, 1942, and later in the year another order demobilized them from the army. Those listed as part-Gypsies released from the latter joined the Second Reserve of the Territorial Army.[37] A similar order covered the navy. The release of servicemen took some time and Gypsies could still be found in the army as late as 1943. Certain classes of Jews with mixed parentage were retained in the armed forces throughout the war.

Pitzo Adler was demobilized in 1940.[38] A German Gypsy arrived in Cork (Ireland) on a raft in 1943 after escaping from a ship.[39] On his way back to Germany he realized the fate awaiting him after demobilization. An Austrian Gypsy, Eugen Hodoschi, has told how he was released from the navy:

"I was a seaman in the navy in Norway until Autumn 1942. One day the Chief mate appeared and said to me in front of the assembled crew:
'You are dismissed. Do you know why?'
It went through my head that if I said no, he would answer –
'Because you are a Gypsy'. I wanted to spare myself that, so I said:
'I know quite well.'
I then came to Kiel. My commander was satisfied with me and did

not follow the instruction to dismiss me. (However he was later dismissed from the navy.) I was sent to Elisabethenpromenade in Vienna and they were intending to send me to Buchenwald but I said that I had served in the forces and asked to be sent to Lackenbach (which I was)."[40]

After November 1939 Gypsies received special work-cards and in many cases their other papers were taken away from them. Richard Rose found that with this new work-card he was unable to continue as a circus artist.[41]

In March 1942 Gypsies found themselves placed on the same footing as the Jews in respect of labour laws. Under these regulations they lost the right to sickness and holiday pay.[42] Those listed as part-Gypsies with at least half-Gypsy blood were to be classed as Gypsies for these laws. From April Gypsies had to relinquish fifteen per cent of their income as a special tax. This already applied to Poles but not until later to Jews.[43] A further restriction forbade the Gypsies to travel to Berlin.[44]

The marriage laws were reaffirmed and strengthened. A secret order from the Minister of the Interior said that 'since Gypsies endanger the purity of the German blood' careful attention must be given to requests by them to marry. Even Gypsies with less than a quarter-Gypsy blood must not be allowed to marry Germans.[45]

The courts became another organ for oppressing the Gypsies. Robert Winter, Zacharias Winter and Josef Köhler were sentenced to death in 1942 for *stealing bicycles*. Zacharias Winter was a juvenile with no previous convictions, Josef Köhler had no previous convictions and Robert Winter had no convictions for serious offences. Part of the judgement read:

> "The accused Zacharias Winter has no previous convictions and during the time that most of the offences were committed he was not quite eighteen years old. In view of his general development however he must be considered as an adult. As his innumerable thefts prove, he is a criminal who represents a constant danger to others. For the protection of the public, the death penalty is necessary in this case."[46]

Discrimination in the field of education had already started in the pre-war years. Back in 1936 an edict of the Ministry of the Interior said that research should be carried out into whether Gypsies were fit for education and whether Gypsy orphans should be fostered.[47] As we have seen above, the racial scientists supplied the desired negative answers.

In Cologne after February 1939 only one class existed for all the Gypsy children in the town,[48] and the Frankfurt Gypsies were dismissed from school in 1941 'because of the shortage of teachers'.[49] Those who did attend had to put up with persecution by other children.[50] Olga Owczarek remembers that she was driven out by the other children who hit her and her brother and shouted: "You Gypsy bandits and Jews, get out of our school."[51] The Ministry of Education announced in March 1941 that persons without citizenship could not attend school. Gypsies lacking German nationality were excluded and the police instructed to expel from the country any of them who became a 'social nuisance' as a result of having no occupation. Gypsy children holding German nationality had the theoretical right to attend classes. However 'if they were a moral or other danger to the German children' they should be dismissed and the police informed.[52] Eugen Friedrich, seven years old, of Frankfurt was excluded from school under these laws in 1942. She was taken to the children's concentration camp at Friedrichstab (Oranienburg) and later to Theresienstadt.[53]

In view of its importance in some laws we shall here give a brief account of the different groups of Gypsies in Germany at the outbreak of the war:

Sinti who had come as early as the fifteenth century and could be called native to Germany. There were 13,000 in 1939, many of them musicians. The name probably comes from the province of Sind in India.

Lalleri or Lalleri Sinti (i.e. 'dumb' Gypsies, speaking a different dialect) were a smaller group, some 1,017 in 1942. They were chosen for preferential treatment because it was thought they were a branch of the 'German' Sinti but linguistically they are a sub-group of the Rom.[54]

Rom had come to Germany from Hungary in 1860–70 and were mainly horse-dealers. In 1940 there were 1,860 and in 1942, 1,585.

Balkan Gypsies who numbered some 8,000 in Burgenland.

Litautikker who were sedentary in East Prussia. Numbering some 2,000 in 1940, they were probably a sub-group of the Sinti but were not classed as such by Ritter.

Others: *Kelderari, Lovari, Drisari, Medvashi,* Yugoslav Gypsies, and Basket-makers who together probably numbered less than 1,000.

The first hint of any distinction in law between different Gypsy tribes came in August 1941 when following classification, a refinement of the earlier division into pure and part-Gypsies was set up:

Z	pure Gypsy (Zigeuner)
ZM+, ZM(+)	more than half-Gypsy
ZM	part-Gypsy (Zigeunermischling)
ZM 1st grade	half-Gypsy, half-German
ZM 2nd grade	half-ZM 1, half-German
ZM−, ZM(−)	more than half-German
NZ	non-Gypsy (Nicht-Zigeuner).

In addition Gypsies of the Sinti tribe were to be noted as 'native Gypsies':[55]

A non-Gypsy married to a Gypsy or a part-Gypsy was to be additionally classified as 'member of a Gypsy mixed family' and a ZM− or ZM(−) was to be classed additionally, where relevant, as 'member of a non-Gypsy family'.

The Central Police H.Q. was to decide the treatment to be applied to classes ZM− and ZM(−) under the various laws. Döring has pointed out that ZM 2nd grade should logically have been classed as ZM−.

As previously mentioned the definition for mixed blood was stronger than that for a Jew. We doubt whether such a detailed classification as the above was ever carried out for the majority of German Gypsies. Such documents as we have seen indicate 'predominantly Gypsy blood' or similar phrases. The classification was not based entirely on genealogy. Ritter explained that he divided Gypsies into pure and mixed on the following grounds:

1. General impression and physical appearance.
2. Belonging to a Romani-speaking community.

3. Links with tribal law.
4. Gypsy way of life.
5. Genealogy.

We find however that when the time came for the Gypsies to be taken to Auschwitz genealogy was of prime importance. Many integrated Gypsies, sought out by the police using information from family trees, were added to the transports.

It has not been established with certainty when and by whom the decision was made to annihilate the Gypsies alongside the Jews. The date was probably in Summer 1942, some time after the Wannsee conference. The available evidence points to a personal decision by Himmler. Other Nazi leaders were of course involved in the discussions leading to the policy.

In the summer of 1942 the Security Central office (Department VI D 7b) was trying to get information about Gypsies living in Great Britain, as the following correspondence reveals:

"Berlin. 14–viii–1942

Nr 66558/42 Secret.
Precisions about the Gypsies living in Great Britain. You are asked to use all your contacts to establish the number of Gypsies living in Great Britain. We are also interested in the British Gypsy Laws and the way in which the Gypsies in Britain are regarded and treated (military service, freedom of movement, restrictions, etc.). When parachutists and other prisoners from Great Britain are interrogated I ask you to add this question. You are asked to give the matter the utmost priority.

Signed Dr. Schambacher"

The only reply we have found was most unhelpful!

"Hague. 15–viii–1942
The prisoners in Haaren camp have been carefully questioned. They declare unanimously that they have never seen Gypsies travelling during their stay in England. Some prisoners who were in England before the war declared that they never saw any Gypsies even then apart from the Gypsy orchestras in night clubs and so on. One prisoner had seen a film in which a Gypsy King living in Yorkshire was shown. The same prisoner said he had also met Gypsies in the Pioneer Corps."[56]

The request for information had been sent from Berlin to various persons including the Police Attachés in Stockholm and Spain, and was obviously considered of some importance. It was a preliminary to the invasion of England and the Germans were attempting to establish statistics of Gypsies similar to those for Jews.

On September 18th, 1942, Himmler, Thierack, Rothenberger, Streckenbach and Bender[57] met at Himmler's field headquarters. The meeting decided that:

> "Persons under protective arrest, Jews, Gypsies and Russians . . . would be delivered by the Ministry of Justice to the SS to be worked to death."[58]

This referred to Jews, Gypsies and Russians who were already under arrest and extended a 1939 agreement.[59] A letter from Thierack to Bormann dated October 13th read:

> "With the intention of liberating the German area from Poles, Russians, Jews and Gypsies . . . I envisage transferring all criminal proceedings concerning (these people) to Himmler. I do this because I realize that the courts can only feebly contribute to the extermination of these people . . . There is no point in keeping these people for years in prison. I ask you to let me know if the Führer approves of this way of thinking. If so, I will in due course present plans through Dr. Lammers."[60]

About 12,000 persons, including Gypsies, were affected by this plan. It amounted to a request for authority from Hitler to carry out what had already been decided between Himmler and Thierack, although it would seem that a decree of August 1942 had already given Thierack power to do this on his own initiative. In fact on October 9th it was already announced that:

> "Any Jews, Gypsies, Russians and Ukrainians who are serving sentences in prisons as asocial persons are to be handed over to the authority of the Head of the SS. Gypsy women are to be included. Foreign Gypsies are not to be classed as foreign and therefore also to be handed over."[61]

By November 5th, 1942, Thierack's proposition had been approved by Hitler.[62] Jews and Gypsies in prison were handed over to the SS. For those still outside prison the same fate awaited them.

To round off the arrangement, it was enacted (on October 6th) that the juvenile penal law should not apply to young Gypsies. They too would be handed over to the SS.[63] On October 10th the Minister of Justice asked for figures on the total number of Gypsies serving prison sentences in protective custody or in penal labour institutions.[64]

It is clear however that well before these discussions Himmler had decided Gypsies should be annihilated. Perhaps only of theoretical interest is the fact that he stated more than once he wished to preserve two groups, the so-called *pure* Sinti and the Lalleri. Other leaders must have known about this intention because on September 14th, 1942, Goebbels is reported as telling Thierack that in his opinion all nomads should be exterminated without any distinction between one group and another.[65]

Himmler went as far as making the necessary preparations for organizing these two groups. Nine representatives were appointed on October 13th by the Security Central Office, eight for the Sinti and one for the Lalleri. The eight Sinti were supposed to work through their local police headquarters while the Lalleri spokesman was responsible to the police in Berlin. Allowed to travel freely, they were to make lists of those to be saved. In the case of the Sinti these included part-Gypsies whom they considered could be attached to the tribes of pure Sinti (as established by Ritter and his team). The racial scientists considered there were no pure Lalleri and their spokesman, Gregor Lehmann, was to make a list of those Lalleri Gypsies whom he believed could be formed into a tribal group to be permitted to follow a nomadic life.[66] We note that the Lalleri had previously been classed as foreign Gypsies.

An edict of August 1941 gave the following classification:

Foreign Gypsies Rom from Hungary
Kelderari
Lovari
Lalleri (belonging to a group which immigrated around 1900)
Balkan Gypsies

As far as possible these groups should lose their German nationalty.

German Gypsies Sinti Gypsies.[67]

By October 1942 the Lalleri had been reclassified as German Gypsies. A passage in an article by Ritter gives a clue to why the change was made:

"The Lalleri came from the German-speaking part of Bohemia and Moravia in earlier centuries. Most of them belonged to a tribe which was living in the Sudetenland when it was annexed to Germany."[68]

Thus the fact they had lived for some years among German-speaking people qualified them for preservation though they were acknowledged to be of mixed race.[69] If the opinions of the racial scientists had been followed to a logical conclusion the Lalleri would have been seen as a greater menace than the pure Kelderari and Balkan Gypsies. The fact that they formed a small easily controlled and homogeneous group must have influenced the decision.

When party leader Bormann found out about Himmler's intentions to exempt two tribes he wrote (December 3rd) to the SS chief:

"Through my expert's conversation with Nebe I have been informed that the treatment of the so-called pure-Gypsies is going to have new regulations. They are going to keep their language, lore and customs in use and be allowed to travel around freely. In certain cases they will serve in special units of the army. All this because they have not behaved in an asocial manner, and because they have preserved Germanic customs in their religion that must be studied. I am of the opinion that the conclusions of your expert are exaggerated. Such a special treatment would mean a fundamental deviation from the simultaneous measures for fighting the Gypsy menace and would not be understood at all by the population and the lower leaders of the party. Also the Führer would not agree to giving one section of the Gypsies their old freedom. The facts have been unknown to me up to now and seem also to be unlikely. I would like to be informed about this."

The reply to this letter has not been found nor has any appeal from

Bormann to Hitler on the subject. Himmler wrote on the bottom of Bormann's letter – "Inform the Führer where Gypsies are".[70]

On December 16th, 1942, Himmler signed the decree sending German Gypsies to Auschwitz. This was swiftly followed by a series of other decrees applying to occupied areas, suggesting in our view that a decision had been taken in 1942 to wipe out the Gypsies throughout Europe. The Ministry of the Interior ruled (January 26th, 1943) that the property of Gypsies sent to concentration camps should be confiscated.[71] This was partly to avoid the confusion of the 1940 deportations when piles of clothing were left for the deportees' relatives to collect.

The movement of Gypsies from Germany to the General Government of Poland had already been prohibited. Three days after the confiscation decree Himmler published instructions for carrying out his Auschwitz order. All Rom Gypsies and part-Gypsies belonging to the Sinti tribe were to be sent to the concentration camp in March. The pure Sinti and the Lalleri were exempted together with those classed as Sinti part-Gypsies who could be attached to the nomadic tribes. Some other categories were also left out theoretically – but not in practice, namely:

Rom Gypsies and part-Gypsies married to Germans
Socially assimilated Rom Gypsies and part-Gypsies
Rom Gypsies and part-Gypsies still in the army or who had been released with decorations or wounded
Those needed in workshops
Spouses and dependant children of the above
Foreign citizens

Gypsies with court convictions and those who had broken the Settlement Law were to be sent to Auschwitz even if they belonged to exempted categories. The police would encourage the exempted Gypsies, other than foreign citizens, to be sterilized. If they refused there were provisions for their compulsory sterilization.

Several cases are known of Gypsies married to Germans being sent to Auschwitz,[72] and a report from the camp speaks of others wearing military decorations on their camp uniforms. They should not have been there and we must conclude that practice was very different from theory. Gypsies were taken from the Daimler-Benz factory although the foreman wanted to keep them. Though Ferdinand Kraus was in Nazi terms 'socially assimilated' and a member of the Nazi Party, he was persecuted as a Gypsy.[73] There is ample evidence that foreign Gypsies did not escape either. In December 1942 two officials, Westphal and Erhardt, had been made responsible for seeing that they were handed over to the police.[74] We know of a family with Croat nationality who ended in Auschwitz.[75]

No mention is made in the law of the smaller tribes (Medvashi and so on). We can assume that they were taken to the camps with the rest. The vast majority of those sent to Auschwitz had been classified as part-Gypsies and belonged to the Sinti tribe. The lists of exempted Sinti and Lalleri were supposed to be ready before the transports to Auschwitz began. But only three of the nine 'spokesmen' had compiled the lists by January 11th, 1943 – Gregor Lehmann, Karl Weiss and one other.[76] Heinrich Steinberg refused to write a list because his wife and son were already in concentration camps. Gregor Lehmann had travelled to annexed Moravska-Ostrava to seek out Lalleri. Survivors claim that he took bribes from persons who wanted to be put on the lists. Arrested after the war, he was handed over to the Russians and sentenced to a term in prison.[77] Himmler ordered the completed lists to be sent to local police stations and checked immediately. Any Gypsies with criminal records were crossed off together with members of their families. The police had orders to be especially strict if the lists were long. Only Lalleri Gypsies proposed by the Lalleri spokesman could be admitted to the lists, and the police were to make lists for the areas where the spokesmen had not done so.[78] Most of this activity proved a futile blind. When the police came to collect the Gypsies at Magdeburg and at a camp near Neubrandenburg they took away everyone.[79] This undoubtedly happened elsewhere. Josef Langryn was on the Lalleri list but still had to join the Labour Brigade (Org. Todt). He fled and on recapture was sent back to the unit to be put on trial for cowardice before the enemy. He was probably shot.[80]

Discussion on the settlement of so-called pure Gypsies and Gypsy research in general took up thirty-five minutes at a meeting on February 10th, 1943, in the Central Police H.Q. (RKPA) attended by Nebe and Sievers.[81] Plans must still have been vague. The original suggestion was apparently to settle the two exempted tribes in the Ödenburg (Sopron) district[82] but as this was part of Hungary it could only remain an idea. Why Himmler proposed in October 1942 to let these groups wander freely throughout Germany we cannot be sure. Advocates of the plan said they were no danger to German racial purity as they did not marry non-Gypsies. Yet it had been stated that ninety per cent of the Sinti and all the Lalleri were the result of mixed marriages. There may have been a propaganda aim in the move, as with the setting up of a 'model camp' at Theresienstadt. We note no attempt was made to select pure Sinti or other groups in the other countries under Nazi domination. This suggests Himmler's sole aim must have been to preserve a limited number for study purposes through Ahnenerbe, an institution founded by the SS in 1939 to investigate the heritage of the 'Nordic Indo-Germanic' race.

The Citizenship Law as amended in April 1943 gave no status to these Gypsies probably because they were to be sent out of Germany after the war. A few Gypsies, it appears, benefited by their status as 'pure' Sinti. One report[83] says the Sinti were allowed to send their children to school, served in the army and were Party members, but this may be hearsay. Many of the exempted Sinti would in this case have been sedentary, not nomadic, which seems to contradict the whole point of the law and the recommendations of the racial scientists.

A law was passed on March 27th, 1943, declaring that those classified as pure Gypsies were to be excused from Labour service and military enlistment. Part-Gypsies were to serve in the Second Reserve.[84] This is the last use of the term 'pure' Gypsies. Bormann however continued to take an interest in them for some time and later the same year wrote to the Minister of Justice asking him to defer a decision on the status of Gypsy juveniles under proposed new laws.[85] Was this still part of his efforts to ensure that no status was given to Himmler's protégés?

Round-ups of German Gypsies had in any case begun in February 1943. Police using dogs surrounded camps to make sure no one escaped transport to Auschwitz:

"On March 9th, 1943, one hundred and thirty-four Gypsies, men, women and children were driven from their beds in the Berleburg camp-site (Siegen). They were assembled in the yard of a factory and their valuables were taken off them. They were loaded into cattle trucks and sent to Auschwitz. Of this group only nine survived."[86]

"The Gypsies were even taken away from their place of employ-ment and sent away without giving their family any idea of what had happened to them. Each authority made its own interpretation of the general order. Some separated the parents from their children by taking the parents into the camps and leaving the children behind or vice versa."[87]

Reports from different towns indicate that to avoid incidents the Gypsies were told they were going to be resettled in Poland. The authorities even promised each would be given a horse, a pig and a cow.[88] We have noted that the arrests were carried out by the police (Kripo) while Jews were seized by the Security Police (SD). The ordinary police held the lists of Gypsies and it was more con-venient for them to handle the deportations.

Nearly ten thousand German Gypsies arrived in Auschwitz within a few weeks and their camp was overflowing.[89] Many of course were already in Sachsenhausen and other camps and prisons. A few continued to live on outside the camps.

Pitzo Adler continued working in a factory until November 1944. Then he was drafted into a Home Guard unit but dismissed again because of his race. He was sent to Auschwitz and died there. Three other men were still working in an ammunition factory in spring 1945 and their families had the special privilege of being allowed to shelter in the toilets of an air-raid shelter.[90] Other Gypsies are known to have been working in the coal mines up to December 1944.[91] Heinrich Franz and his wife lived on un-disturbed off the main road from Lübeck to Tranemunde. They thought they had been spared because of their age but in fact there were older Gypsies in Auschwitz. Once they received a parcel of ashes through the post but did not know exactly to which member of the family they belonged.[92] Another Gypsy still outside the camps was shot on March 30th, 1945, by SS men Karl Hauger and Franz Wipfler after being made to dig his own grave.[93]

Police Headquarters on May 15th, 1943, ordered that Gypsies should no longer be sent to Auschwitz[94] but after a temporary halt the hunts and round-ups began again. Germans were encouraged to denounce Gypsies to the police. Thus Margarete Dickow pointed out two Gypsies, Johann Krause and Heinrich Freiwald,[95] and Otto Gärther denounced Helene Pohl.[96] Frau Baukus of Friedrichsfelde, Berlin, requested the authorities to send two Gypsy families to a camp,[97] and other Germans asked for a Gypsy family to be removed from Lauben (Karlshorst).[98]

Gypsy children were weeded out of orphanages and hospitals. Police Officer Schulz-Lenhardt of Magdeburg wrote in November 1843 to the State Centre for Fighting the Gypsy Nuisance, then in Fürstenberg-Mecke, saying he had discovered three Gypsy children in an orphanage at Schönebeck on the Elbe. Excusing himself for not having found them earlier and failing to send them to Auschwitz, he asked the Centre what he should do. Two weeks later the police dispatched them to the concentration camp. The children were Loni Steinbach, Christel Rose and Seppel Tritschler. Christel Rose was ten at the time. Her guardian, Anna Rose, had been sent to Auschwitz on March 2nd.[99]

The scheme to preserve a group of Sinti and Lalleri was now definitely forgotten. By March 1944 the number of Gypsies remaining free was so small that Himmler issued the following order:

"As far as Poles, Jews and Gypsies are concerned, the accomplished evacuation of these groups by the Chief of Police has made the publication of special decrees for them meaningless."[100]

By the end of the war about three-quarters of the Gypsies living in Germany had perished. In Austria, to which we shall now turn, persecution was if anything more severe.

Nazi-inspired action against the 10,000 Austrian Gypsies started in 1938. A detailed account has been written by Steinmetz[101] and we shall therefore restrict ourselves to an outline of the events. Two months after Austria's absorption into the Reich, it was announced (May 4th, 1938) that Gypsies would be treated as in Germany. A few days later Himmler ordered the fingerprinting of the entire Gypsy community and forbade them to leave the country.[102] Gypsy children were removed from schools in some Protestant parishes,[103] and sporadic arrests began.[104] From October relatives of interned Gypsies were disqualified from receiving social aid. This placed them in the same category as those of interned Jews.[105]

Some of the first arrests occurred on June 22nd when the Germans came to Stegersbach. They intended to take several Gypsies and as one of those on the list was away they took instead a man named Adolf Gussak who worked for the local priest and lived in his house. Taken to Dachau he found conditions were already bad and rules made to make life a burden. They were made to wear coats when it was hot and leave them off in the cold. The guards forced them to crawl and bark like dogs and to sleep under their beds. In March 1939 Gussak was transferred to Mauthausen concentration camp where on one occasion he received twenty-five lashes as a punishment for writing to the priest, his former employer. He survived the war though his wife was to die in Ravensbrück.[106]

That first autumn the Governor of Burgenland ordered that all Gypsy men and women fit for labour should be forced into agricultural work wherever there was a need.[107] Work-camps were later set up in Vienna, Salzburg and in the Tyrol.[108] Then early in June 1939 a decree ordered between 2,000 and 3,000 Gypsy adults to be arrested and sent to concentration camps. This move was similar to action taken in Germany the previous summer; when 440 Gypsy women went to Ravensbrück and some 1,500 men to Dachau. The men were transferred to Buchenwald in autumn 1939, a camp where circumstances were so poor that the majority succumbed to disease and starvation.

The policy established was that the Austrian Gypsies should be deported to the east together with those from Germany. In April

1940 it was arranged to send the largest group, those in the Burgen-land, to Poland. The local authorities elsewhere, however, planned to use the opportunity to rid themselves of Gypsies by dispatching them all to the Burgenland, so it was later decided to send them from each district. Finally, the whole scheme fell through. An express letter dated October 31st, 1940, announced that the 'resettle-ment' of 6,000 Austrian Gypsies to Poland was to be held up 'because after the war another solution of the Gypsy problem is envisaged'.[109] We have suggested earlier why the deportation plan was abandoned.

Nevertheless the Nazi leaders in Austria were anxious to take harsh measures against the Gypsies. As early as 1938 Portschy, the Administrator of Steiermark, sent a memorandum to Dr. Lam-mers, Chief of the Chancellery, from which we need only quote one passage:

> "Because the Gypsies have manifestly a heavily-tainted heredity and because they are inveterate criminals who constitute parasites in the bosom of our people, it is fitting in the first place to watch them closely, to prevent them from reproducing themselves and to subject them to the obligation of forced labour in labour camps."[110]

A similar letter from Meissner, General Public Prosecutor in Graz in 1940 recommended sterilization of all Gypsies in the Burgen-land. As it is not so well-known we give a longer extract:

> "The Gypsies especially in the district of the lower court of Ober-warth where about 4,000 of them live, are a danger less from the political than from the racial and economic point of view. Among them the pure bred (black) Gypsies probably constitute the majority. They subsist almost exclusively by begging and stealing. Their activities as musicians represent more a camouflage than actual earnings. Their existence is an extraordinarily great burden for the honest working population, especially the farmers whose fields they plunder, a burden growing from year to year . . . The mass of the Gypsies still resemble externally primitive African or Asiatic peoples . . . Inter-breeding with this morally and spiritually inferior people will necessarily mean a decrease in the value of the offspring. On the other hand interbreeding is favoured by the fact that the

young Gypsy men are especially sexually aggressive while the Gypsy girls are sexually unrestrained . . . It is not possible to fight this danger merely by guarding them in central camps. Their transfer to a foreign country too is hardly possible. Since they have no means of subsistence they cannot be deprived of it. They are German nationals and will of course be rejected without consideration by any other country. The only effective way I can see of relieving the population of the Burgenland from this nuisance . . . is the universal sterilization of all Gypsies . . . These wandering work-shy beings of an alien race will never become faithful to the Reich and will always endanger the moral level of the German population."[111]

With deportation ruled out, the German Minister of the Interior ordered that the Gypsies should be compelled to live in a number of restricted settlements. Some 700 from Linz, Innsbruck, Salzburg and Klagenfurt were assembled in one place and similar arrangements made for the 6,000 Gypsies from Vienna and Burgenland. These Gypsies, who for several generations had been sedentary (except for summer migrations) were now faced with eviction from their homes. Settlements containing less than fifty persons were broken up and the inhabitants moved to larger ones. Communal kitchens served meals and ninety per cent of earnings were taken for communal expenditure. Many men were allocated to work-camps at Linz and Eisenerz.[112]

The camp at Lackenbach, set up the previous year, was expanded in 1941 and altogether between 3,000 and 4,000 Gypsies passed through there.[113] Two transports went to Lodz ghetto late the same year. No one from these transports survived.[114] In 1942 the local police in Wolbrom, headed by Lieut. E. Baumgarten, led forty Gypsies into a wood and shot them down.[115] Finally, late that year preparations were made for the extermination of the remaining Austrian Gypsies. Anton Schneeberger was set up as representative of the Austrian Sinti, though at no time apparently was any list made of selected members of his tribe.[116] The order to send the Austrian Gypsies to Auschwitz came in spring 1943 and some 2,600 were moved there, including Sinti from Vienna.[117]

In February 1945 the Ministry of Justice sent a letter to the prison at Linz ordering that all Gypsies were to be shot when prisons near the front line were evacuated.[118] The ultimate aim was the death of all Austrian Gypsies. Less than half survived. The more fortunate were those sent at an early stage to Lackenbach. Some communities were almost wiped out. Of the 275 Gypsies in Stegersbach, for example, only twenty-three survived.[119]

The Gypsies in other territories annexed to Greater Germany suffered similar fates. When Eupen, Malmedy and Moresner were joined to the Reich, Gypsies were specifically excluded from citizenship. The 1942 (2nd) Law on Citizenship in the new Eastern Territories made Gypsies there stateless.[120] As for East Prussia, in July 1941 the Security Central Office ordered that the existing settlement in Continerweg, Königsberg, be turned into a guarded camp.[121] Some 200 Gypsies, headed by a man called Dombrowski, lived there under the surveillance of the police but although it was surrounded by a wire fence they could at first come and go as they pleased.

Gypsies from the town of Tilsit were supposed to be sent to Lithuania in December 1941, unloaded there, and left to fend for themselves. But the authorities in Tilsit refused to do this. Instead, all of them – some 120 including children – were taken to Bialystok prison. In February of the following year orders came from Königsberg for the Gypsies living in the country around Tilsit to be sent to the camp in the Continerweg.[122] Edwig Klein was among those taken to Bialystok, on February 11th, 1942, and nine months later he was transferred to Brest–Litovsk camp. Marie Dombrowski also arrived in Brest–Litovsk from Bialystok in late 1942. The centre consisted of an ex-Russian prisoner-of-war camp surrounded by barbed wire and the gate was locked at night. The men and some of the women worked in a concrete factory or on the railway but received no payment. In February 1943 the Jews in Brest–Litovsk were liquidated and the Gypsies put in their houses in the ghetto with a man, also called Dombrowski, as head. No one was allowed to leave the ghetto and at least one person, Hermann Klein, was shot for this offence.[123]

The order to send East Prussian Gypsies to Auschwitz was made as early as July 6th, 1942. A few were sent[124] but not until April

1944 was the first large transport of some 850 male and female Gypsies dispatched. Gypsies from East Prussia were among those in the Todt labour camp at Valogne near Cherbourg in April 1944. Some were aged over sixty, all had been sterilized and they were put to work removing unexploded bombs.[125]

CHAPTER SIX

WESTERN EUROPE UNDER THE NAZIS

Nazi policy in the occupied territories was to intern the Gypsies in holding camps and from there to transport them into Germany and Poland for use as slave labour or for extermination. Bulgaria, Denmark, Finland and Greece were the only countries where the Gypsies escaped this treatment. In Norway there were no Gypsies[1] and the nomadic families there, as in Denmark, were treated as 'asocials'.[2] One group seems to have avoided harassment by painting swastikas on their caravans.[3]

A few Gypsies in Holland managed to merge into the local Dutch travelling population known as 'reisigers'. Gypsies registered by the Dutch police[4] were picked up during a special sweep, imprisoned at Westerbork and later transferred to Auschwitz.[5]

The Nazi-controlled press began a campaign of propaganda against Gypsies in June 1942. *Nord Brabantsche Courant* reported a 'plague' of Gypsies in the provinces of Brabant and Limburg. It was said that the nuisance they caused had increased enormously and that a central caravan camp should be established under police supervision.[6] In the event, this turned out to be the camp at Westerbork used also as a Jewish transit centre. On March 29th, 1943, Himmler ordered the deportation of Dutch Gypsies to Auschwitz. We know that one transport holding 246 persons arrived there on May 21st of the following year. This reduced the surviving Gypsies in Holland to a handful.[7] Some were probably sent to the camp for 'asocials' at Ommen and from there to work-camps and factories in Germany. Of the nomadic groups who did escape the net, the Baba Tshurkeshti obtained Guetemalan passports made available earlier for Jewish refugees.[8]

Gypsies in Luxembourg are known to have been affected by this Auschwitz order. Although no contemporary records survived, their presence in the camp was mentioned at the Eichmann trial.[9] The number involved in Belgium was small. Some were arrested on the road and sent to prepared camps.[10] Eleven men went to Auschwitz in November 1943.[11] Others remained in poor conditions at Malines while the authorities assembled a larger transport.[12] When this left in January 1944 it consisted of 351 Gypsies of mixed citizenship. Most had been nomadic and these included members of a group refused admission to Denmark in 1934.[13] The entry ban proved to be their death warrant. An extract from the list of this transport shows the range of birthplaces:

Charles and Waldemar Modis	Born Norway
Line Russalino	Stockholm
Jean Tchereanen	Oslo
P. Taicon	Barcelona
A. Reinhardt	Lüdebach, Switzerland
A. Grünholz	Harlem, Holland

Marie Maitre was one of the few survivors. Born in 1901 at Dixmuiden, Belgium, she had at the beginning of the war been in France and interned first at Linas-Monthléry (Seine et Loire) and then at Montreuil-Bellay. Later, classified as a Belgian, she was transferred to Malines. After Auschwitz she went to Ravensbrück and Buchenwald and was repatriated in May 1945. Only eight other Gypsies of those sent to Auschwitz from Belgium lived.[14] The French government brought in severe restrictions against the Gypsy community months before the German occupation. The authorities denied Gypsies the right to travel and placed them under police surveillance. Instructions to this effect, circulated to regional authorities on April 6th, 1940, were published in the *Journal Officiel* three days later. They contained the following passage:

> "It is necessary to forbid the movement of nomads and compel them to remain in one place under the supervision of town and rural police."

French rural police received a directive to stop Gypsies on the road and order them to move with their caravans into designated camps. The task was made easier by the fact that since 1912 travelling Gypsies had been required to carry special identity cards marked *nomade* and were obliged by law to report to the police in each district. Once in the controlled camps, Gypsies found themselves placed in compulsory employment. Anyone trying to go away was liable to arrest and those still travelling sought after and detained.

Confusion ensued when the German *blitzkrieg* started and French Alsace and Lorraine were taken. The German administration in Alsace, through several circulars, ordered the registration of Gypsies for the purpose of later deportation[15] and to check that none returned to the province. This was part of racial purification plans in preparation for their incorporation of the two provinces into the Reich. One such circular, headed *Cleansing Alsace of Gypsies*, stated:

> "It is intended to expel the Gypsies. They are to be put in a security camp at Schirmeck. During the operation Gypsies are to be kept separate from asocials and criminals. Non-Gypsy nomads are to be classed as Gypsies."[16]

According to official correspondence, removal of the remaining Gypsies took place before Christmas.[17] We know that in December 1940 the Germans sent a group of 146 'asocial' men and 403 women and children to another part of France. Three weeks afterwards a list of evacuated Gypsies was sent to headquarters.[18] However, this does not end the story. A year later another letter complains the lists are not complete and that the Gypsies are proving a great burden to the community.[19] As for Lorraine the Criminal Police Headquarters decided in 1942 that they would not accept Gypsies from the area into Germany itself.[20] Orders were that Gypsy *bands* were to be broken up, fortune-tellers arrested and those without work treated as asocials.

These measures caused many to move farther into France, only to be caught in the round-ups taking place in the rest of the country. In the early days some Gypsies were even killed by French soldiers as frightened families tried to avoid the rapidly moving columns of both sides.[21]

After the capitulation when France was cut by a demarcation line between the German administered north and the collaborating

Vichy zone under Marshal Petain, the number of internment camps grew. They soon held 30,000 Gypsy internees. Supervision rested with the Ministry for Jewish Questions headed by Xavier Vallat, while French police and military continued arrests and guarded the camps in both zones.

For a lengthy time the Germans and the French collaborators exploited Gypsies for labour. Later, a great proportion were deported to Germany and eventually to the death-camps, notably Buchenwald, Dachau and Ravensbrück. Between 16,000 and 18,000 subsequently died. Official circles in France are still reticent about the subject because of French involvement. The fact that some twenty large camps and numerous smaller ones were under direct French administration has been cloaked as far as possible and often denied.

The camps provided workers for farmers and industrial enterprises. Some centres had their own workshops for manufacturing and repairing various articles. They were not extermination camps but poor food and bad accommodation caused the mortality rate to soar, particularly among children. Conditions deteriorated as the war became prolonged.

The bigger camps stood at Montreuil-Bellay, Angoulême, Rennes, Poitiers and Compiègne. The compound at Montreuil held 800 Gypsies when first occupied in November 1941. A medical examination by the deputy prefect of Saumur during the early days showed adults and children in poor physical condition. His report says:

> "The children below the age of three are very thin, the pregnant women very anaemic . . . There is little wood available for heating."

Over the following nine months sixty-seven people died, due mainly to malnutrition.

The month after the camp opened, the prefect of Finistère received instructions to send there all nomads of 'Romani type'. One party of 212 he dispatched arrived without any luggage or even winter clothes. The German army field commander at Tours also ordered his soldiers to arrest all 'nomads' and travelling Gypsies. Internees arrived at Montreuil from other smaller camps, including nearly 300 from La Morellerie. Another large group came under escort from Mulsanne. With this influx and a transport from Coudrecieux, the camp population rose to 1,026 in April 1942. Gypsies from Barenton were likewise transferred to Montreuil in October but by December of the next year the number there had been reduced to 400.

Despite the armed guard at Montreuil, on the night of December 11th, 1942, five men escaped. From then on visitors were prohibited, roll-calls held twice a day, money confiscated and patrols strengthened. Already Montreuil had been referred to in an official document as a concentration camp. One-way transportation to forced labour and extermination camps in Germany and Poland began to take its toll. A few fortunate inmates, on condition that they remained at fixed places of work under police surveillance, were permitted to live away from the camp at a distance of twenty kilometres or more from the centre of the town.[22]

During allied air-raids in 1944 bombs fell several times on Montreuil, damaging buildings. On New Year's Day the following year the camp was broken up. The remaining inmates were sent to Jargean and Pithiviers and some, with homes to go to, actually released.

The Poitiers camp set up about the same period as Montreuil stood a few miles from the town on the Limoges road. The barracks there had previously housed refugees from the Spanish civil war. A double barbed-wire fence and four watch-towers with searchlights hemmed in the Gypsy occupants, cordoned off from the Jews who remained in another compound. Under French administration some visitors were permitted. One who came regularly for a period from February 1942 onwards was Madame L'Huillier. Concerned selflessly with the families' plight she eventually received permission to give lessons to the children. On occasion she was even allowed to take them for walks outside the wire perimeter. She recalls there would have been serious trouble had any tried to escape while enjoying this privilege. Later a small building was erected for the classes. A Catholic priest, Father Fleury, conducted a service there in May that year and noted the guards seldom ventured inside the prisoners' huts for fear of being infected by typhoid.

Up to 600 Gypsies of those earlier expelled from Strasbourg and the rest of Alsace-Lorraine were confined to a camp at Jargean, near Orleans.[23] Another big establishment at Rennes held French-born *Manouche* Gypsies. For example eight members of the Caseasch family taken there in November 1941 remained in captivity until the liberation of France; Henri Caseasch, his wife and her sister, Rose Debarre, three sons and two daughters, the youngest a babe in arms when interned.

Gypsies collected together from smaller camps at Coudrecieux, Moison-la-Rivière and Monthléry were gathered into the centre at Mulsanne – a former British Army camp – and numbered 700 soon after the opening in April 1942. The daily vegetable ration at Mulsanne amounted to 400 grams of potatoes or 500 grams of other vegetables, sometimes replaced by 100 grams of dry vegetables. The meat ration hardly averaged 126 grams per week. The prisoners lived in their family groups and a 100 men worked in the Renault motor factory at Le Mans. Taken to work by lorry a few managed to escape, helped by the fact that the guards were not always fully armed.

At La Foucadière camp a quarter of the prisoners comprised Gypsies of foreign nationality. As at Montreuil, a very limited number of Gypsies at Barenton camp secured conditional release on being assigned to particular work with local employers. They remained in barrack-type accommodation under control of the police, who in general mildly opposed the system. Paul Weiss was among those imprisoned at St. Jean Picd de Port for leaving his allotted place of work under this kind of scheme.

The camp at La Pierre (Coudrecieux) – at one time holding 300 nomadic Gypsies – had once been a glassworks. Others were located at La Morellerie in east central France, Montsûrs, Arc et Senans (Besançon), Avrille-les-Ponceaux (Indre et Loire), Moison-La-Rivière and Linas-Monthléry (Seine et Loire).

Three special camps existed for Gypsy children, found at Pithiviers and Saint Fargeau, and within the larger compound at Jargean, Orleans. The camp at Noë is known to have contained eleven children at one time, ten of whom were successfully smuggled across the border into Switzerland.[24] German Campos and her family were among thousands simply stopped on the highway and taken from roadside camps to be interned. She recalls their arrest on March 17th, 1941:

> "My father was a naturalized French citizen, having reared a family of thirteen children in France. We were staying at Meysse, Ardèche, when the police from Rochemaure came and arrested us. Even now I don't know why they wanted to take us. The next day they put us in a camp at Rivesaltes, then moved us to Vaccarès and from there to yet a third at Saliers. We were not let out until September 24, 1944."

Jose Santiago, arrested and placed in a forced labour squad in the old fort at Romainville, escaped and went to Amiens. Caught again by the French police he was asked why he was not doing compulsory work. He gave a story which somehow persuaded them to release him and made his way to the Vichy zone, remaining there undetected.

Another family caught by German soldiers – probably a detachment of the *Das Reich* division – were massacred at the roadside in the department of Lot-et-Garonne during 1944. Paul Wanderstein, then aged twelve, survived to recount what happened:

> "It was early morning about dawn at the entrance to the village of Saint Sixte when the soldiers found us. They took fourteen of us into a field to be shot. My mother, two sisters – the younger four years old, the elder Anne, aged nine – my grandmother, an uncle and cousins were among those lined up. Two of them and one of my girl cousins lay only wounded but appeared dead. Three others escaped by running into the village and hiding in the school loft. I don't remember exactly what happened but I was concealed somehow in the village and saved."

Surprisingly, the troubled times failed to prevent in 1942 the great Gypsy festival at Les Saintes Maries in the Camargue, held each year towards the end of May. Though attended by Gypsies from Spain, it was a subdued gathering that year overshadowed by menaces. The remoteness of the region, set with reed-filled lagoons, and the influence of the Italian-occupied neighbouring area militated against a ban – or worse still a round-up. In the following year the festival was suppressed by the Vichy authorities.

Those who realized in time what fascist government would bring had a slender chance to get out of France. Gypsies in the south with relations in Spain and North Africa could slip over the border into Spanish territory. But although the Falangist regime paid little attention to them once in Spain, the way over the Pyrenees was restricted. From northern France a handful reached England.

Without warning everything changed for the worse in 1943. Men and youths were singled out to join the thousands doing forced labour in Germany, others went to the death-camps. During January seventy men were sent from Poitiers to Compiègne and then to German camps.[25] Events elsewhere followed a similar pattern. Michael Weiss, then aged thirteen, was taken from Compiègne to Block 31 in the main camp at Buchenwald while two adults from his family found themselves in Dora camp.

One man, Louis Simon, born at Perigueux, met a particularly bizarre death. It was noticed that his body was richly tattooed – a souvenir from service in the Foreign Legion. First he was given injections which caused him to swell horribly. The next day his dead body was carried to Buchenwald and the skin used as a decoration for a shelf.[26]

Some who stayed free joined the resistance. Jean Beaumarie helped the *Maquis* and his brother was caught and hanged. Armand Stenegry, today president of the Manouche Gypsy Association and well known as a singer and guitarist under the name Archange, became a guerrilla officer. Stenegry and other Gypsies in his unit assisted in partisan attacks planned to coincide with the Normandy landings. His distinguished services earned him decoration both by the British and the Free French.

Finally we must add that in Algeria, then part of metropolitan France, Gypsies did not escape persecution. Although wealthier people passed as Spanish and escaped attention, poorer Gypsies were pushed together into a ghetto at Maison-Carrée near Algiers. The quarter held about 700 and some died there. Others were rounded up at Oran and Mostaganem.

Under Mussolini Italy passed racial laws against Jews on almost exactly the same lines as legislation enacted in Germany. Large-scale round-ups of Gypsies took place some time before the war. Family groups, concentrated first in staging camps, were transported to the islands surrounding Italy.[27] Many of the camps were former barracks or monasteries and most held men or women isolated from each other, though some family camps existed. The treatment by the police and soldiers was rough but not often brutal.[28]

From one of these centres a steamer brought a large party to forced exile in Sardinia. They were landed on the island and turned loose from the quayside without any provision being made for their maintenance. No camp was erected for their stay nor any guards set to watch over them. They were simply left to disperse inland and fend for themselves. Among the poorer villages of Sardinia the Gypsies received little help and few could follow their trades – smithing and horse-dealing – as a means of subsistence.[29]

We know of another group left stranded on one of the smaller islands under Italian control in the Adriatic. They suffered many hardships in exile but survived the war.[30]

Conscription of men and youths into the Italian armed forces must be regarded as a second measure against Gypsies. After conscription many were dispatched to Italian-occupied Albania and forbidden to return. Wives and children, and friends and relations, followed them. Thus the Fascists rid themselves of Gypsies from the mainland at no further expense or trouble.

Gypsies from Yugoslavia, and more particularly from Slovenia and Croatia, who moved across the border into the zones of Gorizia and Udine before 1940 initially underwent internment in Abruzzi and then deportation to Sardinia. Others were detained in the camp at Puglia but many escaped the police nets and lived in the 'macchia'. Some later joining the partisans.[31]

Much harder was the lot of Gypsy groups living in the zone of the Three Venices when the province came under German military control after the Italian capitulation on September 8th, 1943. They were rounded up as in other German-occupied lands to do forced labour in Germany or sent directly to the death-camps. A proportion never survived the long cruel journey, packed into closed cattle trucks.[32]

Others (Istriani and Gadjekani Sinti) who crossed from Yugoslavia to escape the massacres carried out by the Ustashi in the fascist Croat State[33] were sheltered by the Italian authorities. Detention in camps was partly for their own safety because they wanted to return to Yugoslavia to seek relatives and were in danger of falling into the hands of the Ustashi and Germans.

Zilka Heldt has recounted the fate of these Gypsies who habitually moved in the areas of northern Italy, southern Austria and the northern provinces of Yugoslavia. Travelling mostly on foot with belongings on pack animals, they tried to keep ahead of the German forces which invaded Yugoslavia on April 6th, 1941. But many families were overtaken and some transported to camps in Austria. Zilka, only ten years old at the time, succeeded with her family in reaching Ljubljana from Maribor without being caught. After narrow escapes, during which others of the family were seized and never seen again, the remainder fled across the Julian Alps.

Once in Italy they stayed for some time at Talmina where the Italian authorities issued them with Italian identity cards. Other Gypsies arrived and as time went on many of them had their births registered in the town. The Italians could then furnish all members of the family with the Italian identity cards, placing the holders beyond the reach of the Germans.

Despite warnings, Zilka Heldt's father returned to Yugoslavia to assist other Gypsies to reach Italy. He was captured and placed in a transit camp situated in a disused factory in Ljubljana. During the night he succeeded in escaping by removing tiles from the roof. On another occasion, members of the family were caught on a return journey and were only saved by their Italian papers. After questioning, a German officer placed them on a horse and cart and, with a single German guard as escort, sent the party back to Talmina. The Italian authorities took charge of them at a canal near the frontier. This time they were housed in an old people's home. The police commissioner said it was only by his insistence they had been released and brought back. Such was their concern for relatives, however, that when the situation appeared to have eased, members of the family continued to re-cross into Yugoslavia. They found many Gypsies were still being caught in Croatia and sent away. Finally the Italian police com-missioner became exasperated by their movements which involved him in wrangles with the Germans and interned the family for their own protection.

They were sent to Campo Basso. The building was an old monastery. They remained in their family group and life in this camp was easy, according to Zilka Heldt. The internees were allowed out each day to earn a living and shop in the town. The Italian authorities fed them and looked after their needs humanely.

The situation began later to change and deteriorate. The allies invaded Italy and the camp was bombed. During one air-raid both Zilka's parents died. The Germans came and turned the monastery into a military hospital, paying no attention to the Gypsies at this stage. The families scattered at will in the country-side and some got gifts of food from German soldiers.

When the German units began to retreat north, Zilka Heldt with a band of other children moved in the same direction. They feared the Allies because of the bombing raids. Besides they knew German and could communicate with the soldiers who did not molest them, though adults were still being sent to forced labour battalions to dig defences.

On arrival near Udine the children met up with others. Life became more hazardous as together they tried to survive between the rapidly changing lines. Night and day shots came in their direction and several died. At Forti Popali they encamped near a German command post and for a short time were taken prisoner. Released again, the little band set out on the open road to Redi-puglia. Several times when threatened with capture, Italian people insisted they were not Gypsies but Italian refugee children and the Germans chose to believe this. Towards the close of the war in Italy, numbers of Gypsies liberated from the camps in Croatia moved into east Italy, some hiding, others joining the partisans. On one occasion the children narrowly escaped execution. The party were taken by the Germans, the Italian papers they had confiscated and on a casual order the children lined up against a wall to be shot. The village turned out and begged the Germans to spare them. As the Allies were already near, the infantrymen gave way and freed Zilka Heldt and the others.

Not long afterwards, still pursuing their way northwards, the children were stopped by American soldiers. When one of them, a boy aged eight, tried to run away he was shot by an American soldier and died at the side of the road. It was a desolate world for these Gypsy children, with nowhere to go and nobody who cared. No one had come to liberate *them*.

Yet among the Gypsies were those who had sacrificed their lives for the allied cause such as the partisan hero of Vicenza, Walter Catter.[34]

Serving with the advancing British forces was a Gypsy from England, Fred Wood. He has recalled how, while his unit was holding a pass in central Italy, awaiting armour before moving forward again, a large party of Gypsies came towards them from no-man's-land. Moving on foot, some leading donkeys and small ponies, the group was well-armed. They were a partisan band who, accompanied by their women and children, had fought their way a considerable distance over the mountains, engaging the enemy on a hit and run basis.

The decade immediately before the war witnessed in Yugoslavia an upsurge of activity within the largely sedentary Gypsy community which numbered several hundred thousand. But events overtook them. The Yugoslav treaty with the Axis came as a deadly blow, the first serious indication that the fate already befallen the Gypsies in Germany was likely to be visited on them. The palace coup by the young King Peter against the Regent Prince Paul, which followed the realization that the treaty with Germany would involve Yugoslavia in the attack on Greece, brought only a momentary reprieve.

A merciless bombing of Belgrade, which hit the Gypsy quarter in Zemun, preceded the invasion of Yugoslavia on April 6th, 1941, and the blitzkrieg to southern Greece. Thereafter the young state was torn to pieces between the invaders – Germans, Italians,

Hungarians and Bulgarians – the collaborators in Croatia and their opponents, the Partisans.

In all areas unco-ordinated guerrilla bands came into being to attack the occupation forces and their allies, or simply to survive in the mountains while protecting families fleeing from the towns and villages. The murder and wholesale extermination of Gypsies in Croatia and Serbia caused an increasing number of Gypsies to join the National Liberation Front which emerged as the only effective fighting organization. Because of Gypsy participation in the war effort, serious consideration was given within the NLF to the creation of an autonomous Gypsy region in Macedonia as part of the planned new Yugoslavia federation.[35]

The story of the Gypsies in Yugoslavia during the war must of necessity be broken down into its several parts.

Few Gypsies survived the *terror* in northern Yugoslavia. The Catholic-supported Croat separatist movement which took power four days after German units crossed the frontier inaugurated a bloodbath. The victims died in what was popularly termed a 'holy' war' against non-Catholic minorities – Serbs, Gypsies and Jews.

Notices went up everywhere in public places, in offices, shops and cafés, proclaiming: "No Serbs, Jews, Nomads and dogs allowed."[36]

The fascist militia, known as the Ustashi, formed the strong arm of the administration. Gypsies became their prey for two reasons, racial and religious. Many of those in Croatia, numbering 28,000,[37] professed the Orthodox faith and many in adjoining Bosnia-Hercegovina were nominally Moslem.

From an account given by Zilka Heldt we know of the panic and desperation which seized families as they sought to escape capture and death. Those in Slovenia found within days that the once peaceful province had been split between Italy, Germany and the new Croat State. The region was criss-crossed by different civilian and military authorities, each imposing its own controls.

Zilka's aunt Helenka, caught in the street, was pushed into the back of a truck along with her children, and never again seen by her relatives. The round-ups went on everywhere and they moved cautiously from one village to another:

> "We kept to the woods as much as possible but had to go to houses for food sometimes. Some Sinti (Gypsies) were sheltered by peasants they knew or who took pity on us."

Of those who headed for the frontiers, a few reached the comparative safety of Italy and others ended in the concentration camp at Zemun, outside Belgrade. Though given shelter by the Italian local authorities, Zilka Heldt's parents twice went back into Yugoslavia to seek relatives. But most had already perished or were in hiding in the remoter mountains of Bosnia and Serbia from where the men eventually joined the partisans.

The stories that reached them in Italy told of murder and unbearable tortures. Ustashi militiamen pulled children to pieces and beat them to death against trees. Griblo Heldt has recounted how his parents, after being tied to a mountain cable used for conveying hay, were fired at for target practice as they slipped through the air.

Another atrocity has been described by Angela Hudorović[38] concerning the death of her sister and niece:

> "First the girl was forced to dig a ditch, while her mother, seven months pregnant, was left tied to a tree. With a knife they opened the belly of the mother, took out the baby and threw it in the ditch. Then they threw in the mother and the girl, after raping her. They covered them with earth while they were still alive."

One family group, the Wittes, fled *into* Croatia in a bid to get away from Germany. Thirty-four members, many of them children, crossed over only to be taken by the Ustashi. After brutal mistreatment they were locked in a barn and burned alive, the incident being recorded by a priest at the near-by village of Marija Sorica.[39]

The internment camps established included a large one at Ljubljana from where captives were later transferred to another compound at Sarajevo, capital of Bosnia.

The worst, at Jasenovac, held at one period 24,000 children

taken from Serbian, Jewish and probably Gypsy parents. Half died before the International Red Cross intervened. Hundreds more succumbed after release because caustic soda had been added to the bread ration.

Gypsies throughout Croatia faced death not only at the hands of the local Ustashi but, if they survived, transportation to forced-labour in Germany and eventually the death-camps in Poland.

Those placed in closed wagons for transport to destinations outside Yugoslavia sometimes never moved from the sidings. They remained bolted in to die of starvation amidst their own excrement. One lot endured three weeks in a stationary freight train without any food and water being supplied by the guards. Fortunately some sustenance reached them from villagers and a few survived. Children were preferred for this treatment because they died of thirst more quickly and could be handled easily.

While wandering unattached in the mountains, Gypsies inevitably came into contact with guerrilla groups, and sometimes fell under the suspicion of cautious partisans. At times they could approach occupation soldiers and during one lull Chuka Heldt complained to a German command post that partisans had stolen his horses. As a result partisans, and near-by villages, came under punitive attack and many people died.

In revenge, guerrillas shot a Gypsy mother and father with their eight children. A boy named Mario fell at the first volley and feigned death, later crawling to a river and swimming away. The same night he returned to the scene to find children moaning as they died slowly of their wounds. Mario himself was shot, probably by Ustashi, and the tale of the event relayed by another child who survived capture by the Germans.

A mimeographed document from partisan sources tells of another incident in which the lives of Gypsies were taken:[40]

PUBLIC ANNOUNCEMENT

In compliance with the Liberation Front's proclamation of May 28, 1942, concerning action by anti-LF White Guard enemies of the Slovenian people, the individuals listed below were sentenced to death and shot:

Polde, Stane and Natsé Brajdich, Gypsies

The frequent Ustashi murder orgies even appalled the German and Italian military authorities. On occasion they protested, intervened and sometimes took over temporary control from the Croat fascists.

Five weeks after the occupation of Serbia and the creation of a puppet regime, the military administration issued decrees concerning the 150,000 Gypsies.[41] They were compelled to register and wear yellow armbands inscribed *Zigeuner*. Trams and buses bore placards saying: 'No Jews and Gypsies allowed', but as the administration covered only a part of Serbia proper, probably no more than 40,000 came under its effective control.

German army commander General Bohme sent out orders on May 30th, 1941, which included the following text:[42]

Section 18 Gypsies are to be treated as Jews.
Section 19 A Gypsy is a person who has at least three Gypsy grandparents. Gypsy mixed-bloods who have one or two Gypsy grandparents and who are married to Gypsy women are to be classed as Gypsies.
Section 20 Gypsies are to be put on a special register.

Men became liable to forced labour and mass arrests began. Milan Milanović[43] saw his father and two uncles taken from their homes in the village of Jabuce near Belgrade:

"He had only time to say goodbye to our mother and us three children and then he was put into one of the lorries waiting in the street. We never saw them again."

The arrest of 250 others elsewhere in the area has been noted. At one village in the Banat, ninety kilometres from the capital, the Germans appointed a Gypsy named Branko to recruit workers. Between twenty and a hundred were required on different occasions. The men hesitated to leave the district because they feared the Germans would believe they had gone to join the partisans and kill their families.

The work involved digging graves for Jewish victims whom the Gypsies were permitted to strip and dispose of their clothes. They received small payment but no ration cards. The yellow armbands had to be worn and they understood that Gypsies would die in due course. One of the men, Dushano, recalls:[44]

"After a month or two, they said, 'Now the partisans and the communists and the Jews are being killed, then it will be your turn.' The police told us this openly. 'It isn't time yet,' they said, 'Hitler hasn't yet fixed the day when you'll have to be killed.' The Germans took Gypsy women to work in the barracks and they violated young girls. One day other prisoners were sent out to dig graves and we thought they were for us, so I ran away."

He crossed the frontier into Romania, was arrested on returning to Yugoslavia and sentenced to death but found himself instead working in Austria.

A district court judge, Jovan Jovanović, has described his position at this period:[45]

"During the occupation, I had to tell everyone, even persons I knew well, that I wasn't a Gypsy and had no connections with Gypsies. If I hadn't lied I would have had to carry the outcast's label on my arm and who knows if I'd still be alive.

Despite the orders, one day on leaving my judge's office I entered a restaurant. Instead of the waiter, the manager came in person to tell me in rough terms to get out because I was a Gypsy. I calmly showed him my papers . . . Seeing I was a judge he excused himself saying that he'd made a mistake because of the colour of my skin."

An ambush by partisans near Topola provided a pretext for killing Jews and Gypsies already held. The German army commander ordered a hundred prisoners to be executed in reprisal for each soldier killed in the action. From then on hostage shooting and extermination of unwanted racial minorities became one and the same. This police covered the murder of 2,100 inmates of the camps set up in Belgrade and Sabac,[46] and many more followed. The firing squads were composed not of the special Einsatzgruppen used in Poland and Russia but of regular German army units. A hundred Gypsies were taken from the concentration camp at Crveni Krst, near Niš, and shot on Mount Bubanj.[47]

A circular sent out to district headquarters stated:[48]

"... Gypsies represent in general an element of insecurity and thus a danger to public order and safety ... The Gypsy because of his internal and external make-up cannot be a useful member of the community ... It has been found that ... Gypsies in particular are responsible for special atrocities. That is why it is a matter of principle to put ... all male Gypsies at the disposal of the units as hostages."

About the shootings a junior officer reported:[49]

"One has to admit that the Jews are very composed when they go to their deaths – they stand still – while the Gypsies cry, scream and move constantly, even when they are already on the spot where they are to be shot. Some even jumped into the ditch before the firing and pretended to be dead."

He also noted the effect upon the *Wehrmacht* soldiers. At first they appeared unaffected but on the second day it became obvious that one or two did not have the nerve to carry out shootings over a lengthy period. His impression was that while no psychological block impeded action during the operation this set in when a soldier thought about it in the evenings.

Regular troops mobilized for a punitive expedition shot down 250 Gypsies caught on the road and burned their wagons. At Kragujevac soldiers rounded up 200 who happened to have come into the town and machine-gunned the men and boys on a local shooting range alongside 7,000 Serbians in reprisal for ten dead and twenty-six wounded Germans.[50]

Because of the practice of selecting men, the occupying authorities found themselves with numerous bereaved women and children under their charge. The answer was to concentrate them at Zemun, where the internment camp stood on ground forming part of the old Gypsy quarter. The original cottages had been condemned as a source of infection and razed. Within the new compound stood eight long barrack huts, several hundred people filling each. Among them sick and dying lay on filthy straw.[51] Although the camp was established by the German military, jurisdiction of Zemun passed to the Croat regime and the Ustashi guarded the camp under German Security Police command.[52]

To a German officer inspecting Zemun an Ustashi militiaman is said to have explained:[53]

"We are more practical than you Germans. You shoot but we use hammers, clubs, rope, fire and quicklime. It's less expensive."

The decision to move Gypsies into Zemun from other parts of the small Serbian puppet state rested largely with Franz Rademacher, then a Gestapo officer attached to the German Embassy in Belgrade. It was his name that went on the bottom of the report proposing the transfer of women and children there.[54]

Olga Milanović was one of those who suffered in consequence:

"I was only five years old when our family was arrested in Belgrade and taken to the camp at Zemun. My father died later, I believe in Germany.

"After our arrest I was in the camp for three months. They gave us rotten potatoes and water soup. The ration was one hundred grams a day."[55]

A plan was mooted to transfer the camp to an island on the Danube until someone discovered it was flooded at high water level. Instead the camp commander received a consignment of specially constructed mobile gassing vans. Loaded regularly with women and children these were driven to human dumping grounds in the woods. The possessions passed to the German Welfare Agency which transferred them to the Reich for distribution among the German civilian population.

Amidst the concentration and murder of Gypsies in Serbia, the Vatican made a somewhat furtive attempt to raise the question of civilian hostages with the German Foreign Office. An official account runs:[56]

"The Nuncio today groped around the well-known subject of hostages, in order to determine whether a discussion between him and me about the question of shooting hostages – of late in Serbia – would be fruitful. I replied that . . . the Vatican had conducted itself most cleverly, in that it took the hint I had carefully extended to Papal Counsellor Colli upon a social occasion. If the Vatican should nevertheless feel constrained to return to the subject, I would be obliged to give the Nuncio the same answer that Mexico, Haiti, etc., had received already. The Nuncio saw this point completely, and pointed out that he had not really touched on this topic and that he had no desire to touch it."

Repeated orders went to army and police units for action against Gypsies, with reminders that they assisted the partisans both as couriers and combatants. The number held at Zemun and other centres fluctuated as extermination – speeded up by the gassing process – went on unchecked. From a maximum of 16,000 people, including Gypsies and Jews, figures at the Belgrade camp began a rapid decline. Finally the head of the civil administration reported:[57]

"In the interests of pacification, the Gypsy question has been fully liquidated. Serbia is the only country in which the Jewish question and the Gypsy question have been solved."

The gassing vans were returned to Berlin. There was no longer anyone to gas. We estimate that between 10,000 and 20,000 Serbian Gypsies had perished. The remainder survived the war in areas weakly controlled by quisling and German garrisons, which became later the liberated free zones. Many joined the partisans.

The horrors in Croatia, the death-camp at Zemun, these have held our attention most of this section. More needs to be said about events in other, remoter parts of Yugoslavia. In the mountain fastness of Montenegro a large Gypsy group defended their lives against Italian soldiers for many months. They fought protracted skirmishes without support from partisans or Četniks, and succumbed only when an entire battalion was sent against them.[58]

The whole of Macedonia, both Greek and Yugoslav, with the exception of the port of Salonika, came under Bulgarian occupation. Fortunately for the Gypsy population, the Bulgarians – with an enormous Gypsy community in their own country – felt disinclined to take severe measures whatever Germany wished. The dispatch of Jews from Salonika sounded a warning, however. As time wore on, German security police became active in the region and some Gypsies fell into the net.

Several factors hindered the rooting out and enabled Gypsies, despite their great numbers, to avoid detection. Many owned land or worked as farm labourers and most nominally followed the Moslem religion. To ignorant SS and Gestapo men, they were indistinguishable from neighbouring Turks and Albanians of the same occupation and faith.

The situation remained as confusing in the towns. When a population census took place most Gypsies entered themselves under another minority. Not wanting to court trouble with Turks and Albanians, the police allowed false declarations to pass unchallenged. If identity was obvious they closed in. A circus family, who had been performing in Turkey and Bulgaria, came to Skoplje in 1943 and were arrested. Taken first to Crveni Krst, near Niš, then to Zemun, the family ended later in Auschwitz.[59] Others, betrayed by people helping the occupation authorities, had to wear yellow armbands as in Serbia.

Events in Kosovo-Metohija, bordering on Albania and garrisoned by pro-Axis Albanians under Italian command, have been recounted by Raif Maljoku:[60]

"Albanian fascists, known as the Balisti, occupied Kosovo-Metohija and there were some SS troops there. Local Albanians also joined them. Gypsies who had been given arm-bands remained free for a time but when Yugoslav-born Albanians joined the fascist forces Gypsies had to take their places and were forced to work for the families of these collaborationists, both in Kosovo and Albania.

Even some young Gypsies were conscripted, as their identity was not known. Several deserted and were shot. After the capitulation of the Italians, the partisans succeeded in liberating the territory and many Gypsies then joined the Liberation Front."

An outline of events affecting the community in the town of Kosovska Mitrovica is given by Kuna Cevcet:[61]

"At this time there were three or four hundred Gypsy households in the town and we made up about a tenth of the population of Mitrovica. Those above the age of fifteen who had been identified had to wear a yellow arm-band about four inches wide with the word *Zigeuner* on it. We were not permitted to wear moustaches, which were very common. It seems the fascists didn't want to see us wearing them.

On May 6th, 1942, we gathered to celebrate a festival, and began killing sheep for the feast. But at half-past four in the morning SS troops, accompanied by Albanian police came into the town and took away all the slaughtered sheep in lorries for their own use.

Ljatif Sucuri, an uncle of mine who was about 35 at this time, knew the Albanian chief of police, a general. When an order came through for the police to round up Gypsies Ljatif Sucuri told him that if any Gypsies were killed he would personally kill the police chief and the rest of us would burn down the houses of the Albanians. He told the police chief to inform his superiors over the telephone that there were no Gypsies at Mitrovica, and this he did.

At this time there were few Gypsies with the partisans because they feared the fascists would kill their families. But later when the partisans became stronger they joined.

But one of our people at Mitrovica, Hasani Brahim, then aged 36, was in the resistance in 1943. He worked as a mechanic in a garage being run by the military for repairing vehicles and storing petrol. He would get petrol and made petrol bombs for the partisans.

After supplying bombs for a time, the partisans suggested he should blow up the garage and stores. He set to work and using more petrol bombs succeeded in setting fire to the whole garage, destroying many military vehicles and petrol supplies and quantities of other stores. No soldiers were killed but some ammunition supplies also blew up and the reserve tanks exploded during the fire.

Hasani Brahim was arrested and held in prison. He was questioned for a long time but never admitted his guilt. He had been a good worker, a blacksmith as well as a mechanic, and the fascists found it hard to believe that he might have been responsible. There was no proof against him and after a week he was released and continued to work at the depot. A floodlight was kept on the premises and the authorities thought it was impossible to set fire to the place without being seen.

He went on making petrol bombs and later set fire to the military food stores in the town. Then he helped to steal arms and passed them on to the partisans. In 1944 Hasani Brahim went to the mountains with the partisans and remained with them until the end of the war. He received many decorations in recognition for his service and is again living in Mitrovica doing his old job.

Meanwhile, those Gypsies who had been detected and wore armbands were selected to work for the military. They had to build barracks for the army and carry food supplies and munitions for the front.

Ljatif Sucuri went on with his efforts to save his people, using his influence with the Albanian police chief. The day the police chief came with a paper from higher authorities ordering him to kill all Gypsies, Ljatif Sucuri got him to hand over the paper – and then burned it. Again he got him to telephone his superiors and say there were no Gypsies in the town, only Moslems. This was done a short time before the lorries were due to come to Mitrovica to take away Gypsies to be killed. The period was about August or September 1943.

As a result of his intervention, no Gypsies were murdered in Mitrovica itself. But many other people were hanged for helping partisans.

About two or three hundred were selected for forced labour during 1942 and they started off from the town driving animals – cows and sheep – for the soldiers. The soldiers rode on horseback and continually beat the Gypsies to make them move faster. They had to travel hundreds of kilometers across the mountains and into Greece. This work went on for three or four months. Many deserted and made contact with the partisans. Four whom the fascists believed assisted the partisans were arrested when they tried to desert. They were beaten to get information out of them and then hanged in public in a Greek town in front of the other Gypsies and the towns-people. Those hanged were Djemajl Maljoku, Halil Avdija, Ramadan Dibrani and a man called Bajram.

When Ljatif Sucuri heard about their deaths he again went to the police chief, demanding an explanation. This time he succeeded in persuading the chief to have the remaining Gypsies from Mitrovica released, himself going to Greece to see that this was done.

At the end of the war, collaborators trying to cover up their own activities, denounced Ljatif Sucuri and said he had co-operated with the fascists. Neglecting to make proper inquiries as to the truth of the allegations, the partisans took him away in the night and shot him."

When the Germans took over the occupation of Italian-held areas of Yugoslavia and Albania in the autumn of 1943, they had a year to impose their extreme policies against Gypsies. During this period people are known to have been sent to concentration camps in Yugoslavia, and to Buchenwald, Mauthausen and elsewhere.

The number of Albanian-born Gypsies, of whom there were 22,000 before the war, who got caught up in this process is unknown.

CHAPTER SEVEN

EASTERN EUROPE UNDER THE NAZIS

In February 1941 the Hungarian government made plans to intern in work-camps all Gypsies who had no profession.[1] None of the Hungarian Gypsies interviewed by us have mentioned this operation which probably means it was not carried out throughout Hungary. However a family of sedentary Gypsies called Sarkozy said that during the Nazi occupation of Hungary they had been herded into a ghetto and kept there for over three years. One of them, Ferenc, had been condemned to death by the Germans and 'executed' but a Gypsy grave-digger, finding life in the body, had rescued him. All his front teeth had been knocked out.[2] The 'ghetto' most likely refers to one of the labour camps set up for Jews.[3] There is some difficulty in following the story of the Hungarian Gypsies during the war as many of the Austrian Gypsies had been born in Hungary[4] and probably many held Hungarian papers. Thus a transport arriving at Auschwitz[5] on March 16th, 1943, included 'Hungarian' Gypsies, but these had probably been arrested in Austria. No other Hungarian Gypsies are recorded in the Auschwitz documents. A Romani song has been recorded in Hungary[6] which tells of a woman whose husband and son were sent to Auschwitz. The son, Veso, died there.[7]

About 1940 a law was passed expelling from the area annexed from Yugoslavia all Gypsies not resident in Hungary before October 31st, 1918, and their children. Those expelled were allowed to take with them only personal belongings and enough money for the journey.

The newspaper *Eesti Ujsag* proposed the setting up of labour camps for all Gypsies. Another newspaper pointed out that the Hungarian Gypsies cost the country 75,000,000 pengos (22,000,000 dollars) in handling and supervision, as much as the Hungarian Diplomatic Corps annually.

Leading Hungarian personalities expressed their horror at inter-marriage between Gypsies and non-Gypsies producing a stratum of half-castes and in June 1942 the Budapest Chamber of Agriculture proposed the sterilization of all males.

In November 1941 the slogan was launched:

"After the Jews the Gypsies."[8]

In fact however little active persecution of Jews or Gypsies took place as long as Hungary remained independent; although an atmosphere was created which made future persecution easier.

Large-scale persecution of Jews and Gypsies began in 1944 when the Germans occupied Hungary. Although the Germans were in control from March 1944 and began deporting Jews then, the persecution of the Gypsies did not apparently start until October when the Germans had strengthened their hold over the government of Hungary.[9] The Germans and Hungarian fascist soldiers and police rounded up the Gypsies from their settlements. In some cases only the males were taken and in others males and females. It is estimated that 31,000 Gypsies were deported from Hungary within a few months and that only 3,000 of these returned.[10] The deportees included whole tribes of nomadic Gypsies who fled from the advancing front-line right into the hands of the Nazis.[11]

Figures from the Heves region give an idea of the extent of the deportations:

Kerecsend. 22 men out of some 100 were sent to the Concentration Camp at Mezekövesd and about half did not return.

Andornaktalya-Felsö. Most of the 40 families hid in the forests. About 20 persons did not return from Mezekövesd including the daughter of the informant.

Eger (Veroszala st.). Only one man was captured by the Germans and he did not return. The others (40 families) hid in the forest.

Tiszaigar. Many Gypsies taken to Mezekövesd.

From Mezekövesd the Gypsies were deported to Germany or Poland.[12] We can assume there were similar camps to Mezekövesd in other parts of Hungary.

So far we have no records to show where this large number of 31,000 Hungarian Gypsies was sent. The records of Natzweiler (incomplete) show that four Gypsies who died there on January 7th, 1945, had Hungarian Vlax names, Geza Balog, Sandor Bogdan, Ivan Sztojka and Laszlo Raffael. One other, Jozsef Gazsi, was a sedentary Gypsy from Hungary.[13] Joska Nyari of the Budapest settlement (behind Vizmellek st) was taken to Berga-Elster after the Budapest Jews had been deported and died there of illness in the winter of 1944–5.[14] The presence of Hungarian Gypsies in Gross-Rosen has also been recorded,[15] but the fate of the Hungarian Gypsies after their deportation represents one of the gaps in the documentation.

Kallai Janos has told how he escaped:

"In the district of Heves about 700 male Gypsies were collected together in Mezekövesd. They came from the villages of Bogacs, Kal and Andornaktalya-Felsö, as well as from Mezekövesd itself. The males were collected in Laszlo school, and the women and children at another place.

All had to work. Firstly we worked in the fields and then building trenches. We were guarded by Germans and Hungarian 'Pfeilkreuzler' soldiers. Particularly cruel were Sergeant Karoly Toth and Lieutenant Dezso Ujlaki. We stayed about four weeks in the camp during which time about 300 of the Gypsies escaped. In the camp the soldiers took everything away from everybody. They said they would shoot anyone who didn't give up his papers and soldier's book. In spite of that I didn't give up my soldier's book. I had been a soldier in 1941–3 on the Russian front.

From Mezekövesd we marched to Tiszapolgar, the men separately from the women and children. But the Russians were already firing at the village and we were sent back to Egerszalok, then Eger Visonta, Gyöngyös and Nagymaros. At Nagymaros we crossed the Danube and made a forced march to Komarom and Györ. The soldiers, who travelled in a horse-drawn cart, told us we must reach Germany within a week. From Nagymaros we marched together with the Jews. We were distinguished from the Jews by a yellow ribbon on our arm. Anyone who became ill during the march was shot by the German soldiers. I and my friend Adam Paczok fled before Györ.

I was the coachman of the string of vehicles which carried the

German soldiers' property. The soldiers trusted me and when one soldier's horse was lame because the shoe had fallen off he said to me – 'Kallai, go to a blacksmith in the village and get a horse-shoe made. But if you don't come back within two hours we will shoot you like a dog.'

I found a blacksmith in the village. I left the horse there telling the blacksmith that I had to go and get food for the horse. I didn't return but went by a roundabout route to the forest and there I met other Gypsies.

Of the 400 Gypsies who left Mezekövesd on the march only ten to fifteen succeeded in fleeing. I don't know where in Germany the others were taken but no one I knew came back."[16]

A woman survivor recounts:

"In autumn 1944 a list was made of all the Gypsies in Adacs, the men aged 16 to 60 and the women from 16 to 40. In November we were deported by German soldiers. Only about 70 Gypsies were taken as after the lists were made many fled from the village. First we went to Hatvan where we were put in the Jewish synagogue. From there we went with our families to Komarom. There we were put into the town prison and the men and women separated. The men were taken somewhere in Germany, the women and the girls were taken first of all to Ravensbrück and then to Dachau. We had to work all the time, in Ravensbrück we worked in the sand mine.

We were together with Polish, German, Hungarian and Russian Jewesses. Our clothes were a blue and white striped dress, on our feet were wooden sandals. The Germans cut off all our hair. On the left arm of our dress was sewn the number of the barrack with green numbers on a white background. My barrack number was 19. Many Gypsy women and girls died in Ravensbrück but I do not know how many. Those who could not work were shot by German soldiers. When the Russian soldiers approached we marched to Dachau. During the journey many women were shot as they could not walk any further. At Dachau the Russians liberated us. Of my family the following died – Ferenc, aged 60, Istvan, aged 46, Ferenc, aged 21, and Laszlo, aged 19."[17]

One tragic incident should perhaps be recorded. The Russians were driven back temporarily by the Germans after occupying the village of Lajoskomarom and the Germans took their revenge on the villagers who had been celebrating their liberation, by shooting everyone in sight. The 150 Gypsy families (including some from Transylvania and Budapest) were the principal victims of the massacre.[18]

In Romania there was always an ambivalent attitude towards the large Gypsy minority. As elsewhere the Gypsies were admired as musicians and entertainers, indispensable at weddings and celebrations, yet many had to live as distrusted social outcasts.

Once the Romanian government of Antonescu had established itself, the attitude towards minority groups hardened. Even after the alliance with Germany had come into effect, however, the Fascist government was never as strong and imposing as that of other Axis countries and satellites.

Antonescu made a speech on July 8th, 1941, calling for the 'elimination' of national minorities while popular opinion was expressed by a Romanian captain who is quoted as saying:

> "Mice, rats, crows, Gypsies, vagabonds and Jews don't need any documents."[19]

The Romanian Fascist paper *Eroica* said the Gypsy question was as important as that of the Jews. It mourned the "prevailing dangerous opinion that the Gypsies formed part of the Romanian race" as a result of which mixed marriages were increasing, and the number of half-castes had reached 600,000. *Eroica* demanded that such marriages be prohibited.

> "Gypsies must be eliminated from any part they may play in the social life of the state."

The paper suggested all nomadic Gypsies should be placed in labour camps.[20]

The government, it is clear, never planned to exterminate this large minority group itself. Action was limited apparently to expulsion from parts of the Romanian homeland. To those to whom the policy was applied it brought disruption of family life, suffering, hardship, hunger and death.

On August 19th, 1941, Hitler confirmed the Romanian occupation of the Ukraine as far as the River Bug. The following October

Romania took Odessa, though most of the Crimea was taken over by the Germans. Romanian troops were responsible for security up to the River Dnieper and a new name was invented, Transdniestria, which comprised some of the richest farmland of the USSR. Altogether the Romanian military zone extended as far north as the Uman-Cherkassy line, east of the Bug and west of the Dnieper.

Some of this occupied area, copying German methods, was used as a dumping ground for Gypsies. In the years 1941-2 some 25,000 Gypsies from the Bucharest area were transported across the Dnieper to the Stalingrad region. Petre Radita has described the departure of one transport.

Dispatched from Bucharest in cattle trucks, the journey took some weeks and because of the cold nights, lack of blankets and inadequate food supply, many died of hunger and exposure before arriving at the River Bug in the Ukraine. Those that had survived were lodged in huts and made to work digging trenches. Those found with gold teeth had them pulled out. Two children caught carrying messages to the partisans were executed in front of their parents.[21] Towards the end of 1943, after the Germans had been driven over the Bug with their Romanian allies, the Gypsies took the opportunity to return to Romania.[22] The policy of transporting the Gypsies into the Ukraine aroused opposition amongst the local German officials. The Reichskommissar for the Ukraine wrote on the subject to the Minister for the Occupied Eastern Territories in August 1942. After this a letter was sent from the Minister to the Foreign Office in Berlin, dated September 11th, 1942, pointing out the danger that these Gypsies would try to settle on the east bank of the Bug and would then be a bad influence on the Ukrainian population. The Minister said the area set aside for Gypsies was in fact populated by ethnic Germans and asked the Foreign Office to persuade Romania to change its policy.[23]

In 1942 also, as part of the policy of 'purification of the Romanian nation' the sedentary Gypsies of the wholly Gypsy village of Buda-Ursari (now in the USSR) were taken to a camp in the town of Nikolaev in the Ukraine. Many women and children died on the way. One man, Bogdan Nikulaje, lost all the members of his family.[24] An internment camp was also set up at Tiraspol in 1944.[25]

Meanwhile elsewhere in Romania the Gypsies remained comparatively free. As far as we know, no further large-scale activity against them took place and many of those interviewed could not distinguish the period of the war. Others served in the army. Mikhai Dimitraskcu was in the cavalry regiment of the 9th Romanian Division until his capture by the Russians in 1942. He stated that he had been flogged twice by Romanian officers, once for wearing his hair long.[26] Pirvan Regalie, from the village of Clejani near Bucharest, fought at Stalingrad.[27]

The Italian journalist Curzio Malaparte during a journey from Jassy, in Moldavia, to Poduloea, Bessarabia, in June 1941 noted the activities of some Gypsies and peasants after the removal of Jews who had died during a three-day transport in railway cattle trucks. He and the Italian consul from Jassy, Sartori, heard the sounds of a quarrel. Then they saw a crowd of peasants and Gypsies stripping the corpses. A rabbi from Poduloea remarked, "It can't be helped. It is the custom. They will come to us tomorrow to sell the clothing stolen from the dead and we shall have to buy it – what else can we do?"[28]

After the war when the Romanian People's Court appointed an investigation committee to look into war crimes, it reported:

"Tens of thousands of defenceless Gypsies were herded together in Transdniestria. Over half were struck by typhus. The gendarmerie practised unprecedented terror; everyone's life was uncertain; tortures were cruel. The commanders lived in debauchery with beautiful Gypsy women and maintained personal harems. Approximately 36,000 Gypsies fell victim to Antonescu's fascist regime."[29]

There are no reports of Nazi persecution of the Gypsies in Greece, although the authorities were aware of their existence. An article in *Volk u. Rasse* in 1941 mentioned them. It is probable that the Germans were too occupied with their prime victims, the Jews, to have time for the Gypsies.

The fascist press in Bulgaria attacked the Gypsy community,

which numbered at least 100,000 in 1939.[30] It was claimed that the control and police supervision of Gypsies had cost the state 500,000,000 Leva (about £2,500,000) and that this was a waste of money.[31]

The government announced that all Gypsies between the age of seventeen and fifty would be mobilized for the harvest and in August 1943 the Sofia national newspaper *Dnes* reported that thousands of Gypsies had already been deported from the capital and many more would follow. According to the press after the war, plans were being made during the fascist period for the extermination of Gypsies in Bulgaria.[32] However they were left undisturbed throughout the war.[33]

The German ambassador in Sofia, Adolf Beckerle, advised the German Foreign Office in June 1943 that difficulties were being met in obtaining agreement with the Bulgarian authorities on the deportation of Jews. The reason he said was because:

". . . the Bulgarians have lived for too long with peoples like Armenians, Greeks and Gypsies to appreciate the Jewish problem."[34]

There is one report of Bulgarian Gypsies being seen in Maidenek concentration camp in Poland[35] but this is unconfirmed.

Under Nazi rule Czechoslovakia ceased to exist. The fate of the Gypsies varied considerably in the five different parts into which the country was divided, and with the exception of those areas annexed to Germany and Poland, we shall consider each separately.

Bohemia and Moravia became a German Protectorate in March 1939. In November of the same year the Ministry of Internal Affairs considered issuing a special law to control the Gypsies and the police were asked for their views on the subject.[36] Sporadic arrests began in 1941 but only later that year a decree was made under which the Gypsies' movements were controlled until such time as they could be deported to concentration camps. The following are the relevant provisions:

Protective custody

In order to protect the community from all harmful persons, protective custody is herewith introduced. The persons to be placed into custody are ... anyone who, without being a professional or habitual criminal, endangers the public through his asocial behaviour, beggars, vagabonds, Gypsies and persons travelling as Gypsies, prostitutes, persons with infectious diseases who do not follow the regulations of the Health Police ... and work-shy persons.

Persons in protective custody will be held

(a) in concentration camps in Bohemia and Moravia.

(b) In the event of the concentration camps in the Protectorate proving insufficient, camps will be made available in Germany by the German Criminal Police. Hard labour camps will be turned into concentration camps. The length of protective custody is not a fixed period of time. It continues for as long as it is needed. At the latest after one year's arrest, but not before six months have elapsed, it can be investigated whether its continuation is necessary.

The Criminal Headquarters in Prague or the Police Authorities in Brno will decide in which camp the person in protective custody is to be held.

Special regulations for Gypsies

1. Gypsies are forbidden to leave their place of residence without previous permission from Police Headquarters.

2. The distribution of licenses to travel is to be transferred to the Criminal Police Headquarters.

3. The previous agreement of the Criminal Police Headquarters is necessary before permits or licenses are issued for Gypsies to carry on nomadic trades.[37]

This law came into force on January 1st, 1942. Soon afterwards the Nazis began the removal of the Gypsies to concentration camps. There were two camps within the Protectorate, at Lety in South Bohemia and Hodonin nad Kunstatem in South Moravia. The camp at Lety was opened in August 1942; 1,200 Gypsies passed through its wooden barracks, an average of 600–800 at one time. Conditions in the camp were poor and 341 prisoners died there. At first they were buried in neighbouring Mirovice, then in a forest cemetery. An epidemic of typhoid fever broke out in autumn 1942. In August 1943 the camp was closed and 420 Gypsies were transferred to Auschwitz and another ninety-four to a camp in Poland. The remainder were sent to various destinations. After this the Germans burnt all the huts and equipment to prevent the spread of typhoid.

Hodonin camp was set up in March 1942 and at first held 300 persons. Then in July 1942 three huts and a building were erected to hold 800. Once again poor conditions took their toll: 118 corpses were buried in a Roman Catholic cemetery and seventy-six more in a mass grave opposite the camp. About 1,200 Gypsies are noted in the camp records. The camp was closed in September 1943 and the prisoners taken to other camps including Auschwitz. About fifty Gypsies were also imprisoned in a work-camp in Dolni Markovice (Moravia) and another group in Osoblaze u Krnova, though these camps were not specifically built for Gypsies.[38] As the two main camps soon became full Gypsies were deported to camps outside the boundary of Bohemia and Moravia. Some were sent to Auschwitz well before the setting up of the special Gypsy camp. One group from Brno arrived there in April 1942[39] and another, of about sixty men and thirty-seven women, in December of the same year.[40] Certainly there were other transports in between. Included in the latter group was Ignacy Mrnka, no. 80,735, who was shot after an unsuccessful attempt to escape in January 1943.[41]

After the establishment of the special Gypsy camp at Auschwitz, deportations increased. Gypsies from Bohemia and Moravia comprised the second largest group there, numbering nearly 4,000. The following list of transports[42] shows that by 1944 the majority of Gypsies had been rounded up.

7– iii–43	100 persons	(estimated)
8– iii–43	100	(estimated)
11– iii–43	764	
17– iii–43	100	(estimated)
19– iii–43	1,074	
7– v–43	863	
22–viii–43	768	
19– x–43	92	
28– i–44	63	
2– vi–44	5	

Gypsies from Bohemia and Moravia could also be found at Gross-Rosen[43] and other camps. An unconfirmed report speaks of 250 Gypsy children from Brno being gassed at Buchenwald in 1940.[44] This would be very early for such a mass killing and the year is probably wrong.

Only a few hundred of the Czech Gypsies survived the war. One, Ferdinand Bernard from Reichenberg, had been a prisoner at Auschwitz.[45] Anna S. was born in 1943 at Pankrac prison in Prague. Straight after giving birth her mother was killed but Anna was removed from the prison in a sack.[46] Jan Daniel, from Moravia, survived, though injected with typhus and malaria at Natzweiler camp.[47] Leon Růžička has told how after arrest near Kladno in March 1941 he was deported to Auschwitz. There he had the number 21,931. From Auschwitz he was sent to Buchenwald, Dora, Harzung, Erlich and Bergen-Belsen. When he returned to Czechoslovakia after the liberation he found that all the other seventeen members of his family had perished.[48] The whole Oslavany colony of 150 persons were taken to Auschwitz and all but five died.[49]

Barbara Richter, Auschwitz number Z. 1963, has told a fuller story from which we give a few extracts.

"At the beginning of the war my family were in Bohemia. My father had sold his caravan and taken a house. The Czech police came and took us to Lettig [sic]. There were eighteen to twenty families there, all Gypsies. We were kept in barracks and not allowed to go out. This was in March or April 1941. In May I escaped. When I arrived in Prague a ticket-inspector gave me clothes and a hat to hide the fact that my hair had been shaved off." (She set off to escape across the border to Slovakia but returned to Prague and hid with a Gypsy family. Here she was betrayed by a police informer.)

"I was kept six weeks at the police station and then sent to Auschwitz (arriving there March 11th, 1943). Two Gypsies tried to escape but were caught, beaten and hanged. Later my family was released from Lettig because the Richters were a well-established family in Bohemia. My mother came to Auschwitz voluntarily. Once I was given twenty-five blows with a whip because I had given some bread to a new arrival. One day I saw Elisabeth Koch kill four Gypsy children because they had eaten the remains of some food. Another time we stood for two hours in front of the crematorium but at the last moment were sent back to the barracks. I was given lashes a second time for taking bread from a dead prisoner. Three times they took blood from me. Dr. Mengele injected me with malaria. I was then in the sick bay with my uncle. Some Gypsies carried me to another block just before all the patients in the sick bay, including my uncle, were killed."

(Barbara and her mother were taken to Ravensbrück, probably April 15th, 1944. Six weeks later she was sent to a camp in Austria from where she escaped and made her way to Prague. There she was hidden by a Gypsy whom she later married. Her mother also survived until the liberation of Ravensbrück.)[50]

Margareta Kraus, taken to Auschwitz at the age of thirteen, lost both her parents there. While in the camp she contracted malaria and typhus. One day, for taking some potatoes while she was working in the kitchen she was given twenty-five strokes, a customary punishment. During the beating she collapsed and woke up later to find she had been carried back to her own block. She too was transferred to Ravensbrück and after the liberation came to live in East Germany.[51]

Out of an estimated Gypsy population in 1939 of 13,000,[52] several thousand managed to escape to Slovakia before deportations began. Official Czech figures give a figure of 6,540 (including 1,246 children) for the population in 1941. Of these 6,490 were sent to concentration camps and about 500 returned.[53] Thus some 6,000 perished, the vast majority in Auschwitz.

Conditions in Hungarian-occupied Slovakia were very hard. Arpad Krok from Košice relates that his father was sent to a work-camp in Romania while he and his three brothers found themselves in a concentration camp for Gypsies and Jews at Komarno (Vezdova Basa). Their living quarters were underground and the lice were so numerous that, as he describes it, 'the children threw handfuls at each other'. As he was only twelve, Arpad was in the women's camp. On one occasion he saw the guards shoot a new-born baby and its mother. The baby died immediately and the mother some days later, apparently from gangrene in the untreated wound in her breast. Later the Gypsies were sent to Dachau.[54]

Ludovi Bihari from Rastice told how the Milashi (Hungarian fascists) caught him and put a rope around his chest. They tied the other end to a horse's saddle and he was dragged along the ground. He was then sent to Mauthausen where he spent twenty-eight months. On his lower leg he still carries a large scar from medical experiments performed on him in the camp before he escaped.[55]

The treatment of the many Gypsies within the puppet fascist state of Slovakia, though hard, did not reach the level of the systematic extermination practised in Bohemia and Moravia. For this reason it was considered a place of refuge by the Gypsies from other areas although the Slovak fascist leader Mach, addressing the Hitler Youth in May 1942, promised that the solution of the Gypsy problem would follow after that of the Jews.[56]

An edict dated January 18th, 1940, imposed compulsory labour upon Jews and Gypsies.[57] A second law, in May of the same year, fixed the labour service at two terms of two months twice annually.[58] In 1940 also Gypsies were forbidden to enter parks, cafés and restaurants or to use public transport. In 1941 local authorities received instructions to expel Gypsies from the quarters they occupied in nearly every town and village in Slovakia.[59]

As with many fascist decrees, the orders were executed differently from one place to another. At the village of Smizany the Gypsy community of 500 had become well-integrated and here no one was sent to perform forced labour. At Letanovce the mayor tried to protect the Gypsies but the Hlinka Guards (Slovak fascist police) ordered him to send Gypsies to the forced labour camps. However he selected only two, both men with a bad reputation for drinking and anti-social behaviour. They worked at a railway construction camp near Presov, survived the war and returned to the village afterwards. Again, in the settlement of Rakusy the Gypsies were left alone until 1944 when Gypsies and Slovaks had to dig trenches against the advancing Red Army.[60] Work-camps for Gypsies existed at many places including Čemerný, Dubnica, Hanušovce, Ilava, Kremnica and Petra.[59]

A Gypsy from Janova relates how towards the end of the war he too was sent to dig trenches for four months after which he was transferred to a camp in Poland. They received very little to eat and the bread was so thin that 'you could see the whole length and breadth of the country through it'.[61]

In 1944 pressure on the Gypsies increased. A law in June accused the Gypsies of spreading typhoid through the country and for practical purposes banned them from using the state railways. In order to travel they first had to get a doctor's certificate that they were clean and free from typhoid, then this certificate had to be presented to the district office to obtain a travel permit. The travel permit was valid only for the outward journey and the whole procedure had to be gone through again for the return.[62]

The Ministry of Internal Affairs wrote to district offices pointing out that they had not all complied with the 1941 law concerning the evacuation of Gypsies from towns and villages. All Gypsies had to be shifted to places well away from roads and execution was to be the punishment for any refusing to move. The order ended with the ominous words,

"I wish to add that arrangements for concentration working camps for Gypsies are being prepared."[63]

A number of pogroms by local fascists took place. Every member of a community of 112, men, women and children, were killed at Ilija. At Križa nad Honom the Gypsies were locked in a hut which was then set on fire. Those attempting to escape from the burning building were shot. Other murders took place at Kremnička, Podlavice, Skubina and Liubetov.[64] In the village of Cierny Balog fifty to sixty Gypsies met a similar death in two huts, after being forced to carry the cans of petrol themselves. Later other Gypsies had to dig a collective grave for the dead. A massacre in Neresnice left only two families alive.[65]

The Gypsies actively supported the Slovak National Uprising against the puppet government in the summer of 1944. As a result, when the fascist regime called in German troops and the rising was brutally suppressed, the Gypsies suffered. Among Gypsy partisan officers was Tomas Farkas who led a mixed group of

Gypsies and Slovaks. His unit held up the German counter-attack in a gorge near Tisovec, some seventy-five kilometres east of Banska Bystrica, the centre of the rising. As the Germans pressed forward the unit had to retreat to the mountains. In consequence, Tomas Farkas's family was punished and his son was sent to a concentration camp. Fortunately he survived the war. Tomas Farkas and Anton Facuna, who was dropped as a parachutist to act as a liaison officer between the partisans and the U.S. military mission, were decorated after the war.

The Gypsies from Tisovec had earlier in the war been forced out of the village and had set up camp in the woods. The men joined the partisans but when their group had to move to another area the unit commander left heavy weapons and machine-guns hidden near the Gypsy camp. After the Germans had reoccupied the area an intelligence officer who spoke Russian was sent there disguised as a Russian partisan. After making some of the Gypsies drunk with vodka, he asked them how many weapons they had. They began to boast about the machine-guns. Shortly afterwards, the Guardists (Slovak fascists) surrounded the settlement and shot the men in front of their families and then killed the women and children. The bodies were thrown into a lime quarry. The victims of this massacre are commemorated in a memorial at Banska Bystrica.

The fascists suspected the Gypsies of another village, Slatina, of giving food to the partisans. On November 23rd, 1944, they killed all the persons they could find in the camp, and only three members of the community escaped.[66]

It is generally accepted that only the end of the war saved the Gypsies of Slovakia from sharing the fate of their fellows in Bohemia and Moravia.[67] One writer has mentioned that accusations of cannibalism were made against the Gypsies as part of the preparation for a campaign against them.[68] In fact, only a few hundred of the wartime Gypsy population of Slovakia, estimated at 100,000,[69] died at the hands of the fascists.

The order for the expulsion of the Gypsies from communities where they were already largely sedentary, accepted and integrated had an effect which is still being felt today. Forced to leave their houses and make primitive camps for themselves in wood and scrubland usually several kilometres away, they existed for several years as outcasts, the children denied education and the parents barely able to scrape together the necessities of life.[70]

On September 1st, 1939, German troops invaded Poland. Later in the month Russian troops entered the country from the east and on September 29th Poland was partitioned between Germany and the Soviet Union. Two groups of Gypsies were shot in cold blood by the Germans during this invasion in the Berent (Schoeneck) area of East Prussia. Some others from the local prison were shot in the cemetery in October.[71]

For the Nazis Poland was a convenient place to dump Germany's unwanted Jews and Gypsies and nearly 3,000 of the latter were sent there during 1940. In June 1941 Germany attacked the Soviet Union and soon occupied the rest of Poland. Persecution of the Gypsies then began in earnest.

At first the policy was to put the Gypsies in ghettos and work-camps:

"The numerous Gypsies living in the 'General Government'[72] will be forced to positive work as far as possible."[73]

One reason advanced for putting the Gypsies under control was that they were responsible for attacks on German troops.[74] The administrative machinery seems to have been unsettled by the large deportations into the General Government of Jews and Gypsies from Germany. No real provision was made for the Gypsies who arrived in 1940 and some of them ended up in the ghettos together with the Polish Gypsies.

Ghettos with Gypsy sections included Belapodlaska, Chelm, Kielce, Kostopol, Krakau, Lodz, Lublin, Radom, Praga (Warsaw), Sanck, Siedlce, Tschenstochau and Wengrow. Conditions varied from comparative freedom in some ghettos to concentration camp conditions in others.[75] Usually the Gypsies had to wear a white armband with a blue Z on it.[76] There were also work-camps in Rabka-Zaryte and Warsaw-Marimont.[77]

One survivor has recounted how his uncle was shot in Warsaw in front of the whole family for buying trousers from a Russian.

On another occasion he himself was put in front of a wall with ten other Gypsy children and some Jews to be shot. At the last moment an SS officer came and took the Gypsies away.[78]

In 1942 the Nazis intensified their anti-Gypsy campaign. On June 1st it was ordered that all Gypsies in the Warsaw and Ostro-Masowiecki regions must move to the ghettos. There were also some Gypsies imprisoned in the Gesia St. jail in the (large) Warsaw ghetto.[79]

In Lemberg the authorities tried to work up public opinion against the Gypsies. Towards the end of 1942 the *Lemberger Zeitung* and the *Krakower Zeitung* broke out with a rash of articles whose burden was that it was intolerable to let an entire race of parasites go on eating while Europe was suffering hunger as a result of the Allied blockade.[80] However the Gypsies were kept in the ghetto at Lemberg until 1944[81] and allowed to go about freely and practise their traditional trades.[82]

From 1942 large-scale massacres of Gypsies, often by Polish and Ukrainian Fascists, took place in many parts of Poland while other groups were sent to concentration and extermination camps.

In all 115 Gypsies were killed at Lohaczy in 1942, 96 at Szczurowa and 15 at Berna in 1943; 104 were killed at Zahroczyma, 30 at Grochow and about 50 at Karczew. All the Gypsies in Olyce were shot and other murders took place at Pyrach, Zyradow, Targowka, Radom, Sluzeca and Komorow.[83] Dogs were let loose on the Gypsies of Poznan.[84]

Mass executions took place in Wolyn (Wolhynia) and the Carpathians. In the Wolyn province about 3,000 to 4,000 Gypsies died at the hands of German and Ukrainian fascists. Only the adults were shot. The children were often murdered by seizing them by the legs and smashing their heads against tree-trunks.[85] Transportable gas chambers were also used. Another group was drowned when they were driven on to a river covered with thin ice.[86]

Apart from the many thousands killed indiscriminately, Gypsies faced transportation to Auschwitz, Belsen, Chelmo, Maidenek and Treblinka. About 600 Polish Gypsies, as well as 2,600 from Bialystok, are known to have been sent to Auschwitz.

Finally, from September 1944 the majority of the Gypsies remaining in the ghettos were killed.[87] It is estimated that some 35,000 persons (two-thirds of the Polish Gypsies) lost their lives during the Nazi occupation.[88]

Apart from Germany and Austria, Poland was the only country where the German authorities appeared to have tried to deal with representatives of the Gypsies (as with those of the Jews). Although Janusz I Kwiek, who had been elected King of the Polish Gypsies, was arrested early in the war, there were some dealings between the German authorities and Rudolf Kwiek, his rival: In a letter written as early as 1941 he offered to point out the hiding places of Polish Gypsies in exchange for safe conduct passes for sixteen members of his family, expressing his wish to be of service to the German cause. In 1947 he was put on trial as a collaborator. Witnesses testified that Kwiek had arrived in a Gypsy settlement with the Gestapo before the inhabitants were taken off to be executed. Other witnesses however supported Kwiek and he was found not guilty. The letter mentioned above was not found until after his death in 1964.[89]

Hanna Brzezinska was born in Poland in 1928. The Germans came to her village and all the men including her father were shot after being made to dig their own graves. The women and children were driven into lorries and taken to Auschwitz. Her number was Z. 4517. One day she was taken with some other Gypsies to clean an empty Jewish camp. When she returned to Auschwitz she found all the remaining members of her family had disappeared. Then taken to Ravensbrück she worked making rings, but after a while was transferred to Rechlin and then to Maidenek. She was chosen for the gas chamber and tied up with a Jewish girl for twenty-four hours while awaiting her turn. Spared at the last minute, she was taken to a war factory at Hamburg where there were some other Gypsies. She stayed there until the end of the war.[90]

Another survivor tells of his escape:

"They put us behind barbed wire and imprisoned us at Jadowa. Then all the men were collected and locked in the synagogue. I was still small, a child, so they let me stay with the women. Later they hauled all the men out of the synagogue and shot them all. So in the night we cut the wires and escaped. From there we went to Karczew but there was no peace there either. Not long after, the Germans began to kill the Gypsies. There were two houses full of Gypsies. They threw small children out of high windows on to the cobble stones and there was a lot of blood. I jumped out of a window and as I fell I smashed my knee. I hobbled to a restaurant where two of my brothers were drinking vodka. They hadn't yet heard what had happened to the Gypsies. I told them and we escaped. One brother had a revolver and when the Gestapo started to chase us, he shot two of them."[91]

The Nazis murdered almost all the Estonian Gypsies. Included in the massacre was the whole tribe (about ninety persons) of Lajenge Roma, distinct from the other Estonian Gypsies, living in Lauise, forty miles north of Tartu.[92] Sixty Gypsies were killed in Harku concentration camp on October 27th, 1942.[93] The only reference to Lithuania we have found is the arrival of a transport of twenty persons at Auschwitz. It seems likely that the Lithuanian Gypsies suffered the same fate as those of Estonia.

Soon after the German invasion in 1941 all the Gypsies in East Latvia were assembled in three towns, Rezekne, Ludza and Vilani. At Ludza they were locked up in a synagogue where they died in hundreds of hunger and disease. The survivors were 'deported to the forests', that is to say shot in the forests. Gypsies were also killed at Libau, Bauska, Venspils,[94] and Hargla near Tallinn.[95] Of the 150–200 Gypsies of Daugavpils only sixteen survived the war.[96] Sasa Aleksejonko of Daugavpils was one of those killed. Two Nazis seized his arms while another pair disembowelled him. He died two days later.[94] In these massacres of 1942 a total of 1,500–2,000 were killed, about a third of the population.

Two educated Gypsies, Vanya Kochanowski and Janis Lej-manis[97] tried to get the orders to exterminate the Gypsies altered. This was done but too late to save many, including eight members of Kochanowski's own family who were murdered two hours before the order for their release arrived.[98] There was then a pause in the massacres. Kochanowski himself was called up by the

Germans and put in a Transport Section. He escaped and was captured by the Russians. They delivered him back to the fascist Lettish police and he was put in prison at Kaunas. Accused of attempting to escape he was sent to a disciplinary camp at Saka-spils and then to a prison in France. Here he escaped again and was helped by French Gypsies to hide.[99]

Some Letts were apparently pleased to be rid of the Gypsies. As one said, "From the Jews we do at least get some trade, but what can these parasites the Gypsies give us."[99]

"It has not yet been discovered by whom and when the order was given to kill Gypsies in the Soviet Union."[100] Nor is it possible to say with any accuracy the total killed. We have however collected a considerable amount of material which sheds light on these questions.

No written orders have been preserved authorizing the mass killing of Gypsies and Jews in the Soviet Union.[101] The Commissar Order of June, 6th, 1941 ordered the special treatment of political commissars and the Barbarossa Jurisdiction Order[102] gave a general right to deal harshly with the civilian population but did not in itself justify the mass murder of Gypsies and Jews.

However at a briefing conference for the leaders of the Einsatzgruppen (the special units which were to carry out these murders) Brigadier Streckenbach[103] gave orders that 'all racially and politically undesirable elements seized who were considered dangerous to security' were to be killed.[104] It is possible that Streckenbach did not mention Jews and Gypsies specifically[105] but the implication was understood by the heads of the Einsatzgruppen.

Ohlendorf, Commander of Einsatzgruppe D said:

> "On the basis of orders which were given to me by former Brigadier Streckenbach . . . a number of undesirable elements composed of Russians, Gypsies and Jews and others were executed in the area detailed to me."[106]

We may note here that 'a number of undesirable elements' refers to at least 90,000 persons in the speaker's own estimate.[107] It seems likely that Streckenbach did not call for the killing of Jews and

Gypsies on his own initiative, but that the orders originated with Heydrich, then Chief of the Security Police and Security Service.[108]

The Einsatzgruppen were certainly not obliged to kill Gypsies, in particular women and children, and they must have done so for a mixture of three reasons:

1. A generally sadistic and bloodthirsty attitude to non-Germans.
2. Knowledge that the Gypsies were a legitimate object of persecution and 'could be hunted like game'[109] with the approval of their immediate and higher superiors.
3. Indoctrination that the Gypsies were an undesirable and dangerous people.

During the campaign the theoretical justification was that they were spies, partisans, helpers of the partisans, looters, etc. To some extent such a justification was needed for the ordinary soldiers (apart from the Einsatzgruppen) who took part in the shootings, but it was also part of a general policy of not calling things by their right names.[110] It was later advised that innocent Gypsies should be killed as well as guilty ones as they would become disaffected after their fellows had been killed.

Gypsies were of course active in the USSR in partisan bands[111] but the wandering tribes of men, women and children executed by the Germans could not by any stretch of the imagination be considered partisans.

Ohlendorf in his defence at his trial used the argument that the Gypsies were spies:

"(The Gypsies participated) in espionage organisations during campaigns ... I want to draw your recollection to extensive descriptions of the Thirty Years War (sic). In the Yaila mountains such activity (i.e. espionage) of Gypsies has been found."[112]

The Einsatzgruppen contained 500–1,200 men each and were reinforced as required for special actions by the army. They were active from May 1941 to July 1943. Their records are not complete but those that have been found mention the following killings of Gypsies.

Einsatzgruppe A. Covering the Baltic States and attached to Army Group North.

1–ii–42 38 Gypsies and Jews killed at Loknya[113]

10 to 24–iv–42 71 Gypsies killed in Latvia[114]

These figures only represent a fraction of the some 5,000 Gypsies killed in the Baltic States.

Einsatzgruppe B. Covering the Moscow region. Attached to Army Group Centre.

6 to 30–iii–42 45 Gypsies killed in Klincy region[115]

33 Gypsies killed in Mogilev region[116]

Once again these figures are indicative only. Smolensk, where some thousands of Gypsies were killed, was in the region covered by Einsatzgruppe B.

Einsatzgruppe C. Covered the Kiev area and was attached to Army Group South.

Sep (Oct), 1941 32 Gypsies killed in the vicinity of Vyrna and Dederev[117]

Nov. 1941 414 Gypsies killed[118]

Einsatzgruppe D. Covered South Russia, South Ukraine and the Crimea. Attached to 11th Army.

16–xi to 15–xii–41 824 Gypsies killed[119]

16 to 28–ii–42 421 Gypsies killed[120]

1 to 15–iii–42 810 Gypsies killed[121]

15 to 30–iii–42 261 Gypsies killed[122]

Many books and articles mention the shooting of 800 Gypsies at Simferopol on Xmas Eve 1941.[123] Although this would have been a typical action of the time, similar to the use of Jewish festivals for special executions and the killing of Poles and Russians on their name-day, it does not appear to have happened. The confusion may have arisen because the Commander of the Second Army said to the Chief of Einsatzkommando 11b that the army expected him to kill several thousand Jews and Gypsies *by Christmas*. Report no. 153 of January 9th, 1942, said that 'In Simferopol the Gypsy problem has been cleared up'.[124] It seems that the mass killing of the Simferopol Gypsies took place at the beginning of December 1941 as shown by the report cited above (that 824 Gypsies were killed in the first half of December) and also by an exchange that took place at the Nuremberg Trials.

Prosecutor. When were the Jews, Krimchaks and Gypsies executed in Simferopol?

Braune. In the first half of December 1941.[125]

We may note that the Simferopol Gypsy community was already settled in 1874[126] and possessed a cultural club with 300 members. Some of the Gypsies killed were living outside the Gypsy quarter.[127]

The Einsatzgruppen were not the only units that killed Gypsies. 128 Gypsies were shot in the Novorzhev region by the 281st Security Division on June 7th, 1942,[128] and the German gendarmerie took part in actions in Kamenez-Podolsk in the Ukraine around June 1942.[129] From these and other reports[130] we can build up a picture of the fate of Gypsies during 1941 and 1942.

Post-war trials expand the story of the 45 Gypsies killed in Klincy. In March 1942 some 30 Gypsies and 270 Jews were killed there. They were brought in lorries to the side of a ditch where their money and outer clothes were taken off them. Then they were shot in groups in front of those waiting their turn for execution.[131] In Spring 1942 a group of 10–15 Gypsies came into Klincy with horses and carts. They were arrested and orders were given for them to receive 'special treatment'. They were shot in the neck at the edge of a trench.[132]

Soviet sources dealing with German atrocities do not normally mention that the persons concerned were Jews or Gypsies but a few survivors have told their story:

"The Germans went to one kolkhoz (collective farm) which was all Gypsies. They shot the president Andrej Massalskij and sent the Gypsies to the ghetto of Roslav. Many Gypsies were killed in Kiev. Near Smolensk the Germans shot and buried alive about 1,000 Gypsies, men, women and children. There is a monument in Smolensk with the names of the victims of the Fascists and many

Gypsy names are on it. The actor Sergej Leonov of the Moscow Gypsy Theatre lost seven members of his family there."[133]

Valentin Ivanov was born in 1930 in Ostrov (Pskov region). His parents were sedentary and even after the arrival of the Germans he continued to attend school together with Russian children. Then in 1943 the Germans collected all the Gypsies of Ostrov and took them to a camp near by. A few months later they were taken to another camp near Saulkrasti in Latvia. Here the parents were separated from the children and transported to another camp. Separate barracks existed for Jews, Gypsies and Russians. They once saw Jews executed but no Gypsy children were killed in that camp. The guards used to beat them and one Russian guard threw cigarettes among the children for them to fight over and poured water over them as they were struggling on the floor. The Gypsy children were then taken to the special Gypsy camp at Konstanty-now near Lodz. This was the children's branch of the Lodz ghetto camp. In 1944 he was taken with other Gypsy boys to Auschwitz and three months later to Mauthausen where he stayed until the camp was liberated by the Russians. His mother was in Stutthof camp and was among some thirty Ostrov Gypsies who survived the war. His father never returned.[134]

Some army officers disapproved of the shooting of Gypsies. The Commander of Army Group North ordered on November 21st, 1941, that the shooting of Gypsies without cause should be stopped[135] and the attention of at least one unit was drawn to this after they had killed some Gypsies in Summer 1942. However as we have seen the Einsatzgruppen took no notice of this order.

In 1942 pressure against the Gypsies was increased. A report from the Chiefs of the Army Field Police on the development of the partisan movement was sent to all Army Groups on August 25th, 1942. It contained amongst other items the following recommendation:

"The appearance of Gypsy bands is a major threat to the pacification of the territory as their members are roaming the country as beggars and render many services to the partisans, providing them with supplies etc. If only part of those Gypsies who are suspected or convicted of being partisan supporters were punished, the attitude of the remainder would be even more hostile towards the German forces and support the   artisans even more than before. It is necessary to exterminate these bands ruthlessly."[136]

In the following year there was some easing of the position as regards sedentary Gypsies. A letter from the 218th Security Division to Field Command 822 in March 1943 said that non-nomadic Gypsies who could prove a two-year period of residence in the place where they were found should be exempted from destruction.[137]

There was also a change in the official policy at higher level. Lithuania, Latvia and White Russia had come under civilian rule in September 1941 and Estonia in December of that year. The civilian governor Lohse issued a confidential order to the SS on December 24th, 1941:

"The Gypsies wandering around the country are a double danger.
(i)   They carry disease especially typhus
(ii) They are unreliable elements who cannot be put to useful work.
Also they harm the German cause by passing on hostile news reports.
I therefore determine that they should be treated in the same way as the Jews."[138]

This meant a policy of extermination. The order was apparently made by Lohse at the suggestion of SS leader Jedicke[139] without authority from Berlin, although he had written to Himmler on the subject.[140] In June 1942 the Minister for the Eastern Occupied Territories wrote to Lohse asking for information on the Gypsies in order to establish a general policy.[141] In May 1943 the Minister put forward his proposals for dealing with the Gypsies to Himmler, the Nazi Party, the Army and the Governors of Ostland (The Baltic States and White Russia) and the Ukraine. He proposed that the Gypsies should be put in special camps and settlements. They should not however 'be treated as Jews' (be killed). No distinction was to be made between nomadic and sedentary Gypsies. Part-Gypsies should generally be treated as Gypsies.[142]

A final decision was held up awaiting Himmler's approval. He modified the proposals to exempt the sedentary Gypsies and the order was published in December 1943:

Order of November 15th, 1943
(i)   Sedentary Gypsies and part-Gypsies are to be treated as citizens of the country.
(ii) Nomadic Gypsies and part-Gypsies are to be placed on the same level as Jews and placed in concentration camps.
The police commanders will decide in cases of doubt who is a Gypsy.

This official distinction between sedentary and nomadic Gypsies was only made in the USSR and the Baltic states. In other occupied countries there was no such distinction. Sedentary Gypsies in the Soviet Union were however drafted to serve in labour brigades and cases are known of their being sent to concentration camps.

This order applied to the Baltic states and White Russia which were under German civilian rule but not to the Crimea and the Caucasus which remained under the military authorities. In the latter territories indiscriminate slaughter was practised.

Deportation to extermination camps began. There were two small transports to Auschwitz – twenty persons from Grodno and Orel (November 28th, 1943) and eighteen from Vitebsk (June 17th, 1944). Another group went on foot from Bessarabia to Treblinka where they were exterminated on arrival.[143] It has also been said that Gypsy children were deported from the Leningrad area[144] but nothing is known of their fate.

Finally, an unknown number of Gypsies were murdered with the Jews at Babi Yar:

"It is known that in the Ukraine the Gypsies were victims of the same massive immediate destruction as the Jews. The passport was of decisive importance. They examined the passports in the streets, they examined them when they searched houses. Physical appearance was in second place. People with black eyes and hair, with a long nose, did their best not to show themselves in the street. The Gypsies were led to Babi Yar by entire camps and, apparently, until the last moment they did not understand what was going to be done to them."[145]

The 1926 census in the USSR showed 60,000 Gypsies of whom 42,000 lived in the European part of the Soviet Union. The post-war census of 1959 gave 132,000 for the whole country. Both these figures are underestimates but they do indicate that a considerable proportion of Gypsies survived the war. We estimate that about 30,000 Gypsies were killed by the Einsatzgruppen army units and in the extermination camps.

CHAPTER EIGHT

CONCENTRATION CAMPS
AND MEDICAL EXPERIMENTS

Andr oda taboris,
ay, phares buti keren,
mek mariben chuden . . .

In that camp,
oh, they work hard,
they work hard and they get beaten.

Do not hit me, do not beat me,
or you will kill me.
I have children at home,
Who will bring them up?[1]

Few camps did not have their share of Gypsy prisoners. In this chapter we cover those for which some documentation has been found. It should be remembered that only in Auschwitz was any form of preferential treatment given and that even here such arrangements – keeping family groups together to avoid trouble – merely meant postponement of death.

Auschwitz camp, built in 1940, received the first prisoners in June that year. Himmler made a visit in 1941 and ordered the construction of a second camp near Auschwitz – Birkenau, large enough to hold 200,000 persons. Gypsies were amongst the prisoners in the main camp. At least two transports of Czech Gypsies arrived during 1942[2] bringing the probable total to between two and three thousand. During the week ending October 18th seventeen died.[3] When later a special Gypsy compound was constructed at Birkenau the authorities tried unsuccessfully to find block leaders from among the Gypsies in the old camp. Gypsies arriving at Auschwitz in January the following year were placed in Block 18 and later transferred to the new camp.[4]

After the establishment of the special compound, some Gypsies still stayed in the old camp. On January 20th, 1944, 479 remained on the lists.[5] During that year Gypsies fit for work were transferred to the old Auschwitz camp prior to the liquidation of the Gypsy camp though some came back clandestinely to join their families.[6] Block 11 at Birkenau, though in a non-Gypsy section, had a Gypsy prisoner as block leader. He had two rooms, in one of which his two daughters sometimes stayed, presumably having come to the Gypsy camp before being brought to his block. The girls distributed the rations to the prisoners but the block leader stole the bulk of them. He obtained newspapers and cigarettes while the girls owned a gramophone and one record. One day he sent a prisoner from his block into the women's camp with some sardines to exchange these for some lipstick for his daughters. The daughters were killed with the rest when the Gypsy camp was closed.[7]

Following Himmler's decree,[8] a special section of Birkenau was set aside for Gypsies and from February 1943 they came in from all over Europe. The table below shows the rate of arrival:

26–ii–43 to	25–iii–43	10,776 (plus 1,700)[9]
26–iii	25–iv	4,072
26–iv	25–v	2,140
26–v	25–vi	27
26–vi	25–vii	69
26–vii	25–viii	812[10]
26–viii	25–ix	51
26–ix	25–x	140
26–x	25–xi	95
26–xi	25–xii	220 approx.
26–xii	25–i–44	424 approx.
26–i–44	25–ii	138
26–ii	25–iii	129
26–iii	25–iv	956
26–iv	25–v	408
26–v	25–vi	60
26–vi	21–vii	41

To the above must be added some 360 children born in captivity and given numbers. Designed to hold 10,000 prisoners, the camp was completely full.[11] The thirty long huts should have housed 300 each but at times some of them had over twice this number crammed into them.[12]

Contrary to clauses in the Auschwitz Order[13] many assimilated and ex-service Gypsies soon showed up there:

"Persons were arrested who could not possibly be regarded as belonging to the category that it was intended to intern. Many men were arrested while on leave from the front, despite high decorations and several wounds, simply because their father or mother or grandfather had been a Gypsy or part-Gypsy. Even a very senior Party member whose Gypsy grandfather had settled in Leipzig was among them. He himself had a large business in Leipzig and had been decorated more than once during the First World War. Another was a girl student who had been a leader in the Berlin League of German Girls (the feminine equivalent of the Hitler Youth). There were many more such cases."[14]

"At the end of March 1943 a Gypsy was brought to the camp who, according to official documents and photographs had served as a lieutenant of the German army in this war."[15]

"Some of the men walked around wearing war decorations awarded to them by the Nazis for their courage at the front."[16]

According to Broad, a member of the SS staff, the camp authorities received a telegram from Berlin just as the camp was opening saying the Gypsies should not be treated the same as Jews.[17] We cannot say for certain on the basis of existing knowledge that the Gypsies were sent to Auschwitz to be killed. Those unfit for labour were not gassed on arrival and only a few Gypsies worked during the first months, so there was no policy of 'Annihilation through Work'. Also the Gypsies in other camps were not transferred to Auschwitz.

On the other hand we cannot believe it was merely intended to intern Gypsies in Auschwitz until after the war and then release them as the Camp Commander, Höss, has suggested.[18] Since even the privileged *Rom* Gypsies, exempted from the Auschwitz order, faced sterilization, it is clear that the 'less desirable' Gypsies in Auschwitz would not be left to procreate. Possibly they were to be kept at Auschwitz and used for various experimental purposes until they died out.[19] The whole family camp was perhaps an attempt to see what could be done with other non-Aryan races the Nazis would have met if German expansion had been continued.[20] The records of medical experiments show Gypsies were freely available for these.

If we accept that the intention was to kill them, why was there a delay of more than a year? One writer suggests they were left alive for the benefit of Red Cross Commission visitors and because their execution would have been bad for morale as many of the assimilated Gypsies had relatives outside the camp.[21] Another factor – the gas chambers were possibly too busy with the Jews. Meanwhile they may have been left in families to give them a sense of security as well as to circumvent trouble. The Germans had already found out in Russia and Serbia that Gypsies did not go quietly to their deaths as did the religious Jews. We may also believe the SS wanted to annoy the other prisoners by letting them think the Gypsies led an easy life[22] – a prejudice common enough outside the camps. Again one can note an element of favouritism from Höss who claimed to be fond of his Gypsy prisoners.

Höss himself puts forward another explanation:

"In July 1943[23] Himmler visited the camp. He made a most thorough inspection of everything in the Gypsy camp noting the overcrowded barrack huts, the unhygienic conditions, the crammed hospital building . . . He noted the mortality rate which was relatively low in comparison with that of the camp as a whole . . . He saw it all in detail and as it really was and he ordered me to destroy them. Those capable of work were first to be separated from the others as with the Jews. I pointed out to him that the personnel of the Gypsy Camp was not precisely what he envisaged being sent to Auschwitz. He thereupon ordered that the Central Police H.Q. should carry out a sorting as quickly as possible. This in fact took one year.[24] The Gypsies capable of work were transferred to another camp. About 4,000 Gypsies were left by August 1944 and these had to go into the gas chamber."

Höss said:

"I made a report to the Police H.Q. As a result the Gypsy camp was constantly under examination and many releases took place. But these were scarcely noticeable so great was the number of those who remained."[25]

Broad however gives a contrary view:

"From the camp some letters were sent to the Central Gypsy Office asking for certain cases to be released (settled and educated Gypsies) but these were all refused. The police refused to release anyone from Auschwitz. The Central Office knew it was Hitler's aim to wipe out all the Gypsies without exception and the exemptions in the Auschwitz order were only a blind. (They) wrote to Auschwitz asking them not to send any more requests to release Gypsies."

Broad quotes one specific case. The family Dikulitsch-Todorowitsch had Croat nationality and the Croatian embassy asked for their release. However Grabner, the head of the Political Section in Auschwitz, did not want them to go as they would spread word about the conditions. So he said release was impossible as there was a danger of their carrying typhus. While discussion continued eight of the family died in the camp. The ninth, a four-year-old boy, was gassed in August 1944.[26]

Now let us consider the general conditions in the camp:

"In the Gypsy camp were large barracks that had a hole in the front and rear. Those were the doors. On single planks in large wooden boxes lay five to six persons. The sanitation was catastrophal. There was no paint on the walls. The water facilities were as good as non-existent . . . The hygienic conditions were indescribable . . . It was a bog with horse stables without windows . . . The people waded up to their ankles in slime."[27]

On arrival the Gypsies were tattoed with a camp number. Their heads were shaved but the hair allowed to grow again.[28] They received no special clothing[29] but wore in the early period a black triangle, as asocials. Possessions including jewellery were taken from them[30] but they were for a time allowed to keep their musical instruments.[31] The families were not separated but the guards tried to control in which barrack people slept. Thus Block 7 was at first reserved for ex-soldiers who had some privileges. Later, however, they were split up amongst the other blocks.[32] A sick barrack and a quarantine barrack and also a special barrack for sick children existed, though in fact no different from any other.[33]

Some had to work from the beginning. Elisabeth Guttenberger wrote that fourteen days after her arrival their group was allotted to labour commandos. She had to carry stones.[34] Two hundred women toiled transporting stones in their hands or sorting clothing in Birkenau III camp. Between April and June 1943 the Gypsies did some canalization work[35] and another commando cut trees in the forests.[36] The majority however were not employed and this gave other prisoners the impression that the Gypsies were excused forced labour.[37]

Food in the Gypsy camp was totally inadequate:

"The Gypsies were all undernourished. I controlled and tasted the food in the kitchen. It was a sort of grain soup, no, rather it was a water soup with a few grains swimming in it."[38]

"The imprisoned Gypsies were often shrunken to skeletons. I went to the kitchen and found that the food did not contain the prescribed 1,680 calories. I wrote a memo immediately but Hartjenstein (Commander of Birkenau) said 'Oh, they are only Gypsies after all'."[39]

Guttenberger said she had received parcels from outside but after these were stopped, her mother, sister, father and brothers died of starvation.[40]

"It was quite impossible to provide proper food for the children . . . The Food Ministry laid down that no special children's food might be issued to the Concentration Camps."[41]

As a result of the poor food and unhygienic conditions, disease was rife in the camp. From May 1943 typhus raged, along with scurvy, diarrhoea and water-cancer.[42] Six hundred were sick with small-pox that month and 1,000 the same summer. Others suffered from a form of chicken-pox resembling bubonic plague.[43] We know that several thousands died from these diseases.

Adelsberger, a prisoner who worked as a nurse in the Gypsy

Camp, describes the minimal hospital facilities.[44] The sick barracks, like the other buildings, had previously been horse-stables. They had no windows but some small covered openings in the roof for light and there were holes in the walls and ceiling. Inside, each side was lined by three-storey wooden bunks strewn with straw sacks and thin blankets. In the middle stood two wooden tables and a stove, used as a couch for examining patients. Ten persons slept in places designed for four. Water dripped from the roof on to the bunks. On the bottom row in their own dirt lay the patients who could not move. Most of the nurses were untrained Gypsies whose job was to measure temperatures and give out food. The doctors main task was to keep check on the numbers of dead and make sure they t 'lied. For medicines the staff had two ampules of camphor and a bottle of digitalis each week plus sacks of bolus alba. Every day twenty to thirty died and their bodies were placed in one corner of the barrack and collected each evening by a special commando.

Dr. Mengele set up an experimental barracks in the Gypsy camp. Here research was done on twin births, dwarfs and giants and also on gangrene of the face (Noma or water-cancer). Non-Gypsy twins were also brought to him here. When the final gassing of Gypsies took place the bodies of twelve sets of twins were saved from burning in the crematorium for autopsies. Dr. Mengele had marked ZS on their chests with his special chalk before they went to the gas chamber. A Dr. Bendel and Dr. Epstein, employed by Mengele for these experiments, said he judged these more important than attending to the sick Gypsies.[45]

Most had come in families and a high proportion of children existed in the camp. As one report said 'the camp was overflowing with children'.[46] The orphans were kept separately in Blocks 22 and 23.[47] There was a children's playground between the wash-room and the kindergarten with a roundabout and other apparatus.[48] Höss described it as "a large playground where the children could run about to their heart's content and play with toys of every description'. The purpose was propaganda. The special playground displayed a large notice 'Children's School'. On occasions the children were driven into the playground and photographed.

The children however were badly clothed and inadequately fed. Although butter was included in the 'rations' it was nearly always stolen before it reached the children.[49] The camp doctor, Mengele, gave them sweets when he came and from November 1943 they received some oat biscuits with sugar.[50] This was not sufficient to stop under-nourishment and consequent disease:

> "The children were all skin and bone. The thin skin rubbed on the bones and became infected. The sick children would drink the washing-up water as there was often no other water. Sometimes the children's blankets (in the sick barracks) were washed and put back still wet on the beds."[51]

> "The children were suffering from Noma . . . which reminded me of leprosy . . . their little bodies wasted away with gaping holes in their cheeks big enough for one to see through, a slow putrefaction of the living body."[52]

Over 300 Gypsy women were pregnant when transported to Auschwitz and gave birth at the camp. The monthly figures are not without interest:

Dates		Recorded births
26–ii–43 to 25–iii–43		15
iii	iv	45
iv	v	48
v	vi	38
vi	vii	47
vii	viii	41
viii	ix	40
ix	x	23
x	xi	18
xi	xii	7
1– i–44	24–i–44	7
25– i	ii	3
ii	iii	4
iii	iv	5
iv	v	11
v	vi	9
vi	–	0

In the first eight months (26–ii–43 to 25–x–43) 297 births were recorded and in the last eight months (26–x–43 to 24–vi–44) only sixty-four. The dramatic drop had many causes. First, the general debility of the women and the removal of many young men caused a drop in the total of pregnancies, while shortage of food and rampant disease resulted in many miscarriages and still-births. It is also likely that many newly born children were killed in the latter period.[53] The slight rise in the last two months could be due to the abandonment of the policy of murdering babies, less over-crowding and slightly better food given in the period just before the liquidation of the camp.

Langbein, a prisoner, describes the barrack where the mothers who had given birth lay:

"The only anxiety the SS took was to see that the newly-born had their prisoner number tattooed immediately on the upper thigh. There was no special food, hardly any water. The floor was of clay and at one end there was a curtain. There I saw a pile of children's bodies, and among them, rats."[54]

Of course, the child mortality rate was extraordinarily high and not many new-born babies survived more than a few weeks[55] as some examples taken from the official records show:[56]

Girl Z. 8893	born 14–vi–43	died 25–vi–43
8894	–do–	27–vii–43
8895	11–vi–43	3–vii–43
8896	12–vi–43	17–vii–43
8897	14–vi–43	17–vi–43

Apart from killing by neglect, there was deliberate cruelty and murder in the Auschwitz Gypsy Camp, in spite of higher instruc-tion to treat the Gypsies differently from Jews. Morning roll-call lasted from 6 to 8 a.m. – sometimes all day.[57] Often during the roll-call 'Sport' was called and the weakened prisoners had to do exercises while Hofmann, Camp Commander for part of 1943, hit many people. In midsummer 1943 all room orderlies and barrack secretaries had to do 'Sport'. Then they had to sing 'Das kann doch einen Seemann nicht erschüttern' (That can't worry a sailor) and then do Sport again. During the second Sport seven or eight people died.[58]

Bednarek, a prisoner who was a barrack leader, beat a Gypsy to death.[59] Broad beat up a Gypsy while questioning him about the theft of a goose before he had come to Auschwitz.[60] Eighty-two Gypsies are known to have been imprisoned in an underground cell during 1943 for various offences against the Auschwitz rules.[61] Once a month everyone had to go through the Sauna for delousing at a temperature of 50–60° centigrade. Several Gypsies suffered heart attacks and some died.[62]

Many prisoners tried to escape from Auschwitz although they knew well the fate that awaited them on recapture. As the entries in *Auschwitz-Hefte* laconically put it:

> "On May 4th, 1943, Jozef Cerinek (Z. 1904) and Franz Rozycka (Z. 2035) tried to escape from a work commando. They were put in Block 11 bunker and shot on May 22nd."

Two more Gypsies at least faced death by shooting after attempting to escape from the main camp.[63] On April 7th, 1943, Stefania Ciuron escaped from the camp. We do not know whether she was recaptured or not.[64] Two successful escapers were Paprika Galut and her fiancé, Jean.[65] Soon after the erection of the barracks, the Gypsy camp was completed by an electrified wire fence and a watch-post built at the gate.[66] These measures did not deter Gypsies from trying to break out and by August 1943 more than a score had been shot after recapture, torture and detention in the notorious Bunker 11.[67] At least twenty-nine Gypsies fled from the camp and a few were not recaptured.[68]

At the end of 1943, after Höss left Auschwitz, the camp authorities did not treat those recaptured so harshly. Three caught escaping in November and December were merely locked up, as were some non-Gypsies recaptured about the same time.[69] An SS man who captured an escaped Gypsy that summer received three days extra leave as a reward.[70] A witness at the Auschwitz trial, ex-SS officer Casar, told of the mutiny of a forest work-party during which four or five Gypsies were shot down. This is probably a reference to an attempted mass break-out on February 1st, 1944, when three Gypsies died from gun-fire as they tried to flee from a Punishment Company.

Little relief to the hard life at Auschwitz existed. After morning roll-call those not joining work commandos were left alone for the rest of the day to walk up and down the 'main street' between the barracks or to sit outside them until the evening curfew. Höss wrote that "if one went into their camp they would often run out of the barracks to play their musical instrument or to let their children dance or perform their usual tricks".[71] An ex-prisoner says Gypsies went silent whenever SS men came into the camp, which is probably nearer the truth.[72] SS officer Broad got up an orchestra in the Gypsy camp[73] and once a full-scale concert was arranged. But this was interrupted by a curfew during which the SS came to fetch many hundreds of Gypsies to be gassed.[74] Later all instruments were taken away, and this loss spelt the end of an interest in life for many. The SS men came sometimes in the evenings and took girls off to dance in their barracks.[75] Through this contact the Gypsies knew of their coming annihilation. An SS officer called Palitsch was killed because of his liaison with a Gypsy girl though no details are known.[76]

Before the final liquidation, two large massacres took place. In March 1943 1,700 Polish Gypsies arrived from Bialystok. They received no numbers and were isolated in Blocks 20 and 22. A few days later during an evening curfew they were all gassed 'as suspected typhus cases'.[77] Then on May 25th, 1943, 1,042 Gypsies were dragged out of the blocks and gassed. The SS came to each barrack, including the sick bay, and looked for the numbers they had on a list, as these people had already been dispersed among the different barracks.[78] They comprised passengers on the following two transports which had arrived on May 12th or 13th:

From Bialystok	468 males	nos. Z.7,666 to	8,133
	503 females	8,331	8,833
From Austria	45 males	8,134	8,178
	31 females	8,834	8,864

One man managed to avoid this gassing but was shot on May 31st.[79] Those gassed on May 25th are marked in the Control

Book with SB (Sonderbehandlung, special treatment) or + and given dates of death ranging from May 25th to June 11th. Suspected typhus may have been the main reason for these two mass killings but the overcrowded state of the camp could also have been a factor.

As mentioned above, Himmler decided in 1943 that the Gypsy Camp must eventually be done away with. After it was resolved in April 1944 to use Jews for work in aircraft factories[80] we can presume the decision went through to use those Gypsies at Auschwitz fit to work and to murder the remainder. Up to this point there had only been two transports out of Auschwitz. A few hundred healthy young Gypsies had been sent to Natzweiler on November 9th, 1943,[81] probably for medical experiments, and in 1943 some Gypsies were sent to Mauthausen to work in the stone mines.[82]

After April 1944 selections were made of healthy Gypsies in the Gypsy Camp. On April 15th 883 (or 884) males were sent to Buchenwald and 473 females to Ravensbrück; May 25th 82 males (aged 20–25) went to Flossenburg and 144 females (aged 18–25) to Ravensbrück; August 2nd 918 males (including 105 boys) were taken to Buchenwald and 490 females to Ravensbrück. The 1,408 were loaded into a train, took their farewell through the wire and left at four o'clock in the afternoon. The arrival of these transports at their destinations is recorded on August 3rd.

Dutch Red Cross reports say 2,500 left in the last days of the Gypsy camp. This figure may include a transport of a thousand males to the main camp which is mentioned by one source.[83] Also a group of ex-servicemen was sent to Ravensbrück for sterilization.[84] Steinberg, Broad's secretary, says that two or three months before the liquidation she was instructed to draw up a list of all the Gypsies by blocks. She worked on these lists for some days. Broad then told her who was to be crossed off. These included a small number of Gypsies with German citizenship who had no crimes recorded on their papers. They were sent to the main camp quarantine block on the very day of, or one day before, the liquidation.[85]

The last males entered in the record book are for July 8th, 1944, and the last females July 21st. The order had obviously gone out that no more Gypsies were to be sent to Auschwitz.[86] From July 28th extra food was allocated to the children's barracks.[87] The day now drew near for the end of the Gypsy Camp.

The story of the final liquidation is well documented though there are some discrepancies. These will be explained after the general picture has been given. During the last day more selections were made. These included a large group of adults. And at four in the afternoon Dr. Mengele went round the children's block and sent some twins to the main camp. After this a strict curfew was imposed. The lorries arrived at 8 p.m.[88] As previously noted, the Gypsies knew what was in store for them but the Germans tried to allay suspicions. Everyone was given a ration of bread and salami as they came out of their quarters and some believed at first they must be going to another camp.[89] The lorries drove off in another direction and only when darkness had fallen did they drive them directly to the crematoria.[90] During the transfer the majority of Gypsies resisted as best they could:

"We were within easy earshot of the terrible final scenes as German criminal prisoners using clubs and dogs were let loose in the camp against the women, children and old men. A desperate cry from a young Czech-speaking lad suddenly rent the air. 'Please Mr. SS man, let me live.' Blows with a club were the only answer. Eventually all the inmates were crammed into lorries and driven away to the crematorium. Again they tried to offer resistance, many protesting that they were Germans."[91]

"Terrible scenes took place. Women and children were on their knees in front of Mengele and Boger crying 'Take pity, take pity on us'. Nothing helped. They were beaten down brutally, trampled on and pushed on to the trucks. It was a terrible gruesome night. Some persons lay lifeless after being beaten and were also thrown on to the lorries.[92] Lorries came to the orphans' block about 10.30 and to the isolation block at about 11.0 p.m. The SS and four prisoners lifted all the sick people out and also 25 healthy women who had been isolated with their children."[93]

"At 23.00 the lorries stopped at the hospital. 50 to 60 people were

put into one lorry and thus the sick were brought to the gas chambers."[94]

"Until far in the night I heard their cries and knew they were resist-
ing. The Gypsies screamed all night . . . They sold their lives dearly."[95]

"Afterwards Boger and others went through the blocks and pulled
out children who had hidden themselves. The children were brought
to Boger who took them by the feet and smashed them against the
wall . . . I saw this happen five, six or seven times."[96]

"We heard outside cries like 'Criminal, Murderer'. The whole lasted
some hours. Then an SS officer came whom I didn't know and dic-
tated to me a letter. The contents were 'Special Treatment Carried
Out'. He took the letter out of the machine and tore it up. In the
morning there were no more Gypsies in the camp."[97]

"At dawn I noticed the scattered pots, the torn garments."[98]

The reports by eye-witnesses show how the Gypsies, even
though the active adults had been removed, struggled to the last.
One woman threw herself on to an SS man clawing him with her
bare hands.[99]

A woman and two children hid themselves in Block 29 but
were found next day and shot.[100] One Gypsy who tried to claim
he was pure German was sent to work during the liquidation but
shot later.[101]

"Four Gypsies were delivered to the Punishment Company and
were overlooked when the Gypsy Camp was liquidated and realized
that they would be gassed. They begged everyone they thought had
some influence to help them. When they asked Bednarek he hit
them. Some time later these Gypsies were taken to the crematorium."[102]

Thus ended the sixteen months' life of the Gypsy Camp at
Auschwitz.

One or two points about the liquidation are still in doubt.
The first concerns the transports on the last day. Many documents
confirm the movement of 1,408 persons to Buchenwald and
Ravensbrück. A witness at the Auschwitz trial spoke of 2,000
persons fit for work being sent to the main camp, just before the
end.[103] Dr. Beilin said that Mengele selected 600 persons on the
morning of the final extermination.[104] A survivor from a trans-

port fills in some of the details but the date of departure from the Gypsy Camp is not given. An announcement was made during roll-call that all men and women fit to work should step forward. The SS men said their families would come later to join them. The numbers of these people were read out, they were loaded on to trucks and taken to the main camp. Sometime later the German Block Leader came and told this group what had happened to those left behind. These Gypsies were transferred together with a few hundred ex-soldiers to Ravensbrück.[105] Almost certainly then, there was one large transport to Buchenwald and Ravensbrück on the very afternoon of the liquidation and probably one or more smaller removals to the main camp in the days before.

The date of the liquidation varies from one account to another but this is not of great importance. The night of 2nd to 3rd is generally accepted,[106] while July 31st[107] and August 6th[108] have also been advanced. Estimates of the number killed vary from 2,000 to 4,500. An attempt to calculate the total deaths at Auschwitz is made below.

Before leaving the subject we must mention that Schwarzhuber, Commander of Birkenau in 1944, told Höss that the killing of the Gypsies in the camp had been more difficult than any previous mass destruction of Jews. It had been particularly hard on him, he informed his colleague, because he knew many individually and had been on good terms with them.[109]

Further information is available about the transports out from Auschwitz. The 918 men sent to Buchenwald arrived there on August 3rd, 1944. Some were used for sea-water experiments, some sent to Ellrich (Mittelbau) camp on September 3rd, others to Camp S-III on December 18th and a fourth group back to Auschwitz on September 26th. In addition a number of boys were apparently returned to Auschwitz on October 10th.[110] The 490 women sent to Ravensbrück also arrived there on August 3rd. The majority went at the end of the month to Wolkenburg (Flossenburg) and their names have been preserved. Those still alive were probably evacuated to Mauthausen or Theresienstadt about April 15th, 1945.[111] The ex-soldiers dispatched to the main camp went later to Ravensbrück and were sterilized there. Some volunteered to rejoin the army and avoided the fate of the remainder – probably gassing.[112]

Two hundred Gypsies sent back from Buchenwald who reached Auschwitz on September 28th, 1944, were immediately gassed.[113] A train-load of 800 Gypsy children came from Buchenwald on October 10th and died crammed into the gas chambers of Crematorium 5. They probably included some of the 105 boys aged nine to fourteen who had been sent to Buchenwald from Auschwitz earlier and found unsuitable for work.[114] A week later forty-nine Gypsy women arrived from Kommando Altenburg (Buchenwald) and 168 from HASAG-Taucha (Buchenwald). Their fate is not known to us but they had been in Auschwitz before.

Few Gypsies were left by 1945. A roll-call on January 17th showed four male Gypsies.[115] There may have been some women plus a few registered under other nationalities. We know of one Gypsy who took part in the evacuation of the camp on foot and survived.[116] One Gypsy was also among the 4,000 ill persons left when the survivors were counted after the liberation.[117]

Some statistics of the Gypsy Camp have been discovered including entries in the official register:

Males registered	10,094
Females registered	10,839
	20,933

The highest female number was Z. 10,849 but ten numbers were not used (10,814 and 10,819–27). Since some 360 children born in the camp lived long enough to be given numbers the total of admissions must have reached 20,570. This is by no means the whole number of Gypsies brought to Auschwitz but simply those registered in the special Gypsy Camp. To these must be added 1,700 gassed soon after arrival in March 1943 and not given numbers and several thousands in the main camp, both before and after the life of the special compound. The total number of Gypsies at Auschwitz over the whole period is unknown. The nationality of prisoners in the Gypsy Camp was approximately as follows:[118]

Austria	2,650
Bialystok	950 (plus 1,700 not registered)
Belgium	100
Czechoslovakia	4,000
Germany	9,700
Hungary	100 (possibly arrested in Austria)
France	100
Holland	300
Lithuania	20
Norway	60 (probably arrested in Belgium)
USSR	40
Yugoslavia	270 (probably Croatia and Slovenia)

Finally, our estimated statistics of the Gypsy camp at Auschwitz are set out below:

Transports out	4,300[119]	
Killed	5,000	1,000 on 25–v–43
		4,000 on liquidation, August 1944
Died	11,700	This figure includes a small number of individual killings[120]

Survivors fall into three categories: successful escapers such as Paprika Galut (Z. 9171), workers in the camp office who were not included in the liquidation and those who were transported to other camps and remained alive there until the end of the war. In the last two groups are Max Friedrich (Z. 2894), Elisabeth Guttenberger (Z. 3991), Paul Morgenstern (Z. 5439), Waldemar Schröder (Z. 2987) and Hillie Weiss (Z. 4609), all witnesses at the Auschwitz trial. Out of more than twenty thousand only a few hundred lived through their experiences.

We now turn to the story of other camps, beginning with Belsen. Several thousand Gypsies were interned at Bergen-Belsen and almost all were put to death, among them Luluvo la Sidako, a Gypsy leader known as King Josef XIII.[121] A great number of children died there in the years 1943 and 1945.

More is known about Buchenwald where special barracks were allocated to Gypsies, though on entry they were not always registered as such. This makes it impossible to give an accurate figure for the number that passed through, dying there or going on to other camps. Certainly there were several thousand. As early as June 1938 1,000 Gypsy men and boys from Germany entered Buchenwald. In autumn the next year they were joined by 1,400 Austrian Gypsies transferred from Dachau, in addition to numbers of Gypsies committed individually. Even before the war, life in the camp was strict and brutal, as this description of the death in spring 1938 of one Gypsy who had tried to escape shows:

"He was locked in a large box with iron bars over the opening. Inside, the prisoner could only hold himself in a crouching position. Koch (the Camp Commander) then had big nails driven through the planks so that each movement of the prisoner made them stick in his body. Without food or water, he spent two days and three nights in this position. On the morning of the third day, having already gone insane, he was given an injection of poison."[122]

At the end of 1938, at SS Major Rödl's command, a camp band was formed. Most of the musicians were Gypsies. At first they played guitars and harmonicas. Then a trombone, and later a drum and trumpet were added. The prisoners had to pay for the instruments themselves and worked by day in the lumber-yard or carpenters' shop, rehearsing only after work:

"It was ghastly to watch and hear the Gypsies strike up their merry marches while exhausted prisoners carried their dead and dying comrades into camp, or listen to the music accompanying the whipping of prisoners. But then I remember New Year's Eve 1939 . . . suddenly the sound of a Gypsy violin drifted out from one of the barracks far off, as though from happier times and climes – tunes from the Hungarian steppe, melodies from Vienna and Budapest, songs from home."[123]

In the winter of 1939–40 many Gypsies died because of the bad conditions, lack of clothing and blankets, poor food and overwork.[124] They were meant to die. During 1942 at least three transports went from Buchenwald to the Auschwitz main camp before the opening of the special Gypsy compound. Two hundred were transferred on September 26th and two other mixed transports of Gypsies and Jews also left.[125] By 1944 few Gypsies remained in Buchenwald and these were mostly from Germany with a few from Poland and Bohemia. They lived in Block 47 alongside prisoners classified as asocials. Like them they wore black triangle badges. Gypsies still had places in the band and one looked after the bear in the camp zoo. In April more began to arrive from Auschwitz where the special Gypsy camp was already being disbanded. Initially put into the 'Little Camp' (quarantine quarters), some moved illegally from the quarters into the main camp and others were transferred officially. These Gypsy inmates had to sleep in the open air and beg food from better-off French inmates.[126]

About 1,800 Gypsies arrived from Auschwitz in two large transports. Many had to be moved to Dora, an overflow camp for Buchenwald, and died there.[127] Some French Gypsies were also sent to Dora.[128] The children were sent in autumn 1944 – on a return journey for some of them – to Auschwitz for extermination:

> "Even hardened prisoners were deeply moved when the SS in the fall of 1944 singled out and herded together all Jewish and Gypsy youngsters. The screaming, sobbing children, frantically trying to get to their fathers or protectors among the prisoners, were surrounded by a wall of carbines and machine pistols and taken away to be sent to Auschwitz for gassing."[129]

The Gypsies at Buchenwald at this time came from widely separated parts of Europe, including Bohemia, Carpathia, Croatia, northern and eastern France, southern Poland and Ruthenia.[130] Three Gypsy women were on the death list for January 1945.[131] In February 200 men went to Dora and on to Bergen-Belsen. Not more than forty of them survived. One prisoner wrote that he met no Gypsies when he returned to Buchenwald in March 1945,[132] while other witnesses say there were a few.

The Polish War Crimes Commission reported that 5,000

Gypsies were murdered at Chelmno,[133] but full details have not been uncovered and estimates vary. Another source puts the figure at 15,000 out of 1,300,000 people exterminated there.[134] Several thousand Gypsies came from Lodz when the city's ghetto was liquidated. Others were brought from elsewhere in Poland. The Germans used poison gas and machine-guns to dispatch some groups.[135]

One of the early concentration camps, Dachau, was the first to hold Gypsies. In 1936 some 400 were shut up there on the grounds that they constituted an asocial element.[136] Joseph Kramer, who worked in the camp office the same year, said that at that time there were "only political prisoners, criminals, beggars and Gypsies in the camp. The guards had orders to shoot if any prisoners attempted to escape."[137]

Arpad Krok recounts that he was arrested at the age of twelve in the Hungarian-occupied part of Slovakia. After a period in a Hungarian camp he was sent to Dachau. There he contracted typhus and was thrown on to a pile of dead bodies, but an SS woman doctor saved him and gave him food. As a result he survived and was liberated from Dachau by the Americans.[138]

Lackenbach camp was for Gypsies only and the first arrived in 1940. The next year mass deportations of Austrian Gypsies to the camp began. Because Lackenbach came under the Criminal Police and not the SS it was never officially classified as a concentration camp but conditions hardly differed. No high-voltage electric fence was built but the usual roll-calls, corporal punishment and forced labour went on. The prisoners were permitted, however, to stay in family groups.

Rosalia Karoly has stated:

"On a Sunday in August 1941 we were collected by the police and sent to Lackenbach. I was 12. On the following day I was sent to work digging a canal. I was already beaten on the first day. My mother was beaten with a rubber truncheon by Camp Commander Langmüller."

Josef Hodoschi was sent to Lackenbach on September 19th, 1941. He escaped but was recaptured, returned to the camp and given twenty-five strokes with the rubber truncheon. His mother and brothers and sisters all died at Auschwitz.[139] Another survivor, Franz Karall, recalls that both the Camp Commander and a Gypsy Kapo,[140] Sarkozi, ran through the camp with whips and beat anyone they wished. People who could not work were sent to Lodz and other parts of Poland.[141] Among the inmates were settled Gypsies (Rom) from Vienna and the Burgenland and at least one Jenisch.

Knobloch, an Austrian who visited the camp in the spring of 1943 to obtain specimens of Romani dialects, has provided a description of the conditions:

"The Gypsy Camp at Lackenbach was under the control of the Security Police (SD). The main part of the camp consisted of three long barracks which were divided by a corridor into two halves. In these further divisions separated smaller rooms, which gave enough space to the inhabitants. One barrack was intended for the Sinti, one for the Rom and one for those of mixed race . . . I discovered that efforts were being made to set up a Gypsy genealogy. I asked the purpose of this work and was told that it was intended to stop marriage between those of mixed race and further mixing. When I asked if it was intended to keep the Gypsies in the camps for ever I was told this was only a necessity because of the war and that after the war the Gypsies would be able to continue their nomadic life again and earn their living as previously by music and other activities. In fact there was an orchestra in the camp that had played once during an inspection by higher authorities from Vienna.

Apart from this, the men were occupied in two work parties, one building roads and the other felling trees in the forest. There was also a teacher in the camp (Mrs. Wajbele) who taught the children. She was a Gypsy and asked me for pencils . . . The spokesmen enjoyed a superior position in the camp. For the Sinti 'Lumpo' Schneeberger was the spokesman and for the Rom of the Burgenland Alexander Sarkozi.

The food in the camp was not bad. Of course there was also horse-meat which the Gypsies avoid when they are free to do so."[142]

At his trial after the war Langmüller was accused of responsibility for 287 deaths. In one incident 35 to 40 children were poisoned, possibly deliberately but more likely during some medical experiment. Sarkozi also faced trial.

The Nazi authorities in Austria seem to have regarded the prisoners in Lackenbach as being on the same level as those in other camps. Gerland[143] offered them to Himmler for use in medical experiments.[144]

After the plan to move German and Austrian Gypsies to Riga had been dropped[145] it was decided to use part of the Jewish ghetto at Lodz. A consignment of 5,000 were to be sent there but the mayor of Lodz protested:

"The Gypsies as born agitators and arsonists would start a conflagration."[146]

Biebow, the German head of the ghetto, also objected in a letter dated September 24th.[147] Ubelhör, Nazi civil chief in the area, was also opposed to the plan.[148] Himmler would not change the orders and suggested to Ubelhör that he should announce that for every fire in the ghetto, ten Gypsies would be shot. He would then discover that Gypsies will be the best firemen he ever had. Heydrich, Chief of Police, had been put in charge of the operation and he made the final choice to go ahead with the deportation.[149] Eichmann visited the ghetto and claimed at his trial that he sent the Gypsies to Lodz to save their lives.[150]

The first transports came in October 1941 and by the middle of November the whole consignment had arrived.[151] The 5,000 included over 2,600 children[152] from Austria and other countries. The senior Jewish ghetto representative, Rumkowski, was ordered to make room for the Gypsies. Jewish occupants had to vacate the houses in one quarter. This was then surrounded by a double and in some places a triple wall of barbed wire and an excavated ditch filled with water.[153]

In the small sectioned-off area the Gypsies were again interned in their family groups. The whole first day cries and lamentations filled the air and every evening the Jews saw cars full of soldiers going in the direction of the Gypsy quarter. That bitterly cold winter the Germans smashed all the windows of the houses. Two weeks later a typhus epidemic broke out. The Germans accorded no medical aid whatever. But two Jewish doctors volunteered to go in and help. One of them, Dr. Glaser, died of the disease. During the first two months 613 people perished.[154] Each day carts loaded with bodies had to be taken from the quarter. Some of the corpses were atrociously disfigured, with missing limbs. In March and April 1942 the remaining Gypsies were deported to Chelmno and gassed there.[155]

The first mention of Maidenek we have found is in the account of a young German Gypsy who was taken there in 1940. In June 1942 the Senior Prisoner[156] was a Gypsy named Galbavy from Holić.[157] Hannah Brzezinska came there from Rechlin at the end of 1944 or early 1945. She met Gypsies from Czechoslovakia, Germany and Poland in the camp, all of them slowly starving to death.[158]

The Nazis tried to destroy the official records of Mauthausen but some lists of prisoners have survived. These contain the names of Gypsies[159] who were generally accommodated in Block 6.[160] In July 1941 a transport of ninety-one Gypsies was sent from Buchenwald to Mauthausen, of whom one at least, Robert Schneeberger, survived.[161] The records for February 1945 state ten Gypsies died in the camp that month.[162] A Gypsy woman, chosen as an overseer, was, when her race was discovered, transferred to Auschwitz.[163]

No complete picture has come to light concerning Neuengamme but several references to Gypsies there exist. Gypsy internees had to wear brown triangles while the asocials carried brown and black badges.[164] Though called 'Zintys' by the other prisoners they may not have all been Sinti Gypsies.[165] Several men, given the rank of work foreman, formed an authority within the camp. They improved their position by stealing, sometimes from each other. A large-built man from this group was for a time Kapo of the Punishment Company and those sent to the company had to bribe him not to beat them.[166] There were also small Gypsy children, some born in a concentration camp and many of them orphans. They kept the parade ground and streets clean, starting work as soon as the other prisoners left the camp in the morning.[167]

The first large party of Gypsies to go to Ravensbrück concentration camp came from the Austrian Burgenland and arrived on June 29th, 1939. Women holding their small children close had to remain sitting on the ground for two days while the process of admission went on.[168] From time to time other groups of children were placed in the camp, many in the period 1942–3 being of Polish nationality. They were separated from their parents and relatives and dispersed[169] though other children were allowed to remain with their families.[170]

The Gypsies wore black triangles like the so-called asocials but formed a separate group.[171] They occupied Block 22 where conditions were the worst in the camp.[172] Starvation compelled them to beg outside the barracks of the Norwegian prisoners who received food parcels.[173] Gypsy women worked in the clothes factory[174] and two little girls, aged nine or ten, worked in the masseur and hairdressing salon early in 1942.[175]

Selections and mass killings appear to have begun late in 1943 : Eighty pregnant women were packed into one railway wagon and dispatched to Mauthausen[176] but the party was switched to Bergen-Belsen as Count Bernadotte of the Swedish Red Cross was taking an interest in the inmates of Mauthausen. They were exterminated on arrival at Bergen-Belsen.[177] Erdely Kapoline (no. 35726) was among a group gassed, probably in autumn 1944.[178] Mass executions took place during February 1945 and 1,356 Gypsies appear on the list of those murdered.[179] In addition Gypsies were sterilized at Ravensbrück and information about this is given below.

A Norwegian inmate of Sachsenhausen has described the arrival of Gypsy children from Ravensbrück on March 4th, 1945.

"The children from Ravensbrück were Gypsy children, fantastically beautiful and charming, hungry and musical. A group of them were given food in Norwegian Block 16 and gave a concert in gratitude."[180]

Other Gypsies had been in Sachsenhausen much earlier. An account from 1942 tells how they formed a community apart:

"When it was a question of standing in a queue in front of the clinic, Norwegians, Dutch and Germans always had to stand in front.

Right at the bottom came Jews and Gypsies. Then there were the middle classes, from Frenchmen and Belgians down to Ukrainians."[181]

No total figures are available for Treblinka nor can any estimate be made of the total number of Gypsies murdered there. But a few fragments of information remain:

"A number of Bessarabian Gypsies appeared. Two hundred men and eight hundred women and children. The Gypsies came on foot. Behind them came their wagons drawn by horses."[182]

Afterwards they were made to undress for 'baths' and then driven by guard dogs and blows into the gas chambers. We know that others came from Poland:

"Once a transport of seventy Gypsies from near Warsaw was brought in. These men, women and children were destitute. All they had were some soiled underwear and ragged clothes . . . Within a few hours all was quiet and nothing left but their corpses."[183]

A group of Gypsies recaptured after trying to escape from the Warsaw ghetto were sent to Treblinka and killed by machine-guns.[184]

Finally, other camps at which the presence of Gypsies is attested included Belzec,[185] Deutmergen,[186] Gross-Rosen,[187] Gusen,[188] Natzweiler,[189] Niederhagen,[190] Rechlin,[191] Sobibor,[192] Stutthof,[193] Theresienstadt,[194] and Zwodau.[195]

Gypsies interned in the concentration camps were regularly used as guinea-pigs for experiments. Usually these led to death, maiming and disfigurement. Rarely was any regard paid to the pain and suffering of the patients except by the prisoner nursing staff. Often the experiments were of doubtful or no scientific value and sometimes were simply another way of murdering unwanted human beings. The centres for experiments were squalid and lacked medicines, the circumstances mitigated heavily against recovery.

Below is a short account of some of the experiments, representing only a fraction of those which took place. We have indicated where possible who was responsible for this hideous maltreatment of Gypsy prisoners.

Authority to use Gypsies seems to have rested with Himmler. For example, he gave agreement to serological experiments under Prof. Fischer on June 9th, 1942.[196] But SS General Oswald Pohl, from March 1942 head of the Inspectorate of Concentration Camps, appears to have given permission for at least one set of experiments. No record exists to indicate that any difficulties were met in getting permission and it is obvious to us that authorization was in fact freely given.

At one stage, on May 15th, Himmler asked Grawitz (Chief doctor of the SS) to obtain the opinions of Nebe and other Nazis on the use of prisoners for sea-water experiments.[197] Grawitz replied[198] giving among others Nebe's ideas:

"I agree to the proposal to make an experiment to make sea-water drinkable. I suggest using the asocial Gypsy half-breeds in Auschwitz."

He said there were Gypsies healthy enough but not suitable for work, and that he was going to make a special suggestion to Himmler about it. He added:

". . . I think it right to choose the required number of guinea-pigs from these people. If Himmler agrees I will name the persons to be experimented upon."

In his communication to Himmler, Grawitz pointed out:

". . . because the Gypsies are partly of a different racial composition they may produce results which cannot immediately be applied to our men. So it is desirable that such prisoners who are similar to the European population should be made available for the experiments . . . I request your approval."

Brandt replied on behalf of Himmler, on July 8th, 1944, saying he had agreed to Nebe's proposals.[199]

One aspect of this field of activities was particularly horrible because of its widespread implications for Gypsies. This was experimentation with sterilization, one of the methods used in the attempt to destroy the Gypsy people. The Nazis wanted the labour of the living generation but were determined to prevent them from reproducing.

The Deputy Gauleiter for Lower Austria, Gerland, wrote to Himmler on August 24th, 1942, requesting that Dr. Fehringer be permitted to conduct experiments with caladium on the Gypsies in Lackenbach camp. This method of sterilization, however, could not be adopted on a large scale because the climate in Germany was unsuitable for growing this plant.

During the Auschwitz trial evidence was shown Dr. Lucas carried out sterilization of men and women at Ravensbrück.[200] Witness Bruno Stein said when he was in Auschwitz it was announced that ex-soldiers could volunteer to be sterilized and would then be freed. According to Stein, these ex-soldiers were put into a work party and built a platform, but they were not sterilized at that time. Later all were sent to Ravensbrück and sterilized there by Dr. Lucas at the end of 1944. Stein himself was not released but transferred to Sachsenhausen at the same period.[201]

Another witness said Dr. Lucas came to Ravensbrück in January 1945. This witness was sterilized on January 4th and had to stay in the sick bay for a week afterwards. He recalls that at this time six persons were being sterilized daily.[202] One Gypsy has recounted how he was sterilized without anaesthetic on January 10th. When he screamed Dr. Lucas said to him, "Be quiet you swine!" He was in the hospital block for six weeks after the operation.

Dr. Lucas himself claimed he only operated three times for sterilization. On other occasions the operations were a pretence and could be reversed. He claimed that Gypsies were so anxious to be sterilized so they could be released from the camp he could not resist doing the operations. One witness states that after the operation Gypsies were allowed to volunteer for military service. Those who did not were gassed.[203]

In 1945 Professor Clauberg sterilized between 120 and 140 Gypsy girls who had been brought to the camp from Auschwitz.[204] This was probably done by an injection into the uterus. The mothers of the girls signed forms of consent after being promised release. Several died and the survivors were not freed but transported to another camp. One twelve-year-old girl operated upon did not even have her abdominal wound sewn up after surgery. She died after several days of agony.[205] Dr. Schumann sterilized Gypsies in Auschwitz from March 1941, using X-rays.

Sterilization also took place outside the camps, for example 123 persons at Stettin.[206] Gypsy women married to Germans were operated on at Dusseldorf-Lierenfeld. Julius Adler and his family from Scheidemuhl were sterilized. His wife died soon after the operation.[207] Elfriede Dinschmidt was sterilized in an institution near Bielefeld in 1940 on the orders of the Eugenics Court: The reason given – she was a half-breed.[208] Lucia Strasdinsch, as a condition for being permitted to reside in Libau in the USSR, had to undergo sterilization on January 9th, 1942, on the orders of Lieutenant Frank.[209] There are many other Gypsies alive today who cannot bear children as a result, among them Tickno Gardner who carries a tattooed Auschwitz number. Lined up to be gassed with other Gypsies she escaped death by moving into another group of naked women near by and was then put to work sorting clothes.[210]

From the above information it is clear the practice was carried out in widely separated places and at different periods. In fact, sterilization was one of the first measures suggested against Gypsies and the choice between this and internment faced some even in the pre-war Nazi period. Towards the end of the war hospital facilities of every kind were needed for the increasing number of air-raid victims and this stopped sterilization being practised on a really large scale.

At Natzweiler experiments with typhus took place. Both Gypsies and Jews, sent from Auschwitz and elsewhere, were infected with the disease. Those selected travelled for two weeks during mid-winter locked in goods wagons. They had no heating and enough food for only four days so that many perished and others became seriously ill even before arriving at Natzweiler.[211] Dr. Chretien, a prisoner who worked in the camp hospital, relates how eighty Gypsies were used for these experiments early in 1944. Divided into two equal groups they were placed in two separate small and cramped rooms. Those in one room received vaccination against typhus while the others did not. Then the entire number were injected with typhus, returned to their rooms and locked in.[212] Another report says six men including Gypsies were injected in the arm at the hospital. In consequence the whole length of the arm was scarred, pus erupted everywhere on the skin and the sores did not heal.

Also in 1944 Gypsies came from Sachsenhausen, Buchenwald and elsewhere to a centre at Dachau for experiments involving injections with a solution of salt. It was claimed some were volunteers. A witness reports that two volunteered only in order to get out of a punishment squad. Beiglböck, who was among those conducting the research, found some of the Gypsies had been drinking water and he flew into a rage, reproaching them with first volunteering and then disobeying the rules.[213] A prisoner, Franz Blaha, an eye-witness of these experiments, says in his account that in the autumn of 1944 a group of forty to eighty Gypsies and Hungarians were locked up in a room for five days and given nothing except salt-water. None died, probably because they received food smuggled in by other prisoners.[214]

Gypsies were used at Sachsenhausen for experiments with mustard gas.[215] An anti-gas injection was also tested by Eickenbach at Natzweiler early in 1944. After injections, prisoners were put into a gas-filled room and four died. When the experiment was repeated with a group of ten Gypsies in June, evidence shows that two who were not injected, as a control to the experiment, died. One of the survivors was killed and dissected for an autopsy.[216]

At Buchenwald twenty-six Gypsies received injections of spotted fever virus on the orders of Pohl. Six of them died.[217] At the same camp during 1942 four Gypsy women were used for chilling experiments.[218] Not enough is yet known about the activities of Dr. Mengele who is still alive and believed to be in hiding in South America, but it has been stated that he killed some Gypsies because their eyes were of a certain colour. He sent the eyes to a Berlin institute.[219] We also know he used Gypsies in experiments at Auschwitz for injections with phenole and was particularly interested in twins and blood groups.[220]

Some tests carried out on Gypsies were part of an attempt to prove their inferiority to Germans. With this aim Himmler dispatched a selection of forty Gypsies to Sachsenhausen in spring 1942 for investigation by Prof. Fischer.[221] Prof. Fischer and Dr. Hornbaek, both of whom had acquired experience while working on black prisoners of war, received permission to perform experiments on Gypsies. Hornbaek soon dropped out however because he was sent to the Eastern Front.[222] We must mention lastly that euthanasia took place outside the camps in old persons' homes and elsewhere.[223]

To conclude this section we quote extracts from the personal stories of several German-born Gypsies.

In 1938 Kurt Ansin entered Buchenwald with his father. Dr. Ritter and Eva Justin[224] both came to interview the Gypsies about their families, bringing them one by one into the camp office. They brought written family trees with them. Himmler visited the camp and asked about the food. Afraid to complain they said it was good. Later Kurt was released from Buchenwald and went to live at the official Gypsy camp Am Holzweg in Magdeburg. Questioning on family connections continued and they were taken into town by car to be interviewed, being left to find their own way back to the camp. So-called Gypsy experts came in 1943 and took skull and other anatomical measurements. A few days later police with dogs surrounded the camp, driving everyone out with sticks. The police said they were to be settled on the land and would each be given a house, a cow and a horse. In fact their destination was Auschwitz. While Kurt was there his brother who had been five years in the army arrived and was shot on the same day. Later, Kurt was sent to Buchenwald, then to Ellrich and Harzung camps. When this last camp was evacuated he and other prisoners took part in a forced march to Czechoslovakia.[225]

Eichwald Rose's story is now amongst the Nuremburg Trial documents:

"I was born in 1908 in Upper Silesia and worked as a horse-dealer in Stettin. In June 1938 I was arrested by the police for having relations with an Aryan girl. I was taken to Sachsenhausen and put in the Jewish section. My father was a Gypsy, my mother half-Jewish, half-Gypsy. I remained in Sachsenhausen until December 1940 and was badly treated there. Then I volunteered to search for unexploded bombs. As a reward for my work I was released and sent back to Stettin before Christmas on condition that I would be sterilized at Wendorf hospital near Stettin. I had to sign a paper signifying that I submitted voluntarily to sterilization. If I had not done this they would have sent me back to a concentration camp. The operation took place in May 1941. I was separated from my wife and four children and sent as a farm-worker to Pomerania. In September 1942 I was arrested again, together with my father, four brothers and two sisters. I was taken to Sachsenhausen and the others to Auschwitz. Of the seven of us only one sister returned. While I was in Sachsenhausen the second time my eldest daughter Martha, then twelve years old, was taken to hospital and sterilized. I worked in the tailor's shop until the camp was liberated in May 1945."[226]

Richard Rose relates:

"In 1937 or 1938 my father was told he could not run his own little circus any more. My ordinary papers were taken away and I was given special papers so I could no longer work as an acrobat. In 1941 they forced me to work in a factory but two weeks later I was released from the labour corps because I was not pure German. Later in the year I was arrested and put in prison. In 1943 I was sent to Buchenwald where my number was 22,736, and then to Dora. Here I received a letter from my mother in Auschwitz.

'Brief news. I cannot complain. We are here in the family camp. We are well. It won't be long and we shall certainly meet again after the war.'

In fact my mother, father and four of my brothers and sisters died. In 1945 I was transferred to Sachsenhausen and was on the 'death march' to Wittstock after the camp had been broken up."

Lina Steinbach was sent to prison in 1941 or 1942 for fortune-telling. From the prison she went to Ravensbrück and other camps – Schieben b.Herzberg, Sachsen-Altenburg and Tauchern b.Leipzig. She also worked for HASAG making armour plate. She vividly remembers one particular incident:

"A Gypsy woman tries to escape and was caught. The others had to stand and watch as she was beaten and had dogs set on her. Then the German guards put her in the punishment block and told the other prisoners there they could do what they liked with her as they had had to stand in the freezing cold because of her. Some prisoners in the punishment block beat her to death."

Lina's mother and son died in Auschwitz and her brother in Mauthausen.

Paul Weiss was born in Neubrandenburg where the authorities compelled the Gypsies to encamp in a wood four kilometres from the nearest village. They went to work by train and returned to the camp each night. They were banned from public houses, their children not admitted to local schools. Soon after Loli Tschai (Eva Justin) paid a visit to them, all were taken to Neustrelitz and assembled in a workhouse. From there they moved on to Auschwitz where Paul fell ill with typhus. Later he was sent to Dora camp at Buchenwald where he received twenty-five strokes for fetching food without an escort although told to do so by a camp officer. He was then put in the punishment company where they all wore a special mark on their clothes – which they called a shooting target. The company had to march eighteen kilometres to work in the morning and back again at night. He survived three months of this and then volunteered for a transport to Niedersachswerfen. Going from there to Ellrich as a miner, he was later evacuated to Sachsenhausen. When the group reached there they found the camp full and were abandoned on the railway siding. Many were killed in an air attack and the remainder then let into the camp. After three days in Sachsenhausen Paul was reclassified as a German and enrolled as a soldier. Each new recruit was allowed to fire five shots for practice and was then to be sent to the front. At the last moment the plans were changed and they were marched through woods and lanes to Fregenstein im Wald. Here Paul served on a special unit burying bodies until he was freed.

Natascha Winter lived in Karlsruhe before the war. In about 1940 she and her family were sent to Sobkow in Poland and put in houses. For fourteen days they were guarded and then this precaution was dropped. Nine months later they made their own way back to Karlsruhe with two other families. Natascha was later taken to Ravensbrück with her mother who was not a Gypsy. Loli Tschai visited them in Ravensbrück and suggested the mother should leave the camp and send them food parcels from outside. But she would not leave her children and later on was sent to Auschwitz as she refused to divorce her Gypsy husband. Natascha went from Ravensbrück to Berlin-Haselhorst and then to Sachsenhausen. Her father died in Dachau.[227]

Below we give a table of deaths during the war period. It should be remembered that these figures do not represent the full measure of Gypsy suffering during the Nazi period. Of those not killed thousands were interned in camps and prisons or suffered other restrictions on their liberty. Many had mental breakdowns as a result of this confinement, worse perhaps for nomadic Gypsies than for sedentary citizens. Others were engaged in forced labour on the land, in mines and factories. Many survivors still bore the marks of experiments carried out on them and others were unable to bear children after irreversible sterilization operations. The birth rate dropped not only through direct interference but also through the separation of young men from their families.

Country	Population in 1939	Deaths	Source for deaths figure
Austria	11,200	6,500	Steinmetz
Belgium	600	500	Estimate
Bohemia	13,000	6,500	Horvathová
Croatia	28,500	28,000	Uhlik
Estonia	1,000	1,000	Estimate
France	40,000	15,000	*Droit et Liberté*
Germany	20,000	15,000	Estimate (See Sippel, *Spiegel*)
Holland	500	500	Estimate
Hungary	100,000	28,000	Nácizmus Üldözötteinen Bizottsága
Italy	25,000	1,000	Estimate
Latvia	5,000	2,500	Kochanowski (1946)
Lithuania	1,000	1,000	Estimate
Luxembourg	200	200	Estimate
Poland	50,000	35,000	Estimate

THE DESTINY OF EUROPE'S GYPSIES

Country	Population in 1939	Deaths	Source for deaths figure
Romania	300,000	36,000	Romanian War Crimes Commission
Serbia	60,000	12,000*	Estimate
Slovakia	80,000	1,000	Estimate
USSR	200,000	30,000*	Estimate
Total		219,700	

* These figures may prove to be much higher when further documentation is available.

PART THREE

CHAPTER NINE

THE AFTERMATH

U bar dikhila xoymi, oprundus,
sviymi vastinsa bari armayasa.
Liska ozistar sesi garadu
mangila pali ti inkil ziyasa.

The upright stone stares angrily
with clenched fists and a great curse.
From within a hidden voice
tries to send out a song.

The roads where we still travel
wait to hear it.
The Gypsies await the call
together with their horses.

But they are quiet, all are asleep.
Our brothers lie among the flowers
and no one knows who they are
or on which road the victims fell.

Hush, Gypsies! Let them sleep
beneath the flowers.
Halt, Gypsies! May
all our children have their strength.
                              Dimiter Golemanov

"We faced something terrible. Heaps of unburied bodies and unbearable stench. When I saw the surviving Romanies, with small children among them, I was shaken. Then I went over to the ovens and found on one of the steel stretchers the half-charred body of a girl and I understood in one awful minute what had been going on there."

So relates British serviceman Frederick Wood, first president of the Gypsy Council. He was with the spear-heading 6th Airborne

Division, elements of which overran Belsen as Allied forces penetrated the collapsing Third Reich.

The opening of the concentration camps brought no immediate release. Few had the reserves even to walk out. Weak and destitute, a desperate uncertainty surrounded them. Outside, they could only stumble on unwanted news of missing relatives who had perished and the realization of just how immense had been the destruction of the Gypsy people. Scattered fragments were all that remained of great families and entire *vitsi* (clans).

Even those outside the camps, who had escaped internment and the murder squads, had lived for the most part in appalling conditions deprived of normal human contact. They had been denied every basic right, outlawed and isolated in remote areas. This isolation caused a breakdown and reversal of the process of *natural* integration, producing a generation further handicapped by war-weary parents. Thus the holocaust had touched everyone, killing many, blighting all. Many suffered mental breakdown as a result and some committed suicide.

For ex-internees and others reduced to the status of refugees there now began an indeterminate period in displaced persons' camps where they had to share accommodation with all classes including former SS men, police of various nationalities and other pro-Nazis who submerged their identity in the herds of refugees. Remnants of the families who had been put behind barbed wire at the Dusseldorf-Lierenfeld holding camp before the war found themselves in the same barracks when they returned.[1]

The sorting process was tough and the Displaced Persons camps administration necessarily firm. At Auschwitz Gypsies refused to give details about their families. They were reluctant to impart any information even for indemnification claims which could be used to trace and detain relations because they suspected persecution would recommence. Convinced the administration would use the data later to check and harass them, members of a Hungarian Gypsy family, well-known musicians, would not allow forms to be completed. There could be no guarantee that the claim forms would not be scrutinised by police agencies.

Some of the single survivors and orphaned children soon fell into difficulties under the military occupation authorities and new German civil law. Anyone who lost their Displaced Person's card or whose records in the UN relief agency UNRRA or IRO[2] archives had been misplaced or who had served a term in prison for any offence could be refused the papers they needed after release. In this situation when next picked up by the police they were liable to deportation on a court order or would simply be told on police authority to quit Germany. Some Gypsies, unable to obtain admission to another state, became caught in a vicious circle, were re-imprisoned and served further terms. The number of stateless Gypsies in Europe today is said to be 30,000. The military courts, determined to make stern examples to re-establish order and authority, passed the death sentence and long prison terms on numbers of people, including Gypsies, who, unhinged by their ordeals in the camps, sought revenge and assaulted and murdered known Nazis.

During the Nuremberg war crimes trials not one Gypsy was called as a witness by the Allied prosecutors during the long-drawn-out processes of the tribunal. But an incident within the precincts of the court momentarily drew attention to the feelings of the Gypsy people. Soldiers who volunteered for guard duty at the military tribunal included two English Gypsies. One of them has recounted the incident:

> "There was a glass panel between us and the sergeant on duty who had to indicate through this window when each prisoner was to be brought forward. Five SS men were brought into the room. Four stood along one wall while we two escorted the fifth. This SS man was told to move forward towards the court to stand trial, but instead he stood to attention and gave the Nazi salute, shouting 'Heil Hitler!' This infuriated me. All that I had seen came back to me and on the spur of the moment I turned on him and bayoneted him."[3]

The other guards, caught up in the spontaneous violence, killed the remaining four prisoners on the floor of the ante-room.

The trials could not alter the past and did nothing to change the situation of Gypsies in post-war Europe. Denazification – though it broke the Nazi party structure, failed to exorcise deepseated prejudice which continued to taint the legal and civil administration in reconstructed Germany. This is evident in the obstruction and opposition to claims for war crimes indemnification. The modest number of applications from Gypsies listed for hearing in German courts, under laws enacted in implementation of the Bonn convention, have been undermined by the judiciary.

The Convention provided that 'persons persecuted by reason of nationality' should be compensated. It covered Jews who had held German citizenship before the Nazis came to power. But a circular from the Interior Ministry of Württemberg state published on May 9th, 1950, said that in all restitution claims presented by Gypsies:

> "It should be borne in mind that Gypsies had been persecuted under the Nazis not for any racial reason but because of an asocial and criminal record."

One such claim came from Erik Balasz. At first hidden by Polish peasants, he and his family had been arrested in 1940. Interned from August that year, at the age of sixteen, he contracted tuberculosis and received treatment at Benninghausen. Meanwhile his mother remained at Ravensbrück and was shot with others when the camp was evacuated. The Compensation Claims Office at Detmold in October 1955 stated in its findings that this was not a case of racial persecution. Balasz's arrest had been made by police in occupied territory on security grounds. He had failed to prove, according to the presiding judge, his internment could be attributed to his Gypsy origin. The court would go no further than to accept that racial motives replaced police security measures after Himmler's decree of December 16th, 1942, which consigned Gypsies to Auschwitz.

A high proportion of the entire Gypsy population in Germany and Austria had been rounded up before late 1942. Outside the Reich, throughout occupied Europe, tens of thousands suffered restrictions, internment and death before the decree. In Serbia the Gypsy *final solution* had been declared completed and the 'Gypsies

Forbidden' signs taken down from trains and cafés. At one stroke the survivors were neatly excluded from receiving any compensation.

But this artificial division of the Nazi persecution into two distinct phases was not the only loophole which has enabled the West German government to evade liability. Another escape clause was invented when a somewhat similar case the same year came before the courts at Luneburg, Lower Saxony. Polish-born Gypsy, Wacslaw Mierzinski, claimed for impairment of health and loss of freedom. Deported from Poland to do forced labour in Germany, he had later been transferred to a concentration camp.

The Lüneburg restitution court would not accept that he had been interned because he was a Gypsy. His father had been arrested for alleged membership of a Polish underground organization; hence the son might be considered an enemy of the state. The question of race, the court held, 'played no part in the arrest'. The fact is, in order to lend a quasi-legality to the destruction of Gypsies in the occupied territories, as noted earlier, German troops had been instructed to treat them as bandits, partisans and couriers for the guerrillas, any of which warranted instant death.

These rulings at district and state level received endorsement by the Federal Supreme Court. This came about after another lower court, in North Rhine-Westphalia, had actually upheld the compensation claim of a Gypsy woman deported from Germany to Poland in 1940. The North Rhine district judge found she *had* suffered racial persecution.

The Supreme Court reversed this decision, annulled her award and invalidated other such claims. The court ruled that the deportation of Gypsies, including the claimant, was not a case of racial persecution but a measure justified by the demands of national security. The presiding judge summed up:

> "The resettlement action was contrary to the principles of legal justice. But though the manner of its execution must be described as cruel and inhuman this should not suggest that the action was in itself a measure of racial persecution ... The National Socialist

rulers committed innumerable deeds of inhumanity which disregarded the principles of legal justice but this does not entitle anyone to compensation under the present law."[4]

The hope of finding lost relatives and later better opportunities brought an increasing number of Gypsies into West Germany. By 1970 there were perhaps as many as 30,000 Sinti and 8,000 foreign-born Gypsies in the country, including many migrant workers from Yugoslavia. But wherever they came from they were not wanted. Those who escaped from East Germany or left Poland, crossing the minefields and barbed wire of divided Europe, faced arrest, fines and imprisonment when they arrived in the west. West German border guards at Buchen unhitched railway coaches chartered by Michael Kwiek to bring three hundred Gypsies from Upper Silesia in 1959 and detained them after they had unsuccessfully struggled to leave. A plea to be permitted a temporary stay in the refugee camp at Friedland was rejected and a church mission hall was opened to accommodate them only when the Red Cross intervened. Eventually four members of the group, who carried papers proving they had been concentration camp inmates, were allowed to go on to Friedland.

A smaller party had been sent back to Poland the previous month. The Federal Ministry of the Interior had said on that occasion they could not be allowed in because they had undetermined nationality. When the Red Cross took up the issue with the Polish government they were told the party had been permitted to travel without passports because of their position as stateless persons. In other words Poland was prepared to cut red tape in order to see the back of them. But West Germany was equally determined not to admit Gypsies. When in November 1965 a party of twenty-six arrived by air at Munich by way of Yugoslavia, intending to join relatives already in Germany, they were held in prison and deported back to Poland. Three men, including Ferko Czory, who had helped to make arrangements on the west side, were heavily fined for providing forged papers.

Those eventually accepted into West Germany, through the

intervention of the Red Cross and others, have had to live under special restrictions. A group in Dortmund, for example, have passes which permit them to travel only within a certain radius from their city homes. Nomadism continued to be outlawed and Gypsies harassed by the authorities. One law, dating back to 1938, commonly invoked, empowered the courts to deport anyone without citizenship papers considered undesirable. Gypsies brought into Germany in the latter part of the war as forced labourers and then classified as displaced persons came within this category. Not until 1965 was this piece of legislation revoked. Another, still in force, restricted Gypsy families from travelling with school-age children. Constant attempts were made to register Gypsies for police purposes and frequent visits and raids made on the few authorized camps, mostly inhabited by fragmented survivors of the war. Little provision has been made for nomadic Gypsies and in one case when a house was allocated to a Gypsy family in a provincial town, it was ransacked and burned by local residents before they could take up occupation.

The same anti-Gypsy prejudice has been virulent throughout Europe. Constant harassment has to be borne like bad weather. In Western Europe the total neglect – except in a few countries – of the human rights and social needs of Gypsies, is manifested by a policy of constantly moving families on from one town to the next, from one state to another. This policy has been condemned by the Council of Europe which points out that it deprives them of basic security and education for their children, theoretically guaranteed under the European Convention on Human Rights.

East European communist governments, including Russia, have followed a diametrically opposite policy – outlawing nomadism and attempting assimilation by compulsion. In some instances generous resources have been allocated for re-settlement and education schemes. Czechoslovakia, for example, budgeted to spend eight million pounds. But much work, though well intentioned, has been marred by an over-emphasis on conformity with the norms of the dominant society.

A brief survey of what has been happening in different parts of the continent soon forces one to conclude that few governments can escape criticism, if not condemnation, for their attitude and actions towards Gypsies in recent years.

On the road in Italy and Austria Dennis Marriner and his wife Zilka suffered move-on operations during the late forties by police and military authorities. Mounted police in Austria rode through a camp and toppled their wagons over. Around Trieste early in 1951 when the British Army controlled the civil police force three hundred Gypsies were driven out of the zone. The survivors of several Sinti families had come together for security. But they could find no work and the women were constantly arrested for begging. In an early morning raid scores of police descended on the camp in jeeps and cars, bringing dogs. The men led away mules and horses and the police began to haul out the wagons by hand. Two, in bad condition, were broken up as women and children stood in confusion, shouting and crying.

Dennis Marriner, who afterwards protested in vain to the British military authorities, recalls:

> "The fire brigade was then summoned and the firemen ordered to direct jets of water on to tents and wagons. The flimsy rag tents collapsed under the pressure hoses – bedding, clothes and belongings were soaked. Bundles rolled away under impact of the jets."[5]

Twenty years later, the central government in Italy has itself done nothing for the 60,000 Gypsies in the country. The Ministry of the Interior in 1966 sent out a circular asking local authorities to look into the situation and not to refuse help. But five years later there were still only seven official camping sites set aside for nomadic families and by-laws against the stationing of caravans continued to be enforced.

At Centocelle, a suburb of Rome, in October 1969, an encampment consisting of wooden shacks and tents built near the airport, was surrounded at 5 a.m. by armed police. A hundred Gypsies, including thirty children, were turned out of their miserable homes and taken in lorries to the local police headquarters.

After examination of papers, half were ordered to return to

their 'place of origin'. In most cases this meant to remote villages where they had no homes and no chance of making a living. Sixteen with foreign citizenship were deported. Only one person, a youth, was charged with any offence and that was a minor misdemeanour.[6]

Many Gypsies in Spain suffered similar treatment but on a greater scale – because the authorities believed they made a bad impression on foreign tourists. A drive to break up shanty settlements on the outskirts of several cities has been described by Professor Walter Starkie who gives this close-up of the destruction of a Gypsy quarter in Barcelona:

> "As soon as the order came from Madrid . . . the police went to one of the settlements which consisted of wretched shacks perched on a bank beside the railway line . . . they sprinkled the huts with petrol and set fire to them."

The police took away some of the women and shaved their heads, and warned everyone not to return or try to re-erect the shelters.

The poorer nomadic Gypsies officially number 60,000, but there are several hundred thousand settled in Andalusia and other provinces.

Nomadic Gypsies in France – roughly a third of the 145,000 total – are compelled to carry special registration cards. These cards must be signed by a police officer or the mayor in each district entered. Until recently this routine was often followed several times a week and brought endless difficulties and often deliberate delays which upset the family work pattern. The head of the family also has to get a paper signed by the local school-master attesting to the children's school attendance. This schooling usually consists of an unwelcome couple of hours on irregular days spent at the back of a crowded classroom. The result is ninety per cent illiteracy.

Most districts prohibit camping by Gypsies and there are signs everywhere saying 'stopping by nomads forbidden'. Families frequently have to trespass on municipal land and the police order them to leave. Refusal may bring a night visit when police have been known to beat on caravans with their rifle butts and rock them from side to side until crockery crashes to the floor.

As in Italy, the Ministry of the Interior during 1966 asked the prefectures to allow families to stay a reasonable period of time but this circular had little effect. The few districts responding have usually designated stopping places on rubbish tips and other undesirable spots, with no water supply or sanitary facilities.

The *pass* law was modified in 1969 but failure to produce the 'carte de circulation' brings prosecution as before. One man was fined after leaving his card in his lorry parked three hundred yards away. Every Gypsy-owned vehicle has to carry distinct blue and white number plates, so the police can recognize them at a glance.

The recent destruction of Gypsy shanty towns around Paris and other large cities caused more hardship. One of the largest 'bidonvilles', in the Paris suburb of Rosy-sous-Bois, held over 3,000 Gypsies. It was razed to the ground in 1966 to make way for flats. Bulldozers, under heavy police guard, entered the land while many people were absent at work. A child was injured by falling debris, fires started in several places and much personal property was ploughed into the ground or burned.

The French police use their powers to enter private ground and evict families living in caravans. Numerous small Gypsy-owned yards have been closed in recent years and even those who want to take houses outside the Gypsy quarters, such as that in Marseilles, meet opposition. One family who bought a house at Schalkendorf in the Bas-Rhin region found local shops refused them service. Parents organized a school strike when Gypsy children tried to attend classes and finally a mob of residents, some armed with pitchforks, surrounded the house. The family reluctantly agreed to sell out and quit.

A similar process has been going on in Britain since the war. It was once possible for families to buy land and set up winter quarters. But legislation enacted in 1960 (The Caravan Sites and Development Act) empowered local authorities to close down existing sites, forcing many back on the road to face relentless hounding from one county to another. Evictions from vacant plots and slum clearance land have brought about ugly scenes and frequent violence, causing injury and even death.[7] Extreme political groups around Birmingham exacerbated prejudice, as can be gauged from the words of one local politician:

"We must remember that although we are dealing with people who members of this council would not look upon as human beings in the normal sense, they have children who are likely to grow up to become a kind of sewer of society."

Another put it more bluntly:

"There are some of these people who you can do nothing with and you must then exterminate the impossibles."[8]

John Connors, in November 1966 encamped near Dudley outside Birmingham, within hours had to face council employees accompanied by police who came to tow his caravan and three others from the land.

"They refused me time to telephone the hospital about my wife who was expecting a baby and in poor health with suspected TB. A police sergeant coupled my trailer to the Land-Rover. The wheels hit a pothole and my son, aged two, was thrown on to the floor but they refused to wait while I got him treatment."

The next day the child was admitted to hospital with blood poisoning. In neighbouring Walsall three children were burned to death after their caravan had been towed by the council on to the street from a car park.

Legal discrimination is written into the 1959 Highways Act. Section 127 read:

"If without lawful authority or excuse . . . a gipsy . . . encamps on a highway he shall be guilty of an offence."

Circulars, on the same lines as those sent out by their counterparts in Italy and France, have been issued by the Ministry of Housing and Local Government and proved ineffectual. A survey carried out in 1965 counted 15,000 Gypsies on the roads in England and Wales and revealed shocking indifference on the part of local government.

The Caravan Sites Act, placing an obligation on councils to establish proper caravan parks after April 1970, was openly defied by Walsall and other Midland authorities. A few sites were added but at a rate that would take twenty years to bring adequate provision.

The situation in the Irish Republic and Northern Ireland is closely linked with Britain. An Irish government commission urged the need for sites in 1963 but harassment continued, causing resentment and unrest among families around Dublin. The record of Dublin Corporation, since redeemed by provision of two sites accommodating together some seventy families, was among the worst. A small number of families, on surrender of their wagons for burning, were housed. But in general *tinkers* (Irish travellers) were driven from the city.

The situation in other parts of Ireland has been as bad. Michael McInerney, aged forty-one, the father of ten children, was shot dead in front of his family when two young farmers attacked a roadside camp in Co. Kilkenny. A jury found them not guilty of murder and sentenced them to two years for manslaughter.

In Northern Ireland, still only planning three sites in 1970, constant harassment has reduced the number of *itinerant* families by half. They have in desperation sought refuge in the Irish Republic and Britain.

Belgium, with 8,500 Gypsies, has a community similar in size to that in Ireland. The government has been reluctant to admit their existence though signs on cafés and bars, saying 'Gypsies Prohibited', bear witness to their presence and to widespread prejudice. Whether born in Belgium or abroad, the law defines them as aliens. As in France, they must register with the police and carry a *Carte de Nomade*, to be shown monthly to the authorities.

Rarely allowed to stay more than a day and a night at the roadside, parents are prevented from sending their children to school.

The only temporary stopping place is commonly the local rubbish tip, which contributes to the fact that infant mortality among Belgian Gypsies is twenty per cent above the national average.[9]

A Gypsy who learned to read and write in a concentration camp has written a description of the perpetual harassment:

> "When we have to find a stopping place somewhere at night, we are awakened by police sirens and the arrival of police towing vehicles at seven in the morning. We have to suffer the brutalities of the police on top of having no sanitation, no medical help, few comforts and no water or electricity."[10]

Finally, we turn to two countries whose policies have often been held up as the most progressive. The Netherlands is the one country to have established a network of caravan sites for nomadic families, while Sweden has assisted a small Gypsy community by providing permanent accommodation, education and employment opportunities.

The reason for the Netherlands' adoption of a constructive programme, first suggested in 1948, may be traced partly to the failure over the previous thirty years to compel nomads to give up travelling or depart across the frontier.

Not until 1957 was direct encouragement given to local authorities to set up large jointly-run regional caravan sites. The following year the first of eight properly serviced camps, with space for seventy-five caravans, was created at Hertogenbosch. Many smaller ones have since been established with the help of a government grant of £250 for each caravan pitch. On the larger parks community centres have been built and some have Montessori nursery schools as part of a special system of instruction for the children. Nevertheless, in 1966 half the families were still spending the winter in muddy encampments and the children receiving little or no education.[11]

A criticism from official quarters is that the network of sites has proved too attractive. Few families have any desire to move into houses. This view, of course, exposes the policy underpinning the programme from the start: assimilation of the *caravan-dwellers*.

It is envisaged that as integration proceeds the caravan sites will be closed down.

In Sweden the majority of Gypsies want houses and apartments, if only to escape the nordic climate. Until the present decade, they had been kept constantly on the move and suffered the rigours of tent life, as a parliamentary commission discovered in 1954. Again, the emphasis has been on rehabilitation, a task allocated since 1960 to the National Swedish Labour Market Board. Until 1964, Gypsy families continued to live in appalling conditions in collections of tents and tar-paper shacks on the outskirts of Stockholm. Now most in the capital have decent accommodation and children attend school and some men have begun to take employment as truck drivers and factory workers.

Several thousand Gypsies living in other parts of Scandinavia are receiving far less favourable treatment. Only one child in five is attending school in Finland and little has been done about it. Norway has gone to the opposite extreme and compelled attendance, in some cases forcibly separating children from parents. Travelling is restricted and some families confined to special settlements. Denmark has closed a number of camping sites and on those remaining young people who get married must move into houses.

Gypsies have been prohibited from travelling on the road in Russia since 1956, although the authorities have found it difficult to stop movement entirely. Other east European communist governments have passed similar legislation and the police in some areas of Czechoslovakia, under various pretexts, shot horses belonging to Gypsies. Local authorities have sometimes removed the wheels from caravans to prevent families travelling – which illustrates the extremes of policy carried out on the two sides of Europe.

A proportion have undoubtedly benefited from better conditions, but the majority remain confined to poor shacks and overcrowded tenements. Some Gypsies have refused to move into houses and take factory work – though unable to carry on former trades – and a few have been imprisoned for offences arising out of this resistance.

The existence of Gypsy communities in many villages and small towns in Slovakia has been threatened by a recommendation in 1965 that no commune should contain more than five per cent Gypsies. In one year 1,000 families were uprooted and dispersed to villages in Bohemia. Houses have been built for them but neighbours have shown hostility and work is scarce.

No special schools for Gypsy children, though many speak Romani as their mother tongue, were permitted until 1966. Four small centres for backward children have since been tolerated but the children are still compelled to study through Slovak. As a result few reach even average grades and there is a tendency to regard Gypsy children as less intelligent. The same process has been going on in Poland and Hungary, where officialdom has tried to impose solutions that fail to take into account the different life-style and outlook of the Gypsy people. Romania and Bulgaria – with the exception in the latter of some unpromising settlement of Gypsies in collective farms – have largely ignored the presence of Gypsies as demanding separate consideration and have failed to recognize them as a separate national minority.

In western Europe serious modern studies are lacking and official circles can gain from books only the romantic stereotype image of Gypsies. Since these fictional Gypsies are never encountered, it is commonly thought that the families seen on the roadside are degenerate lay-abouts and drop-outs unconnected with the true Romanies.

The same attitude is found in eastern Europe. But in addition some communist writers have provided a theoretical argument for denying proper recognition to the Gypsy people. The line of reasoning begins with Stalin's criteria according to which national status belongs only to minorities who possess territory and a viable economy, as well as a common language, culture and history. A Czech theorist, Jaroslav Sus, whose work[12] remains the standard text on the subject, provides a short cut by stating that Gypsies have no culture worth the name and therefore pose not a minority question but a social problem. He expresses a conviction widespread in Europe when he writes:

"The state of Gypsy ethnicity leaves only one measure possible – assimilation . . . It would be incorrect and in the end reactionary to act against the progressive decay of Gypsy ethnic unity."

And he adds that the way to achieve assimilation "does not exclude force which would tend to remove whatever differences exist".

The policies we have just examined, whether of harassment, assimilation or simple neglect, reflect the persistent popular attitudes towards Gypsies based in turn upon the stereotypes of Gypsies as parasites and criminals described in the first part of this study. The resulting pressures put upon Gypsies not only to give up a way of life – in the case of nomadic groups – but even their identity as Gypsies, causes deep-seated disturbances and disintegration within the Gypsy community.

The individual cannot indefinitely withstand the continued psychological attack – amounting to a wish to annihilate him as a member of an unwanted minority – and from this the dissolution of the personality may begin. As Gypsies yield to the Gajo estimation of them as objects of distrust, fear and taboo, alienation shows itself in widespread apathy, inter-dispersed with occasional fits of violence. In the process, society – Gypsy and Gajo alike – becomes tainted by ill-will which permeates the whole community fabric.

Faced with a minority shorn of their pride as a separate people, falling apart because of the stresses laid upon them, officialdom finds growing justification for regarding Gypsies only as problem families. The vicious circle is completed by the formal pronouncement of a *Gypsy Problem*. The administration then, with the help of social workers, sets about mopping up the left-over socially inadequate Gypsies.

Harassment and assimilation now become facets of the same policy, aimed at destruction of the Gypsy way of life and forced conformity. Well-intentioned public officials appear to support the Gypsy cause. But in reality they regard Gypsies as unable to represent themselves, and therefore usurp the leadership and monopolize decision-making that ought rightfully to belong to Gypsies. Social workers employ the case-work approach which further fragments the Gypsy community by ignoring its separate culture and identity or regarding these as totally irrelevant to their difficulties. The *enlightened* official approach, represented at state level in the Netherlands and Sweden, snares itself by being too narrow in vision or by displaying an overbearing paternalism – as in France and Ireland – which smothers initiative from within the Gypsy community.

Although government policy appears to be helping individuals, in effect by encouraging them to opt out of the Gypsy community this emasculation actually prevents natural integration; that is, sufficient adjustment of their life-style by Gypsies as a group to remove causes of intolerable friction between themselves and Gajo society. The efforts of Gypsies to make this essential re-alignment on their own terms are constantly frustrated. As we have noted in France and Britain, it is often impossible for Gypsies to buy land and provide themselves with a place to live – either in houses or caravans. A group of twenty-six families in Slovakia who wanted to build brick houses in place of shack dwellings were stopped because official policy demanded their dispersal. Gypsies entering Sweden to join relatives have been expelled, though the government has announced that fifty selected families shall be absorbed from abroad each year. Everything must be done under Gajo direction and control.

When, at certain periods, Gypsies had a recognized role – as smiths, horse-dealers and musicians in eastern and central Europe – they formed an integral part of society. However low their position, they occupied a place in the community, a station in life. To an extent many Gypsies in western Europe today play a part in the economy – as scavenger scrap-collectors feeding back raw material into industry. On this level they have integrated themselves, but socially remain outcasts.

Far more significant than this limited relationship with economic enterprise – anyhow almost vanished in south-east Europe – is the integration *inwards* which results from the conflict with the Gajo world. The realization that the gap is ever widening brings on the common desperation of the have-nots. Stronger members of the Gypsy community, in contrast to the general apathy, begin to assert themselves. As their numbers grow, the policy of forced assimilation is seen to have an effect directly opposite to that intended – the emergence of national consciousness. The new militants carry the name ROM like a standard.

This process of awakening had developed a long way between the two world wars and the Gypsy nationalist movement was already becoming a coherent force when overtaken by the rise of fascism. In the USSR the All-Russian Union of Gypsies, led by Alexander Germano, co-ordinated the work of thirty artisans' co-operatives in Moscow and some fifty collective enterprises in rural areas. The largest was Krikunovo in the northern Caucasus where seventy families ran 4,700 acres, supplying horses for the Red Army cavalry. But when Stalin came to power the union was abolished and its functions transferred to the Commissariats for Agriculture and Public Instruction.

At the same time, in Poland Gypsy nationalism was taking another form. With the pomp of royalty and diplomatic propriety, the influential Janusz Kwiek was crowned king in 1937 by the Archbishop of Warsaw in a ceremony attended by huge crowds at the Army Stadium. In his coronation address, Janos I said the restoration of a Gypsy monarchy had now been fulfilled after a lapse of a thousand years, and added:

"Let us but send our children . . . to be educated, and we shall soon have our representatives in the League of Nations."[13]

Janusz hoped to establish an independent state and asked Mussolini to grant his people a stretch of territory on the borders of Somalia and recently conquered Abyssinia. Events were soon to prove, however, that fascist Italy was no more a friend of the Romani people than it had been to Ethiopians, and Janusz himself died in Auschwitz.

The same year, inspired by Gypsy revolutionary Helios Gomez, many Gypsies participated in the first open combat with fascism – in the Spanish civil war. Gomez saw the struggle as a wider issue which would determine the fate of Romanies everywhere. Following two years in Russia, he worked to build up the Romani movement in western Europe, and in an interview with *Cronica* said:

"... from this war, which will produce so many great things, there must come even in Spain the vindication of the Gypsies."[14]

However, it was in Romania, with the greatest Gypsy concentration in Europe (some 300,000), that the most ambitious pre-war organization took shape. As in Russia and other parts of the Balkans, a few Gypsies were already entering universities and creating a small but growing intelligentsia which formed the nucleus of the new movement. The international congress, under the slogan *United Gypsies of Europe*, which took place in October 1933 was a momentous occasion. Delegations from all parts of Europe gathered in Bucharest and adopted a programme on a world-wide basis. The immediate aims were to revive national consciousness and to fight for civil rights.[15]

The words of Grigoras Nicolescu, on the occasion of the eightieth anniversary of the Romanian Gypsies' emancipation from serfdom, though bravely optimistic, seemed to sound a warning of the net closing in around the Gypsy world.

"So long as we travel on the paths of justice, honour and duty, no one and nothing can turn us from our goal, because we have at our side a devoted and honourable ally – suffering."

After the war, a sense of national identity showed itself still more strongly amongst the survivors. One of the first post-war Gypsy associations – Romano Pralipe – was founded in Skoplje, capital of Yugoslav Macedonia, where the large Gypsy community, as we have already recorded, largely escaped the Nazi net. In neighbouring Bulgaria official recognition was given to the importance of the Gypsy population by the publication of the government-sponsored newspaper *Nevo Drom*.[16] Although no structure was permitted to exist outside this controlled press, run by Gypsy communist party members, it reflects some Gypsy aspirations within the country.

The post-war years witnessed immigration of Gypsies from eastern Europe into France, Belgium and West Germany. Within a few years Paris supported a community of several thousand drawn from different groups which previously had little association with each other. This coming together provided ground for those who wished to see the re-emergence of a recognized movement. One of the immediate issues, besides the need to improve relations with the French civil authorities was the still outstanding question of indemnification for thousands of war victims.

Leulea Rouda, general secretary of the CIT (International Gypsy Committee) has recalled how the movement came to life again in the early 1950s. He was in North Africa at the time and read a newspaper report of a speech by Ionel Rotaru, who had taken the Romanian Gypsy title Vaida Vojvod. Rotaru was outspoken in his demands for justice, reminding the world that the Germans owed an immense debt because of the Nazi crimes and attempted genocide. The United Nations, he said, should assist the Gypsy people to create a Gypsy Israel – Romanestan.

The demand for a homeland has a compelling logic for a people denied the recognition their numbers justify simply because they are without territory. But, as Leulea Rouda says, most working for the movement have come to terms with the limitations imposed by the world scene. Romanestan, however, has a symbolic meaning, crystallized by Ronald Lee, an activist in Canada:

> "What is Romanestan? I will tell you, brothers. Romanestan is our freedom, freedom to live as Gypsies under our laws and our way of life."

Ronald Lee believes it may be possible for Gypsies to exercise this freedom where they now live. But the dilemma he sees is that this may only lead to gradual assimilation.

The same point is made by Dr. Jan Kochanowski, linguist and graduate in oriental studies at the Sorbonne. Borne in Eastern Europe and a convinced nationalist, he stated recently:

> "We must tell the story of the horrors of the war so Gypsies see that today they have their last chance. They are faced with extermination or assimilation – two facets of the same fate."

Kochanowski says Gypsies must work towards acceptance as equals. He views integration into settled society not as a process in conflict with the maintenance of a separate culture but rather as a necessary step towards self-determination. A five-year study of Gypsy tribes in India has enabled him to demonstrate with some conviction that the Romani people once existed as a federated nation with an administration and an army. He stresses that though the struggle by Roms for survival may be hard, he himself remains an advocate of non-violence.

Two new associations came into existence – Organization Nationale Gitane for Gypsies in France and, on the international plane, Communauté Mondiale Gitane. But colleagues became embarrassed by Rotaru's often exaggerated claims–he said 3,500,000 Gypsies had perished in the war – and by his over-zealous call for a Gypsy state, which played on the mass media's taste for the sensational and the bizarre. Moderate leadership prevailed and he lost his position as second President of the C.M.G.

The French Government, then headed by General De Gaulle, chose this moment to make difficulties for the Gypsy movement. Both Communauté Mondiale Gitane and O.N.G. were officially banned. No reason was immediately given but when the issue was raised in the national assembly the only excuse forthcoming was that the organizations had been dominated by Gypsies who did not hold French citizenship. It is known that De Gaulle, at this time engaged in a rapprochement with West Germany, had been embarrassed by Gypsy claims for reparations then being pressed with more determination. But Paris remained the centre of international activity, and the situation in France improved with the establishment of an officially recognized national Gypsy association, Communauté Tzigane de France, under the presidency of the celebrated musician and former resistance leader Stenegry Archange.

As the movement grows, there is everywhere in Europe a bias within official circles towards producing low statistics regarding Gypsies. Often only nomadic Gypsies are counted and the settled communities ignored. This explains, for example, the small official figures quoted for France and Britain. In other countries, among them Yugoslavia and Bulgaria, statistics are distorted because Gypsies reluctant to disclose their identity register for convenience under the heading of other minorities, Albanian, Turkish and so on. But with the establishment of a co-ordinating body, Comité International Tzigane, a collective leadership has been brought together with influence throughout Europe, combating discrimination and giving the Romani people a voice. The Hungarian-born president of CIT, Vanko Rouda, has been instrumental in gaining recognition both from governments and international organizations. Consultation has been maintained with UNESCO and with the Council of Europe, whose report, issued in September 1969, represents a milestone in the struggle for social justice.

Clearly Gypsy nationalism is again asserting itself. Equally evident is the fact that if, just when seeking expression, it is again suppressed there can only be a return to a deeper state of apathy and desperation. More attention therefore must be given to the Romani movement and – just as important – to the mechanisms which has given rise to it. The world must recognize that the Gypsy people hold within them currents of change which, if correctly channelled, will bear them forward to self-realization, responsibility and progress. The cycle of persecution and disintegration can only be broken by sparking their own latent indignation. This indignation is expressed time and again as a conviction that they have a right to somewhere decent to live; the right to send their children to school, and existence as a separate people. These rights exist in theory within the UN Charter. But, by insisting that remedies must be administered from outside, Gajo officialdom in each country runs the risk of imposing solutions little better than the Nazis', killing the spirit of the Gypsy people by robbing them of the right to effect decisions concerning their own fate.

When Gypsies have the opportunity to co-operate in solving the problems of non-integration with the surrounding society they take over part of the responsibility for determining in what way and how quickly progress can be achieved. Once this process

THE AFTERMATH

begins we can at last proclaim 'gipsies are ceasing to exist, and *Roms* are entering history'.

> N'avlom ke tumende
> o maro te mangel.
> Avlom ke tumende
> kam man pativ te den.
>
> I did not come to you
> to beg for bread.
> I came to you
> to demand respect.

CHAPTER TEN

PROSPECTS

Kai jas ame, Romale?
Where are we going, Roms?

Long persecution throughout Europe almost fatally eroded the status of the Romani people. The tide of harassment and neglect reduced *Roms* – once the children of India – to *gipsies*, a phantom species invented by the Gajo.

True, they never ceased to resist the pressures of the alien society into the midst of which they had unfortunately come to live. Roms were as unwilling to become the serfs of landowning nobles in seventeenth-century Romania as they are now to submit to the enslaving restrictions of the capitalist, or for that matter socialist, system. But the legalized brutalities, the hangings, the wish-you-were-dead attitude took their toll, sapping strength and causing psychological withdrawal and even degeneration.

Today it is impossible to hear one or other of the clutter of misnomers – cigano, gitano, tzigane, etc. – without the conviction that an insult is being flung in the face of a re-awakening nation; a collective slice of humanity which by weight of numbers alone – ten million by present estimate – must soon take its proper place in the world.

In the fast-growing ghettos, the Gypsy quarters in the cities and towns of eastern Europe, the *Gitanerias* of Spain and among the hard-pressed Roms still on the road, one is aware of a new mood. The face of apathy is cracking and expectation motivating a hopeful generation. A bulwark is being built against further encroachment that might finally destroy the nation. Roms are on the move; no longer as *gipsies* wandering aimlessly the by-ways of Europe but as a people increasingly convinced of the need to find their own road.

Almost without exception the regimes and the ideologies have failed them, one after another advocating their elimination as a separate entity either by assimilation or, as with the Nazis, by extermination. The religious faiths have antagonized more than they have concerted, treating Gypsies as missionary fodder. While rejecting the overtures of the politicians and priests, their national consciousness has been sharpened by the evidence of history. The catalogue of hate and genocide is enough to bring home to any Rom that members of his once-independent race have been done to death, deported or *re-habilitated* merely in accordance with the changing needs and fashions of Gajo society; and that it is about time this unequal relationship was ended.

The meeting and the departure point for the new movement is the World Romani Congress. With its simple slogan and anthem *Upre Roma! Rise Up Roms!* it is spreading the irresistable doctrine that, after years of passive suffering, the denial of basic rights must everywhere be contested. Crouching in wet tents, trailers and crowded shanties from Stockholm to Barcelona, half a million have-nots have nothing to lose, while for some four million sedentary Roms, concentrated in central and south-east Europe, the prize is nationality status.

The handicap imposed by the conditions of a divided post-war Europe – the impossibility of re-establishing a representative central authority – has been overcome by the first congress, which in April 1971 brought together in London delegates from fourteen countries representing three million Roms. The co-ordination maintained by the Paris-based CIT, which linked the activities of many different groups during the period of separation, also ensured the emergence of a realistic blue-print for progress once liberalization had torn down the Iron-curtain.

The pace and tone of its activities, having inherited the mantle of the 1933 Bucharest Congress – and the nationalist blue and green banner, now embellished with a red wheel – can be gauged by the opening words of Congress President Slobodan Berberski of Yugoslavia.:

"The purpose of this Congress is to unite and activate Roms throughout the world; to bring about emancipation according to our own intuition and our own ideals. Whatever we do will have the stamp of our own particular personality upon it – it will be *amaro Romano Drom*, our Romani road.

The collective desire to be ourselves comes from that well-spring of hope and endeavour which alone can refresh and renew the world.

Our struggle, to evolve according to our own genius, is the same struggle for liberation being waged all over the globe – aiming to prevent the continents being turned into deserts by war, expropriation and misgovernment.

Our people must combine and organize to work locally, and internationally. Our problems are the same everywhere: we must proceed with our own forms of education, preserve and develop Romani culture, bring a new dynamism into our communities and forge a future in accordance with our life-style and beliefs."

The Congress, dividing its work among five specialized commissions, covering social problems, education, culture, language and war-crimes reparations, must now awaken the concern of international agencies, including the United Nations. This task, in its present phase, has fallen to Abdi Faik, son of a blacksmith and MP in the Yugoslav Macedonian parliament, who heads the Social Commission. The commission has under review the plight and needs of Roms in each country and has prepared reports for the Council of Europe and UNESCO.

The compilation of facts is not easy because reliable statistics are still lacking. A plague of misleading information emanates from various governments who have misrepresented the size of the Gypsy communities and hide what is actually going on. This obstacle was foreseen by secretariat president Vanko Rouda who said at the London congress:

"One difficulty is that Gajo official circles have not yet decided who or what we are. In some countries only nomadic Roms are counted, in others the true proportion of Roms is lost under the identity of other minorities – it has been common throughout south-east Europe for Roms to be registered as Hungarians, Romanians, Turks and Albanians. The fashion in western and northern Europe, where through intermarriage there are now fair-skinned Gypsies, has been to call us wagon-dwellers, itinerants and vagrants, making it easier to parcel us up as problem families. But whether we're called *tattare,*

Jenisch or *tinker* we are part of the Rom family and this identity cannot be taken from us."

Without the involvement of these agencies, and an adequate response from governments supposedly concerned with the welfare of their Gypsy citizens, even the first priorities of the Congress cannot be met – for example a mass campaign to combat illiteracy. Nevertheless there is to be no sell-out to government-sponsored policies aimed at assimilation, to which the smaller communities in western and northern Europe are most vulnerable. The employment of Romani teachers in state schools, wherever possible, use of the Romani language and the teaching of Romani history and traditions is demanded as of right – being no more than the facilities granted already to recognized national minorities. Two commissions, those concerned with the standardization of *Romanes* and with collecting together the vast store of songs, tales and music, are ready to assist in devising properly orientated curricula.

A promising lead has been given by the Council of Europe. Following submissions by CIT to the Commission on Social and Health Questions, the Council in 1969 recommended member states to co-operate with Gypsy organizations in the urgent implementation of programmes which would rescue nomadic groups from the worst abuse and neglect.

The Council of Europe found it necessary to preface the Report as follows:

"Deeply concerned that in many cases efforts to improve the situation have failed owing to discrimination against Gypsies, on the ground that they belong to a particular ethnic group, which is incompatible with the ideals underlying the European Convention on Human Rights and the United Nations Declaration on Human Rights, [the Assembly] recommends that the Committee of Ministers urge member governments:

(i) to take all steps necessary to stop discrimination, be it in legislation or in administrative practice, against Gypsies."

This appeal to combat discrimination and in essence to uphold the *individual* rights of Gypsies must be answered. But on a deeper level our concern – and it has been the fundamental subject of this study – is the collective destiny of the Romani *people*. The present ground-swell within the Gypsy world will amount soon to revolution. For a long time that vital margin of territory – the minimum necessary for the survival of any human group – was held by Roms, paradoxically, simply by keeping on the move. Gypsies found their living space on the edge of the road, on the waste-land fringes of industrial society, among the rootless of the great cities. Their livelihood depended upon maintaining a fragile relationship with the Gajo, to whom they provided a service in terms of goods or temporary labour. Of late this narrow and shifting margin has yielded ever lower economic return, and the poorest opportunities to successive generations, until in the richest states Gypsies have become *the rubbish people*, grubbing a living among the filth of civilization. They inhabit a world in which outside of the family they have no stake. The Gajo society remains utterly alien – except in one new and vital respect: mass communications. The message has penetrated, particularly to a restless youth, that we are in an epoch of racial turmoil and resurgent nationalism. It is clear to Roms today, still intolerably confined within their old haunts, that though the first *Blacks* in Europe, they are the last to raise their standard and seek emancipation.

ABBREVIATIONS

CIT	Comité International Tzigane, Paris
Et. Tsig.	*Etudes Tsiganes*
IMT	*Trials of the Major War Criminals before the International Military Tribunal*
IZG	Institut für Zeitgeschichte, Munich
JGLS	*Journal of the Gypsy Lore Society*
NCA	*Nazi Conspiracy and Aggression*
n.d.	no date
NS	Nationalsozialistisch(e)
Nur. Doc.	Nuremberg Document
p.c.	private communication
ZPA	Zigeunerpersonalakten

REFERENCES

CHAPTER ONE

[1] Kochanowski (1967)
[2] Firdausi vol vii sec. 39
[3] Thesleff p. 83
[4] JGLS (2) i p. 197–211
[5] JGLS (3) ii p. 160–7
[6] Ilinski
[7] JGLS (2) iii p. 60
[8] Pott p. 30, JGLS (2) iv p. 83–100
[9] JGLS (2) iv p. 73–4
[10] Tultey
[11] Foletier (1961) p. 20
[12] JGLS (2) iv p. 70
[13] Foletier (1961)
[14] JGLS (2) iii p. 69

CHAPTER TWO

[1] See Mason, Dunstan & Hobson
[2] JGLS (1) i p. 272–5
[3] Champion p. 325
[4] JGLS (3) xvii p. 52
[5] Thesleff
[6] *Daily Telegraph* (London) 14–iv–1969
[7] Borrow (1843)
[8] *Hansard* April 19, 1772
[9] Grellman 1783, Pott 1844
[10] Schechtman p. 52
[11] JGLS (3) ii p. 174
[12] JGLS (2) vii p. 160
[13] JGLS (2) iv p. 66
[14] Foletier (1961)
[15] JGLS (3) xxvii p. 10–11
[16] JGLS (3) xxvii p. 10–11
[17] JGLS (3) i p. 173

REFERENCES

[18] JGLS (2) vii p. 159
[19] Ljungberg
[20] JGLS (3) xiii p. 203
[21] Foletier (1961)
[22] JGLS (3) xiv p. 100
[23] *News of the World* (London) 26-i-1969
[24] *Guardian* (London) 15-iii-1969
[25] JGLS (3) xvii (jub. no) p. 23
[26] Addison
[27] Balys no. 102
[28] JGLS (1) i p. 358-9
[29] Law of Christian V. See Flekstad
[30] Coelho p. 230
[31] Foletier (1961)
[32] JGLS (1) i p. 140 and (3) vii p. 48
[33] JGLS (1) i p. 136, 142-3
[34] JGLS (3) ii p. 175
[35] JGLS (2) vii p. 246
[36] JGLS (2) iv p. 160
[37] Nicolini p. 17
[38] JGLS (3) xi p. 49
[39] Borrow (1841)
[40] Coelho
[41] JGLS (3) iv p. 46-7
[42] Evens p. 3
[43] Foletier (1961) p. 41. See also JGLS (1) ii p. 62-3, (3) ii p. 176
[44] JGLS (3) xvii (jub. no.) p. 119
[45] JGLS (3) ii p. 174
[46] JGLS (1) iii p. 135
[47] JGLS (2) iv p. 67
[48] *Folktro och Folksed på Varmlandsnäs* pt. 1 p. 129 and ib. Pt. 2 p. 35-6
[49] JGLS (3) xi p. 60
[50] JGLS (2) iv p. 199
[51] JGLS (2) vii p. 78
[52] JGLS (3) xii p. 102, xxii p. 68
[53] *Folktro* pt. 1 p. 69
[54] ib. p. 78
[55] ib. p. 82
[56] JGLS (3) ii p. 178
[57] Poissonier p. 33, Borrow (1841)
[58] JGLS (3) ix p. 87
[59] p.c.
[60] JGLS (2) vi p. 58-9
[61] *Times* (London) 26-xiii-1832

[62] JGLS (3) xvii p. 123
[63] *Lacio Drom* 1968 nos. 4,5 p. 51
[64] *Etudes Tsiganes*
[65] 13–vii–1968
[66] JGLS (2) iv p. 155
[67] *Evening Post* 6–vii–1968
[68] *Evening Sentinel* 27–ix–1968
[69] MacRitchie
[70] JGLS (2) iv p. 152–5
[71] JGLS (2) iv p. 69
[72] Maucorps p. 157
[73] JGLS (2) iv p. 69–70
[74] Cf. *Daily Sketch* (London) 2–vi–1970
[75] Arnold
[76] Quiller-Couch
[77] *Antony and Cleopatra* (1606) Act 1 Sc. 1
[78] Foletier (1961), JGLS (3) v. p. 96
[79] JGLS (2) vii p. 246
[80] Pushkin, Lenau and others

CHAPTER THREE

[1] JGLS (2) v p. 202. Picture opp. p. 204
[2] e.g. Arnold
[3] JGLS (3) xxii p. 71–3
[4] 1562
[5] 1637
[6] Ljungberg
[7] Foletier (1961) pp. 167–8
[8] JGLS (3) xxii p. 77
[9] JGLS (2) v pp. 156–7
[10] JGLS (3) xii pp. 128–9. Cf. ibid p. 102
[11] 1683
[12] JGLS (3) vii pp. 93–6
[13] Foletier (1961) p. 52
[14] JGLS (3) ii pp. 81–93
[15] JGLS (3) xii p. 130
[16] Aakjaer vol. 2 p. 99
[17] ib.
[18] Zigeuner Geschmeiss
[19] JGLS (3) xii p. 134
[20] JGLS (2) vi pp. 82–3
[21] Nicolini p. 17, JGLS (1) i pp. 358–362
[22] JGLS (2) v pp. 156–7

REFERENCES

[23] Arnold p. 53
[24] JGLS (3) xii pp. 131–3
[25] non-Gypsies cf. Arnold pp. 41–2
[26] JGLS (3) xvi pp. 154–173
[27] Foletier (1968) pp. 13–22
[28] Coelho
[29] cf. JGLS (2) vi p. 61
[30] Issue of 3–viii–1909
[31] Thesleff pp. 91–2
[32] Taikon
[33] Foletier (1961)
[34] Coelho p. 253
[35] JGLS (3) xxii p. 68 Cf. also Thesleff p. 93
[36] JGLS (3) ii p. 167
[37] JGLS (2) i pp. 321, 322, (3) xxii p. 69
[38] JGLS (3) viii pp. 11–12, Potra
[39] JGLS (3) viii pp. 181–2
[40] *Gypsy & Folklore Gazette* v. 1 no. 1 p. 45
[41] p.c.
[42] JGLS (2) v p. 150
[43] *Le Prix de la Liberté*
[44] JGLS (3) viii pp. 13–14
[45] JGLS (2) viii pp. 54–64
[46] JGLS (2) vii p. 159
[47] JGLS (3) iv p. 88
[48] JGLS (3) xvii (jub. no.) p. 29
[49] Horden
[50] Cf. also JGLS (3) xiv p. 120
[51] Scharfenberg

CHAPTER FOUR

[1] Schutzstaffeln. A para-military organization entrusted with many tasks concerned with security.
[2] See Tenenbaum p. 400
[3] P. Friedman (1951) p. 12
[4] Ib. See also Günther pp. 420, 427
[5] Nationality and Marriage Laws (see below Chap. 5)
[6] op. cit. vol. 1 p. 46. foreign — artfremd
[7] Brandis. See also Krämer, Döring (1964) p. 37
[8] Hilberg p. 608. See also Chap. 8 below
[9] Yates. Cf. Buchheim p. 52
[10] Neuengamme
[11] Zigeuner (Gypsy)

[12] Nachtrichtendienst in Bezug auf die Zigeuner. Later (1929) Zentralstelle für die Zigeunerbekämpfung and then Zentrale zur Bekämpfung des Zigeunerunwesens.

[13] NS Auskunftei

[14] Reichstelle f. Sippenforschung

[15] See below

[16] p.c.

[17] Ritter (1941) p. 479

[18] ib.

[19] ib. p. 480

[20] p. 481

[21] See below

[22] ib. p. 481

[23] Ritter (1942)

[24] *Befehlsblatt des ChSPudSD* 1940. p. 84

[25] ib. 1941 p. 265

[26] Erlass des RKPA 28–iii–1942

[27] *Befehlsblatt des ChSPudSD*1944 p. 6

[28] Ritter (1949)

[29] Classification document no. 21166 (photostat in Wiener Library)

[30] Sch—— p. 23

[31] Rüdiger p. 88

[32] Schubert

[33] Sch—— p. 26

[34] op. cit. p. 192

[35] Rüdiger p. 87

[36] ib. p. 89

[37] Römer (1937) pp. 281–8

[38] Sch—— p. 25

[39] op. cit. p. 70

[40] 1938 pp. 28–9

[41] Rüdiger p. 88

[42] *Volk u. Rasse* 1938 pp. 28–9

[43] Küppers p. 183

[44] Rohne p. 197

[45] (1934) p. 113

[46] JGLS (3) xii pp. 158–9

[47] (1937) p. 282

[48] See below

[49] op. cit. p. 88

[50] See *Volk u. Rasse* 1937 p. 211

[51] e.g. *NS Landpost* 19–iii–1937 and *Volk u. Rasse* 1937 p. 311

[52] Behrendt's italics

[53] unpub. document

REFERENCES

[54] Lundman

[55] See bibliography in Döring (1964)

[56] Ritter (1939)

[57] Ritter (1941)

[58] (1942)

[59] (1941) p. 482

[60] See below

[61] See Hilberg

[62] (1941) p. 482

[63] See Chap. 5

[64] p.c.

[65] Statement of Richard Rose

[66] op. cit.

[67] p. 5

[68] p. 112

[69] p. 121

[70] p. 121

[71] *Allg. Wochenz der Juden* 21–ii–1964. See also *Spiegel* 24–iv–1963

[72] p.c.

[73] p.c.

[74] Gesetz zur Verhütung erbkranken Nachwuchses 14–vii–1933

[75] Massregeln der Sicherung u. Besserung. 24–xi–1933

[76] Photostat in Wiener Library

[77] ib.

[78] Quoted in Arnold p. 67

[79] Unwesen. address Rossauer Lände no. 7, Wien IX

[80] Law of 5–vi–1936

[81] Cramer p. 442

[82] See below. Chap. 8

[83] Wirtz p. 165

[84] p.c.

[85] Höss (1958) p. 105

[86] M. Adler pp. 171–2

[87] p.c.

[88] M. Adler p. 172

[89] Müller (unpub. statement in IZG archives)

[90] Buchheim pp. 56–7

[91] Brandis

[92] Nur. Doc. NG–552. See also Döring (1964) p. 57

[93] Potsdam ZPA 41

[94] Stuckart & Globke

[95] Reichsbürger

[96] Staatsangehöriger

[97] Döring (1964) p. 169

[98] Section A 11 1 e of the Act, see especially the guidelines to the Act published April 4th 1938. National archives. Microfilm T 175 reel 513 frames 9379952–66.

[99] Döring (1964) p. 56

[100] Wölffling

[101] Photostat in Wiener Library

[102] Wölffling

[103] Potsdam ZPA 74

[104] p.c.

[105] Munich

[106] *NS Rechtspiegel* 21–ii 1939

[107] Arnold pp. 68, 69

[108] S. Wolf p.c.

[109] Döring (1964) p. 123

[110] p.c.

[111] Döring, Buchheim

[112] See Chap. 9

[113] Case of Erik Balasz (8–x–1955). See also below Chap. 9

[114] op. cit.

CHAPTER FIVE

[1] Head of the Secret Police

[2] Eichmann Trial Docs. T. 164, T. 165

[3] Festsetzungserlass 7

[4] p.c.

[5] Previously part of Czechoslovakia

[6] Head of the Criminal Police

[7] Wiesenthal p. 216

[8] *Nazi Dokumenten sprechen*. For Capt. Günther see also *Lacio Drom* 1969 no. 4 p. 44

[9] Eichmann trial T.166, Nur. Doc. No–5322, Jüd. Hist. Inst. pp. 51, 52

[10] Testimony of Nowak to Eichmann trial, session 108

[11] Tape played at session 11 of trial

[12] Centre Doc. Juive Cont. CCLXXX–16

[13] Cf. Döring (1964) p. 97

[14] See below Chap. 8

[15] Report of Schleswig-Holstein reparations court 12–i–1959

[16] Reparations case at Schleswig-Holstein court

[17] Reparations case IV ZB 240,62 (1962)

[18] Döring (1964) pp. 97–8

[19] Reparations claim AZ IV ZR 211/55

[20] IZG microfilm MA 1137

[21] Döring (1964) pp. 97–8

REFERENCES

22 IZG microfilm MA 1137 frame 2937926

23 Letter from RKPA 16–viii–1940. (MA 1137)

24 RKPA Reichszentrale z. Bekämpfung des Zig. Unwesens, Berlin 9–viii–1941 Tgb. Nr 299/41 A 2 (MA 1137)

25 Letter from ChdSPuSD Berlin 28–xii–1942

26 Buchheim p. 54

27 Letter from ChdSPuSD, Berlin. 28–xii–1942

28 H. Adler (1955) p. 722

29 Scize p. 93. See also Baraicli-Levy (1962) pp. 80–1

30 cf. Calic Chap. 7

31 p.c.

32 Letter from Ministry of Labour 19–ii–1941

33 Buchheim pp. 56–7, Statement by Müller in IZG

34 Pankok

35 Allg. H. Mitt. 1941 p. 82, Allg. Heeresbestimmungen von OK der Wehrmacht Ziffer 153, 21–ii–1941 (Potsdam ZPA 61)

36 Letter from Minister of Labour 19–ii–1941 ref. Va/5432/909/40G.

37 10–vii–1942

38 M. Adler pp. 174–5

39 p.c.

40 Steinmetz p. 24

41 p.c.

42 Law on the Employment of Jews 3–x–1941 and Order on the Cessation of Holiday pay for Jewish Employees of 13–ii–1942 (See *Hamburger Fremdenblatt* no. 88)

43 Döring (1964) p. 137

44 April 1st 1942

45 20–iv–1941

46 NG–456, NG–709

47 Justin p. 34

48 Döring (1964) p. 130

49 Müller (IZG)

50 For a case in Hamburg see *Tagesspiegel* 14–iii–1962

51 p.c.

52 Edicts of Ministry of Education 22–iii–1941 and 15–vi–1939, *Befehlsblatt des ChSPudSD* 1941, op. 267

53 Friedrich

54 JGLS (3) xvii p. 135

55 Inländische Zigeuner

56 National Archives T.175 reel 461 frames 2980085–6

57 Thierack was Minister of Justice, Rothenberger Secretary of State in the Justice Ministry, Streckenbach Head of the Personnel Division of the Security Central Office and Bender an SS legal expert

58 PS–654, Green series vol. 5 p. 236

[59] Tenenbaum
[60] NG–558
[61] NO–1784
[62] L–179
[63] NG–1014
[64] NG–745
[65] Nur. Doc. PS–682
[66] RSHA V A 2 2260/42
[67] RdErldRFSSuChdDtPol 7–viii–1941
[68] Ritter (1941) p. 484
[69] RSHA VA 2 40/43 11–i–1943
[70] Himmler files Drawer 3 Folder 91/23 (IZG MA 3(9))
[71] See RSHA V A 2 57/43 g. 30–i–43
[72] e.g. Pitzo Adler (M. Adler pp. 197–8)
[73] Potsdam ZPA 56
[74] Nur. Doc. NG–812
[75] See below Chap. 8
[76] RSHA V A 2 40/43 11–i–43
[77] p.c.
[78] RSHA V A 40/43 11–i–43
[79] p.c.
[80] Potsdam ZPA 62
[81] Diary of Wolfram Sievers (Rijksinstituut, Amsterdam). Sievers was the business manager of Ahnenerbe (see below)
[82] Höss (1958) p. 105
[83] Strauss
[84] RSHA V A 2624/42 IV
[85] NG–283. See also NG–1014
[86] *Köln. Rundschau* 22–iii–1950
[87] M. Adler p. 177
[88] p.c.
[89] See figures in *Auschwitz-Hefte*
[90] M. Adler
[91] NI–3006 (F)
[92] Molitor p. 51
[93] Langbein (1963) pp. 109, 190–1
[94] IZG Mat. SS Polizei-Zigeuner
[95] Potsdam ZPA 49
[96] ib. ZPA 104
[97] ib. ZPA 29
[98] ib. ZPA 49
[99] Photostat in Wiener Library
[100] SPo IV D 2 c 927/44 g. 24
[101] op. cit.

REFERENCES

[102] Erfassung der Zigeuner in den Alpen u.Donau Reichsgauen

[103] Steinmetz p. 13

[104] e.g. at Manwörth. See Döring (1964) p. 48

[105] RKPA TgbNr 6001/336/1938

[106] Wiener Library unpub. interviews PIII h (Mathausen) 794

[107] *Volk u. Rasse* Oct. 1938 p. 358

[108] Steinmetz

[109] Nat. Archives microfilm T.84 R.13 fr.40255 (Stadler p. 273, Buchheim p. 54)

[110] NG-845. See Steinmetz and Billig for complete text

[111] NG-684

[112] Schnellbrief des RMdI 31-x-40. Döring (1964) pp. 114-5

[113] See below, Chap. 8

[114] Steinmetz

[115] Yad vaShem M-9/1-9

[116] Steinmetz p. 46

[117] ib. p. 54

[118] NG-030

[119] Wiener Library unpub. interview P III h (Mauthausen) 794

[120] Law of 31-i-42. NO-3521

[121] RSHA Tagb. A A 2 Nr 724/41

[122] rep. claim. Munich EK 3293/1956

[123] rep. claims including EK 2420/55

[124] e.g. a woman from Königsberg who had the number Z. 6036. Reparations claim OH 2104/55(E) E 8072

[125] Wiener Library interviews P III 727 p. 3

CHAPTER SIX

[1] p.c.

[2] See also Bartels and Brun's plea for the Gypsies to be treated as asocial Danes. op. cit. pp. 71, 75

[3] p.c.

[4] cf. Nur. Doc. NO-4037

[5] Wiener Library interview P III b (Theresienstadt) 807

[6] Schechtman p. 56

[7] p.c.

[8] Yoors p. 239

[9] Evidence of Dr. Beilin, session 69

[10] p.c.

[11] numbers Z. 8887-8897 incl.

[12] Novitch (1965) p. 39, Wiener Library interview P III i (Belgium) 274, statement of Alfred Voss (Brussels Min. of Health records)

[13] JGLS (3) vol. xiii pp. 217-8, *Zigenaren* 1968 no. 1-2, pp. 40-2

[14] Brussels Min. of Health records
[15] Nat. Archives microfilm T.175 reel 513 frames 937992, 9379998, 9380004
[16] frames 9380005, 9380006
[17] frame 9380015
[18] frame 9380022
[19] frame 9380049
[20] frames 9380067, 9380068. See also microfilm T.175 reel 432 and Nur. docs. NO–1499, NO–5202, PS–1470
[21] Kochanowski (1963) pp. 136–7
[22] Comité d'Histoire de la 2ème Guerre Mondiale
[23] NOKW–1516
[24] Wiener Library Interview P III h (Gurs, etc.) no. 27
[25] Fleury p. 23
[26] ib. p. 24
[27] Karpati (1962) p.c.
[28] p.c.
[29] Zilka Heldt p.c.
[30] p.c.
[31] Karpati (1962) p. 19
[32] ib. p. 45
[33] See below
[34] Karpati (1962)
[35] Mehmet Čakirovič p.c.
[36] Paris p. 62
[37] Uhlik
[38] Karpati (1965) p. 17
[39] Kratschutski
[40] Adamic p. 95
[41] Estimate
[42] Centre Doc. CCCLXI 95 A
[43] p.c.
[44] Et. Tsig. Dec. 1968 pp. 1–19
[45] op. cit.
[46] NOKW–192, NO–3156, NOKW–905, NOKW–1017
[47] Centre Doc. CDLVIII–50
[48] NOKW–802 Cf. NOKW–840, NOKW–801
[49] Nur. Doc. NOKW–905
[50] Adamic p. 23
[51] Paris pp. 130–1
[52] Hilberg p. 441
[53] Paris pp. 130–1
[54] See Yad Vashem 06–170, Centre Doc. CXCIX–18, Nur. Doc. NG–3354
[55] p.c.
[56] Hilberg pp. 440–1

REFERENCES

[57] NOKW-1486 (29-viii-42)
[58] p.c.
[59] Reparations claim LG Munchen I EK 705/51 (LEA:90406/VII/16843)
[60] p.c.
[61] p.c.

CHAPTER SEVEN

[1] *Volk u. Rasse* (1941) p. 39
[2] Baraicli-Levy (1957)
[3] e.g. Miskolz 1940, Kistarcsa and Budapest 1942. 'Ghetto' is often used in documents for the *Gypsy* quarter.
[4] Steinmetz passim.
[5] Numbers – male Z.3516–3680, female Z.3944-4141. Not all were Hungarian Gypsies
[6] JGLS (3) xlii
[7] The collector (Kamill Erdös) is now dead.
[8] Schechtman pp. 56-7
[9] p.c.
[10] Information from Hungarian War Victims Association (Nácizmus Üldözötteinek Bizottsága) 5,000 claims for compensation are filed in the archives of this organization (SzabadságTér 16, Budapest V) but these are not available for scrutiny at the moment
[11] p.c.
[12] p.c.
[13] Novitch (1968) p. 24
[14] Heimler
[15] Moldawa p. 79
[16] p.c.
[17] Raffael Ilona, p.c.
[18] *Voix Mondiale Tzigane* Jan 1962
[19] *Black Book* p. 163
[20] Schechtman pp. 56-7
[21] Radita
[22] JGLS (3) xxvii
[23] Centre Doc. Juive CDXLIV-9
[24] p.c.
[25] *Kontraste* June 1969
[26] *Soviet War News Weekly* 19-xi-42
[27] Lloyd p. 359
[28] Malaparte
[29] Schechtman p. 57
[30] p.c.

[31] Schechtman pp. 56, 57

[32] JGLS (3) xxvii p. 157

[33] JGLS (3) xxvii

[34] Arendt p. 188

[35] *Welt der Arbeit*

[36] Documents in section 'Gypsies' in Nat. Archives, Prague

[37] Ministry of the Interior no. A–1323/11–41–1. Issued 4–xii–1941

[38] Bubeničková pp. 189–194

[39] Including Vincent Daniel no. 33 804; the transport numbered some 300 persons but they may not all have been Gypsies. *Auschwitz-Hefte*

[40] Photostat in Wiener Library

[41] *Auschwitz-Hefte*

[42] ib.

[43] Nur. Doc. NO–1551

[44] Priester

[45] Friedman (1952)

[46] Reparations claim

[47] Reparations claim

[48] Růžička

[49] Yates p. 457

[50] Richter

[51] Compensation claim

[52] Police report in Nat. Archives, Prague

[53] Jamnická-Šmerglová pp. 79–82

[54] p.c.

[55] p.c.

[56] Schechtman p. 56

[57] *Black Book* pp. 179, 180

[58] Horváthová p. 171

[59] Horváthová p. 171. See also Bubeničková

[60] p.c.

[61] p.c.

[62] Ministry of Internal Affairs, Bratislava, no.501–D/336–1/44 June 13th, 1944.

[63] id. 216–17/7/44. July 19th, 1944

[64] Horváthová p. 171

[65] *Praca*

[66] p.c.

[67] Horváthová pp. 171, 385

[68] Friedman (1950)

[69] Horváthová p. 173. The census of 1927 recorded 62,000 and that of 1952, 150,000.

[70] p.c.

[71] Trial of Arndt and others at Giessen 1959

REFERENCES

[72] Poland excluding the area incorporated into Germany

[73] Gauweiler

[74] Nur. Doc. NOKW–2994

[75] Döring (1964)

[76] ib. See picture in Gauweiler

[77] Döring p. 98

[78] *Die Zeit* 9–v–1946

[79] Ringelblum. Entry for 23–v–1942

[80] Friedman (1951) p. 13

[81] Lohamei haGhettaoth archives (I.Steinberg)

[82] Friedman (1951) p. 13

[83] Ficowski (1965) pp. 98–104, p. 166. See also *Buletyn Glownej Komisji* e.g. vol. x p. 182 items 546, 571, 589

[84] Testimony of Stefan Lehne at trial of Arthur Greiser

[85] Ficowski (1950)

[86] Ficowski (1965) p. 103

[87] Rost p. 4

[88] See however Ficowski (1950) p. 95 for a lower figure

[89] Ficowski 1965 pp. 91–3

[90] *Welt der Arbeit*

[91] Ficowski (1965) p. 100

[92] Ariste

[93] *Nemeckofasisticka okupace Estonska*

[94] Kochanowski (1946) pp. 114–5. See also Lohamei ha-Ghettaoth archives for Ludza

[95] p.c. Those killed included the Mitrowski, Kozlowski and Burkewiecz families

[96] p.c.

[97] translator of the Bible into Romani

[98] Kochanowski (1946)

[99] Kochanowski (1946) p. 113

[100] St. George p. 34

[101] TWC vol. 4

[102] 13–v–41. Barbarossa was the code name for the USSR

[103] Head of the Personnel division of the Security Central Office

[104] TWC vol. 4 p. 93

[105] Cf. Haensch's statement in TWC vol. 4 p. 318

[106] Nur. Doc. NO–2856 Centre Doc. Juive CXXXV–42

[107] TWC vol. 4 p. 255

[108] Cf. evidence of von dem Bach – Zelewski at Eichmann trial

[109] The phrase used by the Nuremberg tribunal

[110] Cf. Buchheim p. 51. Thus in Simferopol the Gypsy question was 'cleared up' (bereinigt)

[111] See Nur. Doc. NOKW–2072 and Lohamei haGhettaoth archives.

Novitch (1965) p. 55 mentions a Gypsy partisan Valya in the Soviet White Russian Brigade who died saving a wounded comrade

[112] TWC vol. 4 pp. 286–7

[113] TWC vol. 4 p. 16

[114] NO–3277

[115] NO–3276

[116] NO–3276

[117] TWC vol. 4 p. 19

[118] NO–2827

[119] NO–2834

[120] NO–3241

[121] NO–3235

[122] NO–3359

[123] The original source is the Nuremberg Trial

[124] NO–3258. In fact there were still some Gypsies in the area in March 1942 (NCA vol. 4 p. 944)

[125] TWC vol. 4 p. 323

[126] JGLS (1) ii p. 75

[127] Ohlendorf said that he required two witnesses to prove that a person was a Gypsy before he accepted this (TWC vol. 4 p. 290). This must refer to persons living outside the quarter. NB. It is not clear whether the execution reported by Heinz Schubert (TWC vol. 4 p. 207–8) was in fact of Gypsies. He says "I went to the Gypsy quarter of Simferopol and supervised the loading of the persons who were to be shot into a truck ... The place which was designated for the shooting of these *Russians and Jews*"

[128] NOKW–2072

[129] NO–5655

[130] e.g. CXXXVI–36, NO–5520, NOKW–1701, NOKW–2004, NOKW–853, NOKW–2856

[131] Trial of Rapp 1964–5

[132] Trial of Matschke 1965–6

[133] p.c.

[134] p.c.

[135] See Nur. Doc. NOKW–2072. Cf. NO 4816 which suggests Himmler also ordered a halt to the killings

[136] NOKW–2535

[137] NOKW–2022

[138] Letter of 7–vii–42 in Yivo file

[139] Letter of 12–i–42 in CIT files

[140] PS–1133

[141] Yivo file

[142] Yivo file

[143] Grossman p. 18

[144] Dvoryetski
[145] Kuznetsov p. 100

CHAPTER EIGHT

[1] Czech Gypsy song. For other songs from the camps see Ficowski (1964) pp. 215–220, *JGLS* xxix, xlii, *Lacio Drom* 1968 no. 1 pp. 4–5
[2] See Chap. 7
[3] NO–1934. Official camp statistics. 13,845 Jews died in the same week
[4] Novitch (n.d.)
[5] *Auschwitz-Hefte* VII
[6] Höss p. 107
[7] Heimler pp. 47–54
[8] See Chap. 5 above
[9] These 1,700 were gassed on arrival and not given numbers
[10] Including one Czech transport of 768
[11] Höss p. 105
[12] Adelsberger
[13] See Chap. 5
[14] Höss p. 105
[15] NO–1934
[16] Kraus & Kulka pp. 202–3. See also Broad p. 41 and evidence of Dr. Beilin session 69 of Eichmann trial)
[17] Broad p. 40 and Nur. Doc. NI–11984. See also IZG film MA 3(9)
[18] op. cit. p. 105. Cf. Kraus and Kulka p. 202
[19] This opinion is held by Kraus and Kulka, p. 204
[20] There were two other short-lived family camps at Auschwitz, one for the Jews from Theresienstadt and the Vitebsk Russian camp
[21] Novitch
[22] Cf. Heimler
[23] Text has 1942. The Gypsy camp was not established then
[24] Text has 'two years'
[25] op. cit. pp. 105–6. We may note here that Höss was sentenced to death in Poland in 1947 and executed
[26] Broad p. 42
[27] Langbein (1965) pp. 106–7, 232
[28] Adler H. p. 159
[29] Cf. Adelsberger p. 44
[30] Adler H.
[31] Rost p. 4
[32] Langbein (1965) p. 107
[33] Adelsberger. Dr. Beilin mentions a special barrack for TB cases (Eichmann trial session 69)
[34] Adler H.

[35] Novitch (n.d.)
[36] Evidence of Casar at Auschwitz trial
[37] Heimler, Nyiszli
[38] Langbein pp. 106–7
[39] Evidence of Dr. Lucas. Langbein p. 601
[40] p. 251
[41] Höss p. 127
[42] Novitch (n.d.)
[43] Evidence of Dr. Beilin (Eichmann Trial)
[44] op. cit. pp. 47–53
[45] Nyiszli pp. 30, 31, 58, 132
[46] Kraus and Kulka p. 203
[47] e.g. 39 children brought from the St. Josefspflege Children's Home in Mulfingen on 12–v–44. (*Auschwitz-Hefte*)
[48] Adelsberger p. 54
[49] Kraus and Kulka p. 203
[50] Adelsberger p. 77
[51] ib. pp. 75–77
[52] Höss p. 106
[53] See NO–5262
[54] Langbein (1965) pp. 594–5
[55] Höss p. 106
[56] From *Auschwitz-Hefte*
[57] Adler H. p. 159, Langbein (1965) p. 108
[58] Langbein (1965) pp. 237–8
[59] Naumann pp. 362–3
[60] Langbein (1965) p. 520
[61] *Auschwitz-Hefte* vol. 1
[62] Langbein (1965) pp. 596–7
[63] Vincent Daniel 33804, Ignacy Mrnka 80735, both Czech Gypsies (*Auschwitz-Hefte*)
[64] *Auschwitz-Hefte*
[65] Unpublished interview
[66] Adelsberger p. 44, Heimler p. 53
[67] *Auschwitz-Hefte*
[68] ib. vol. VII p. 52
[69] ib. entries in Calendar for 27–xi and 3–xii–43
[70] ib. entries for 27–v and 25–vi–43
[71] op. cit. p. 127
[72] Adelsberger
[73] Langbein (1965) p. 515. See also Reitlinger p. 489
[74] Adelsberger p. 54. She gives the date of this concert as May 30th 1943 but it was probably May 25th
[75] Langbein (1965) p. 521

[76] Kraus and Kulka pp. 203–4

[77] *Auschwitz-Hefte* vol. IV p. 85

[78] Adelsberger p. 57. She refers wrongly to 2,500 *Czech* Gypsies and gives the date as May 30th

[79] Z. 7867

[80] Reitlinger p. 488

[81] *Auschwitz-Hefte* vol. VI p. 75

[82] Novitch (n.d.)

[83] Ned. Roode Kruis. See Novitch (n.d.) for a transport in June 1944

[84] Langbein (1965) p. 613

[85] ib. p. 108

[86] Ficowski (1965) gives the last numbers written in the book but some were not used

[87] Adelsberger p. 110

[88] Novitch (n.d.) *Auschwitz-Hefte* has 7.0 p.m.

[89] Nyiszli p. 131

[90] Langbein pp. 526–7

[91] Kraus and Kulka p. 204

[92] Naumann p. 114. Boger was a member of the SS staff at the camp

[93] Adelsberger pp. 112–13

[94] Novitch n.d.

[95] Evidence of Diamanski at Auschwitz trial

[96] Langbein (1965) pp. 108, 417–18, Neumann p. 123. The judge at the Auschwitz trial did not accept this story

[97] Evidence of Steinberg. Langbein (1965) p. 523

[98] Heimler p. 63

[99] Novitsch (n.d.) Probably Frau Novotny, half-Jewish, half-German (see evidence of Diamanski) Cf. also Döring (1964) p. 181

[100] Novitsch (n.d.), Adelsberger pp. 109–115

[101] Novitsch ib.

[102] Langbein (1965) p. 806

[103] Langbein (1965) p. 108

[104] Eichmann trial, session 69

[105] Evidence of Stein. Langbein (1965) p. 108

[106] *Auschwitz-Hefte*, Ned. Roode Kruis

[107] Arnold p. 76, Rost p. 5

[108] Kraus and Kulka p. 204

[109] Höss p. 106

[110] Ned. Roode Kruis vol. VI p. 40

[111] Ned. Roode Kruis. Vol. VI pp. 40, 67, 69, 107

[112] Langbein (1965) p. 107

[113] Ned. Roode Kruis. Vol. VI p. 40

[114] *Auschwitz-Hefte* VIII pp. 55, 76, 117

[115] *Auschwitz-Hefte*

[116] ib.
[117] ib. Vol. VI p. 32
[118] From *Auschwitz-Hefte*
[119] 300 to Mauthausen and Natzweiler
      900   Buchenwald, April 1944
      500   Ravensbrück, April 1944
      200   Flossenburg and Ravensbrück, May 1944
      500   Ravensbrück, August 1944
      900   Buchenwald, August 1944
      1000 main camp, July 1944
      ‾‾‾‾
      4300
[120] e.g. escaped persons recaptured
[121] Yoors p. 115
[122] Kogon (1950) p. 102
[123] Kogon (1950) p. 129
[124] *Buchenwald* (1949) p. 32
[125] *Buchenwald* (1949) pp. 17, 18 (1960) pp. 63, 87
[126] Max
[127] Kamenetsky p. 139
[128] Max
[129] Kogon (1950) p. 47
[130] Max
[131] *Buchenwald* (1960) p. 152
[132] Max
[133] *German Crimes in Poland* p. 111. See also Ficowski (1965) p. 115
[134] *Black Book* p. 377
[135] Chelmo Trial, January 1963
[136] Novitch (1965) p. 36
[137] Phillips p. 721
[138] p.c.
[139] Steinmetz pp. 17–20
[140] A prisoner given certain powers and privileges
[141] Steinmetz ib.
[142] p.c.
[143] Deputy Gauleiter, Lower Austria
[144] Nur. Doc. NO–39
[145] See H. Adler (1955) p. 722
[146] Hilberg p. 142
[147] Yad vaShem 0–6–1247
[148] ib. 0–6–1545
[149] ib. 0–6–1544
[150] Arendt p. 88, Hausner p. 66
[151] Novitch (n.d.) and (1965) p. 47, Ficowski (1965)
[152] Novitch (1965) p. 47

REFERENCES

[153] Friedman (1951). Map in Ficowski (1965) p. 115
[154] Novitch (n.d.
[155] Kermisz
[156] Lagerälteste
[157] anon. account (Wiener Library K4H)
[158] *Welt der Arbeit*
[159] Novitch (1965) p. 39
[160] Valley
[161] Steinmetz pp. 38–9
[162] Berdych pp. 112–13
[163] Novitch (1965) p. 54
[164] Lagergemeinschaft Neuengamme p. 7
[165] Meier, glossary
[166] ib. pp. 3, 83
[167] Thygesen p. 65
[168] Buchmann pp. 30, 34
[169] de Gaulle pp. 76, 77
[170] Vermehren
[171] Dufournier pp. 31, 32
[172] ib. pp. 48, 89
[173] Børsum p. 67
[174] ib. p. 99
[175] de Gaulle
[176] ib. p. 75, Amery
[177] CIT archives
[178] Buchmann opp. p. 64
[179] Buchmann
[180] Nansen vol. 3 p. 250
[181] Seip p. 351
[182] Grossman p. 18
[183] Wiernik p. 26
[184] *Rzeczpospolita*. See also the evidence of Jacov Mornik at the Eichmann Trial and Centre Doc. CDLXXX-1
[185] Ficowski p. 173
[186] Dvoryetski p. 60
[187] Moldawa pp. 73, 79, 160, Nur. Doc. NO–1551
[188] Novitch (1965) p. 39
[189] Novitch (1965) p. 39
[190] Nur. Doc. NO–4764
[191] *Welt der Arbeit*
[192] *German Crimes in Poland* p. 104
[193] ib. pp. 108, 120
[194] Friedrich; Wiener Library interview P III d (Holland) 840
[95] Regnault

[196] Nur. Doc. NO–410
[197] Befehl RFSS 15–v–44
[198] NO–179 (28–vi–44)
[199] NO–183
[200] Langbein (1965) p. 616
[201] ibid p. 613
[202] ibid pp. 616–17
[203] ibid p. 107
[204] NO–440 and Buchmann p. 78
[205] de Gaulle pp. 80–1
[206] Döring (1964) p. 153. See also Bayle pp. 665–725
[207] Novitch (1965) p. 43
[208] NG–832
[209] IMT vol. viii p. 313 (USSR–400)
[210] p.c.
[211] Novitch
[212] NO–3818
[213] Mitscherlich and Mielke p. 114, Nur. Doc. NO–911
[214] PS–3249, US–663, NO–911, NO–3342
[215] NO–372
[216] *De L'Univ. aux Camps de Conc.*
[217] NO–1188
[218] NO–285
[219] Rost p. 5
[220] Centre Doc. CCCLXI–3
[221] Hilberg p. 608
[222] NO–410
[223] PS–3882
[224] See Chapter 4
[225] Unpublished interview
[226] Nur. Doc. NG–552
[227] unpublished interview

CHAPTER NINE

[1] CIT archives
[2] International Refugee Organisation
[3] p.c.
[4] *Suddeutsche Zeitung* 10–i–56
[5] p.c.
[6] *Il Messaggero*, Rome, 8–x–69
[7] See Puxon passim
[8] MacColl p. 23
[9] *Informations Tsiganes*, No. 1, February 1970

REFERENCES

[10] ibid
[11] Speech by Fr Oremus, Social Study Congress, Dublin 1966
[12] op. cit.
[13] JGLS (3) xvii pp. 72–3
[14] JGLS (3) xviii pp. 146–8
[15] JGLS (3) xiii pp. 182–190
[16] Now bearing the Bulgarian title *Nov Put*

BIBLIOGRAPHY

AAKJAER, J. (1903) *Steen Steensen Blicher.* Copenhagen: Gyldendal.

ADAMIĆ, L. (1943) *My Native Land.* New York: Harper & Bros.

ADDISON, J. (1711) 'Sir Roger de Coverley and the Gypsies', *Spectator,* 30–vii.

ADELSBERGER, L. (1953) *Auschwitz.* Berlin: Lettner.

ADLER, H. (ed.) (1962) *Auschwitz – Zeugnisse und Berichte,* Frankfurt/M: Europäische Verlag.

ADLER, M. (1960) *My Life with the Gypsies.* London: Souvenir Press.

Allgemeine Wochenzeitung der Juden, 21–ii.

AMERY, O. (1945) *Nuit et Brouillard,* Paris: Berger–Levrault.

ARENDT, H. (1964) *Eichmann in Jerusalem,* New York: Viking Press; London: Faber and Faber.

ARISTE, P. (1964) 'Estonian Gypsies', *JGLS* (3) xliii, p. 60.

ARNOLD, H. (1965) *Die Zigeuner,* Olten: Walter.

Auschwitz-Hefte (1959) Auschwitz: Panstwowe Muzeum.

BALYS, J. (1940) *Lithuanian Folk Legends,* Kaunas.

BARAICLI–LEVY, J. de (1957) 'Hungarian Gypsies in Comberton Camp', *JGLS* (3) xxxvi, p. 115–21.

— (1962) *A Gypsy in New York.* London: Faber and Faber.

BARTELS and BRUN (1943) *Gypsies in Denmark,* Copenhagen.

BAYLE, F. (1950) *Croix gammée contre Caducée,* Neustadt: Imprimerie Nationale.

BEHRENDT (1939) 'Die Wahrheit über die Zigeuner', *NS Partei Korrespondenz* (NSK) 10, iii.

BERDYCH, V. (1959) *Mauthausen.* Prague: Naše Vojsko.

BILLIG, J. (1950) *L'Allemagne et le Génocide.* Paris: Éditions du Centre.

Black Book (1946) New York: Jewish Black Book Cte.

BORROW, G. (1841) *The Zincali (Gypsies of Spain)* London: Murray.

— (1843) *The Bible in Spain.* London: Murray.

BØRSUM, L. (1947) *Kvindehelvedet Ravensbrück.* Copenhagen: Christensen.

BRANDIS, E. (1936) *Ehegesetze von 1935 erläutet.* Berlin.

BROAD, P. See *Auschwitz-Hefte,* vol. ix, p. 41.

BUBENIČKOVÁ, R. (1969) *Tábory utrepní a smrti.* Prague: Svoboda.

Buchenwald (1949) Weimar: Thüringer Volksverlag (1960)

— (1960) Berlin: Kongress.

BUCHHEIM, H. (1958) 'Die Zigeunerdeportation vom Mai 1940'. *Gutachten des IZG,* pp. 51–9.

BUCHMANN, E. (1959) *Die Frauen von Ravensbrück.* Berlin: Kongress.

238

BIBLIOGRAPHY

Buletyn głownej komisji badanania zbrodni hitlerowskich w Polsce (1946–58). Warsaw.

CALIC, E. (1966) *Himmler et son Empire*. Paris: Stock.

CASSEL, S. (1962) 'Begegnung mit einem jungen Zigeuner'. *Tagespiegel*, 14–iii.

Central Commission for the Investigation of German Crimes in Poland (1947) *German Crimes in Poland*, vol. 2. Warsaw.

Centre Documentation Juive Contemporaine. Paris.

CERVANTES, M. (1612) *La Gitanilla*.

CHAMPION, S. (1938) *Racial Proverbs*. London: Routledge.

COELHO, F. (1892) *Os Ciganos de Portugal*. Lisbon: Imprensa Nacional.

COLINON, M. (1965) See *Atlas* October.

— (1967) 'Le Martyre gitan sous le Nazisme'. *Monde Gitan*, vol. 4. Paris.

COMITÉ D'HISTOIRE DE LA 2ème GUERRE MONDIALE. Bulletin 9. Paris.

CRAMER, J. (1964) *The World's Police*. London: Cassell.

Daily Telegraph. 2–x–1945. London.

DE GAULLE, G. (1962) 'La condition des enfants au camp de Ravensbrück'. *Revue d'histoire de la 2ème guerre mondiale*, no. 45, p. 71–85.

De l'Université aux Camps de Concentration (1947) Paris: Belles Lettres.

DE VILLE, F. (1956) *Tsiganes, Temoins des Temps*. Brussels: Lebègue.

DÖRING, H-J (1959) 'Die Motive der Zigeunerdeportation von Mai 1940'. *Vierteljahrheft f. Zeitgeschichte*, October, pp. 418–28.

— (1964) *Die Zigeuner im NS-Staat*. Hamburg: Kriminalistik.

DUFOURNIER, D. (1945) *La Maison des Mortes*. Paris: Hachette.

DUNSTAN and HOBSON (1965) 'A note on early ingredients of Racial Prejudice in West Europe'. *Race*. London, vol. vi, no. 4, pp. 334–9.

DVORYETSKI, M. (1951) *Europea lelo Yeladim*. Tel Aviv: Yad Va Sherm.

EHRHARDT, S. (1942) 'Zigeuner u. Zigeunermischlinge in Ost-Preussen'. *Volk u. Rasse*, pp. 52–7.

Eichman Trial – transcript and prosecution documents.

ERDÖS, K. (1963) 'Hungarian Songs'. *JGLS* (3) xlii.

Etudes Tsiganes. Paris.

EVENS, E. (1944) *Through the years with Romany*. London: ULP.

FICOWSKI, J. (1950) 'Polish Gypsies of today'. *JGLS* (3) xxix, pp. 92–102.

— (1956) *Piesni Papuszy*. Wroclaw: Ossotinski.

— (1965) *Ciganie na polskich drogach*. Cracow: Wyd. Literackie.

FIRDAUSI. *Shahnameh*.

FLEKSTAD, K. (1949) *Omstreifere og sigøynere*. Oslo: Aschehoug.

FLEURY, J. (1969) 'Lo sterminio nazista degli Zingari'. *Lacio Drom*, nos. 3–5.

FOLETIER, F. de V. (1961) *Les Tsiganes dans l'ancienne France*. Paris: Connaissance du Monde.

— (1968) 'La grande rafle des Bohémiens du Pays Basque sous le Consulat'. *Et. Tsig.* March.

Folktro och Folksed på Varmlandsnäs (1955) Gothenburg: Gumpert.

FRANK, H. (1956) *Dziennik*. Warsaw: Prawnicze.

Frankfürter allgemeine Zeitung. 14–i–1963.

FREUND, J. (1945) *O Buchenwald*. Klagenfurt: Kleinmayr.

FRIEDMAN, P. (1950) 'How the Gypsies were persecuted'. *Wiener Library Bulletin*, nos. 3–4.

— (1951) 'Nazi extermination of the Gypsies'. *Jewish Frontier*, no. 1.

— (1952) *Auschwitz*. Buenos Aires; Soc. Hebraica Argentina.

FRIEDRICH, E. (1968) F 036159. *Zigenaren* (Stockholm) nos. 3–4, pp. 32–3.

GAUWEILER, H. (1941) *Deutsches Vorfeld im Osten*. Cracow: Ost.

GRELLMAN, H. (1787) *Die Zigeuner*. Göttingen: Dieterich.

GROSSMAN, W. (1945) *Die Hölle von Treblinka*. London: INC. publications.

GÜNTHER, H. (1926) *Rassenkunde des deutschen Volkes*. Munich.

Gypsy and Folk-Lore Gazette. London.

HAAG, F. (1934) 'Zigeuner in Deutschland'. *Volk u. Rasse*, p. 190.

Hansard. Proceedings of the House of Commons.

HAUSNER, G. (1967) *Justice in Jerusalem*. London: Nelson; New York: Harper & Row.

HEIMLER, E. (1959) *The Night of the Mist*. London: Bodley Head; New York: Vanguard.

HENKYS, R. (1964) *Die Nationalsozialistischen Gewaltverbrechen*. Stuttgart: Kreuz.

HILBERG, R. (1961) *The Destruction of the European Jews*. Chicago: Quadrangle.

HORVATHOVÁ, E. (1964) *Cigani na Slovensku*. Bratislava: Slov. Akad. Vied.

HÖSS, R. (1958) *Kommandant in Auschwitz*. Stuttgart: Deutsche Verlag.

Il Messaggero. 8–x–1969. Rome.

ILINSKI. *Gramotei bulgarskih tsarei.*

ILTIS, R. (ed.) (n.d.) *Nazi Dokumente Sprechen*. Prague: Jüd. Gemeinde.

Informations Tsiganes. Brussels.

JAMNICKÁ–ŠMERGLOVA, Z. (1955) *Dějiny našich cikánů*. Prague: Orbis.

JOCHIMSEN, L. (1963) *Die Zigeuner heute*. Stuttgart: Enke.

Journal of the Gypsy Lore Society. Liverpool.

JOVANOVIĆ, J. (1967) 'La Criminalité des Tsiganes'. *Etudes Tsiganes*, no. 4, pp. 12–15.

JÜDISCHES HISTORISCHES INSTITUT (WARSAW) (1960) *Faschismus-Getto-Massenmord*. Berlin: Rütten & Loenung.

JUSTIN, E. (1944) *Lebensschicksale artfremd erzogener Zigeunerkinder*. Berlin: Schuetz.

KAMENETSKY, I. (1961) *Secret Nazi Plan for Eastern Europe*. New York: Bockman.

KARPATI, M. (1962) *Romano Them – Mondo Zingaro*. Trento: Artigianelli.

— (1965) 'Il nazismo e lo sterminio degli Zingari'. *Lacio Drom*, no. 3, p. 6.

KAUTSKY, B. (1946) *Teufel und Verdammte*. Zurich: Gutenberg.

KERMISZ, J. (1946) *Akcje in Wysiedlenia*.

BIBLIOGRAPHY

KNOBLOCH, J. (1950) 'Volkskundliche Sinti-Texte'. *Anthropos*, pp. 223–40.

— (1951) 'Ein Liebeslied der Sinti-Zigeuner'. *Anthropos*, p. 1007.

KNORR, W. See *Volk und Rasse* 1938, p. 70.

KOCHANOWSKI, J. (1946) 'Some notes on the Gypsies of Latvia'. *JGLS* (3) xxv, pp. 34–8, 112–16.

— (1963) *Gypsy Studies*, part 1. New Delhi: Int. Academy of Indian Culture.

— (1967) 'Critère linguistique dans l'histoire dynamique'. (Paper read to the International Linguists Congress, Bucharest.)

KOGON, E. (1947) *Der SS Staat*. Stockholm: Bermann-Fischer.

— (1950) *Theory and Practice of Hell*. London: Secker & Warburg.

Kölner Runschau. 22–iii–1950.

Kontraste (Fribourg-Brisgau) June 1969.

KRASCHUTZKI, H. (1954) 'Der Zigeuner'. *Freiburg. Rundbrief*, Sept, pp. 25–26.

KRAUS, O. and KULKA, E. (1966) *Death Factory*. Oxford: Pergamon.

KÜPPERS, G. (1938) 'Begegnung mit Balkanzigeunern'. *Volk u. Rasse*, pp. 183–93.

KUZNETSOV, A. (1967) *Babi Yar*. London: MacGibbon & Kee; New York: Dial Press.

Lacio Drom. Padua.

LAGERGEMEINSCHAFT NEUENGAMME (1960) *Neuengamme*. Hamburg: Kristelle.

LANGBEIN, H. (1963) *Im Namen des deutschen Volkes*. Vienna: Europa.

— (1965) *Der Auschwitz Prozess* (2 vols.). Vienna: Europa.

LASZLO, C. (1956) *Ferien am Waldsee*. Basle: Gute Schriften.

LAURIÈRE, H. (1951) *Assassins au Nom de Dieu*. Paris: La Vigie.

L'HUILLIER, G. (1948) 'Reminiscences of the Gypsy Camp at Poitiers'. *JGLS* (3) xxvii, pp. 36–40.

LJUNGBERG, E. (1966) 'Les Tsiganes en Scandinavie'. *Et. Tsig.*, no. 3.

LLOYD, A. (1965) 'Gypsy Music'. *Recorded Sound*, no. 19.

Lohamei haGhettaoth archives, Israel.

LUNDMAN, B. (1938) Zigeunernachkommen in Dalarna. *Volk u. Rasse*, pp. 299–304.

MACCOLL, E., and OTHERS (1968) *The Travelling People*. Transcript of broadcast, 17–iv.

MACRITCHIE, D. (1894) *Scottish Gypsies under the Stuarts*. Edinburgh: Douglas.

MALAPARTE, C. (1946) *Kaputt*. New York: Dutton.

MANHATTAN, A. (1950) *The Catholic Church against the 20th Century*. London: Watts.

MASON, P. (1968) 'But O my soul is white'. *Encounter*, April, pp. 57–8.

MAUCORPS, P. (1965) *Les Français et le Racisme*. Paris: Payot.

MAX, F. (1946) 'Le sort des Tsiganes dans les Prisons et les Camps de Concentration'. *JGLS* (3) xxv, pp. 24–34.

MAXIMOFF, M. (1946) 'Germany and the Gypsies'. *JGLS* (3) xxv, pp. 104–8.

MEIER, H. (1948) *So war es.* Hamburg: Phönix.

MITSCHERLICH, A. and MIELKE, F. (1962) *Death Doctors.* London: Elek.

MOLDAWA, M. (1967) *Gross-Rosen.* Warsaw.

MOLITOR. J. (1947) 'Fate of a German Gypsy'. *JGLS* (3) xxvi, pp. 48–52.

NANSEN, O. (1946) *Fra dag til dag.* Oslo: Dreyer.

National Archives. Washington (microfilms).

NAUMANN, B, (1966) *Auschwitz.* London: Pall Mall Press; New York: Praeger.

Nazi Conspiracy and Aggression (1946–8) Washington: Govt. Printing Office.

Nemeckofasiśticka okupace Estonska.

NEDERLANDSCHE ROODE KRUIS (1952–3) *Auschwitz,* vols. 5, 6. Hague.

Neue Zeitung. 15–iii–1950. Munich.

NICOLINI, B. (1969) *Famiglia Zingara.* Brescia: Marcelliana.

NOVITCH, M. (n.d.) 'The Gypsy Camp in Auschwitz-Birkenau, etc.' (unpub. typescript in Wiener Library PC 8 VII 96E).

— (1961) 'Le second génocide'. *Das neue Israel.* June, pp. 693–4.

— (1965) 'Il genocide degli Zigani sotto il regime Nazista'. *Quaderno del Centro di Studi sulla Deportazione e l'Internamento,* no. 2, pp. 31–61.

— (1968) *Le Génocide des Tziganes sous le régime Nazi.* Paris.

NYISZLI, M. (1960) *Auschwitz.* New York: Frederick Fell; London: Panther

OFFICE FRANÇAIS DE L'EDITION (1945) *Les camps d'extermination allemands Auschwitz et Birkenau.* Paris.

PANAITESCU, P. (1948) 'Deportation of Rumanian Gypsies'. *JGLS* (3) xxvii, pp. 77–78.

PANKOK, O. (1950) See *Zeitung ohne Name,* 23–iii.

PARIS, E. (1962) *Genocide in Satellite Croatia.* Chicago: Am. Inst. for Balkan Affairs.

PHILLIPS, R. (1949) *Belsen Trial.* London: Hodge.

POISSONIER, A. (1859) *Esclaves Tsiganes.* Paris.

POLIAKOV, L. (1949) 'Dictator of the Lodz Ghetto'. *Commentary,* vol. 7, no. 2, p. 119.

— (1960) *Breviaire de la Haine.* Paris: Calmann-Lèvy

Pomezia. Barcelona.

POTRA, G. (1939) *Contribuţiuni la istoricul ţiganilor din Romania.* Bucharest: Fund. Regele Carol I.

POTT, A. (1844) *Die Zigeuner in Europa und Asien.* Halle: Heynemann.

Praca. Bratislava. 8–x–1968.

PRIESTER. Unpublished document in library of Fighters against Fascism, Prague.

PUXON, G. (1968) *On the Road.* London: N.C.C.L.

QUILLER-COUCH, A. (1941) *Oxford Book of Ballads.* Oxford: Clarendon.

RADITA, P. (1966) 'Tragedia degli Zingari rumani durante la guerra'. *JGLS* (3) xlv.

BIBLIOGRAPHY

REGNAULT, M. (1963) 'Souvenirs d'une deporteé'. *Et. Tsig.*, nos. 1–2, pp. 14–15.

REITLINGER, G. (1968) *The Final Solution.* London: Valentine Mitchell.

RICHTER, B. (1965) 'Auschwitz, matricola Z. 1963'. *Lacio Drom*, no. 2.

RINGELBLUM, E. (1958) *Notes from the Warsaw Ghetto.* New York: Mc-Graw.

RITTER, R. (1939) 'Die Zigeunerfrage u. das Zigeunerbastardproblem'. *Fortschritte der Erbpathologie*, Pt. 1.

— (1940) 'Primitivität u. Kriminilität'. *Monatsheft f. Kriminalbiologie*, no. 9.

— (1941) 'Die Bestandsaufnahme der Zigeuner'. *Off. Gesundheitsdienst*, part 21.

— (1942) (?) Arbeitsbericht (unpublished).

— (1949) Unveröffentlichtes Schreiben an den Oberstaatsanwalt.

ROBINSON, J. (1965) *And the Crooked shall be made straight.* New York: Macmillan.

ROHNE (1937) 'Zigeunerpolizei'. *Reichsverwalt. B1*, no. 58.

RÖMER, J. (1934) 'Zigeuner in Deutschland'. *Volk u. Rasse*, pp. 112–13.

— (1936) 'Fremdrassen in Deutschland'. *Volk u. Rasse*, pp. 88–95.

— (1937) 'Fremdrassen in Sachsen'. *Volk u. Rasse*, pp. 281–8.

ROST, N. (1965) 'Ook vele tienduizenden Zigeuners werden vermoord'. *Buiten de Perken*, See pp. 1–5.

RÜDIGER, K. (1938) 'Parasiten der Gemeinschaft'. *Volk u. Rasse*, pp. 87–9.

RUSSELL, Lord (1954) *The Scourge of the Swastika.* London: Cassell.

RŮŽIČKA, L. (1959) see *Hvézdy Svobody.* Prague. pp. 60–2.

Rzeczpostpolita (1944) Lublin. 6–ix.

SCH——, V. J. (1938) 'Die Zigeuner'. *SS Leitheft.* 25–vi, pp. 23–6.

SCHARFENBERG, J. (1930) See *Arbeiderbladet.* Oslo. Nos. 288, 308, 316, 321, 322.

SCHECHTMAN, J. (1966) 'The Gypsy Problem'. *Midstream.* Nov., pp. 52–60.

SCHUBERT, H. (1941) See *Volk u. Rasse*, p. 216.

SCIZE, P. (1953) *La Tribu Prophétique.* Paris: Table Ronde.

SCOTT-MACFIE, R. (1956) 'Gypsies of the Third Reich'. *Wiener Library Bulletin*, nos. 1–2.

SEIP, D. (1946) *Hjemme og i Fiendelandet.* Oslo: Gyldendal.

SHAKESPEARE, W. (1698) *Antony and Cleopatra.*

— (1711) *Othello.*

SHIRER, W. (1960) *Rise and Fall of the Third Reich.* London: Secker and Warburg; New York: Simon and Schuster.

SIERAKOWIAK, D. (1960) *Dziennik.* Warsaw: Iskry.

SIPPEL, K-H. See *Neue Zeitung* (Munich) 15–iii–1950.

Soviet War News Weekly 19–xi–1942.

Spiegel 24–iv–1963, pp. 45–52.

ST. GEORGE, G. (1967) *Road to Babyi Yar.* London: Spearman.

STADLER, K. (1966) *Österreich 1938–45 im Spiegel der NS Akten.* Vienna: Herold.

THE DESTINY OF EUROPE'S GYPSIES

STARKIE, W. (1953) *In Sara's Tents*. London: Murray.

STEINMETZ, S. (1966) *Österreichs Zigeuner im NS Staat*. Vienna: Europea.

STRAUSS, W. (1960) See *Süddeutsche Zeitung* 30–iv, p. 60.

STUCKART and GLOBKE (1936) *Kommentare zur deutschen Rassengesetzgebung*. Munich: Hoecksche.

Süddeutsche Zeitung 10–i–1956.

SUS, J. (1961) *Cikánská Otázka v ČSSR*. Prague.

TAIKON, K. (1967) *Zigenare är vi*. Stockholm.

TENENBAUM, J. (1956) *Race and Reich*. New York: Twayne.

THESLEFF, A. (1900) Report on the Gypsy Problem. See *JGLS* (2) v.

THYGESEN, P. (1945) *Laege i tyske Koncentrationslejre*. Copenhagen: Thaning & Appels.

Trials of the Major War Criminals before the International Military Tribunal (1949) Nuremberg: IMT.

Trials of War Criminals (Green series) (1949–52) Washington: Govt. Printing Office.

TULTEY, A. (1881) (ed.) *Journal d'un Bourgeois de Paris*. Paris.

UCHAN, J. (1960) 'Les persecutions nazies et les Tsiganes'. *Et. Tsig.*, no. 1, pp. 27–8.

UHLIK, R. (1947) See *JGLS* (3) xxvi, p. 116.

VALENTE (1966) 'L'ultima vergogna d'Europa'. *Domenica del Corriere* Aug.

VALLEY, E. (n.d.) *Guide to Mauthausen*. Vienna: Amicale de Mauthausen.

VAN KAPPEN, O. (1965) *Geschiedenis der Zigeuners in Nederland*. Assen.

Verfolgung NS Straftaten im Gebiet der Bundesrepublik Deutschland seit 1945 (1964) Bonn: Bundesjustiz-ministerium.

VERMEHREN, I. (1947) *Reise durch den letzten Akt*. Hamburg: Wegner.

Voix Mondiale Tzigane. Paris. No. 27   p. 13, Jan. 1962.

Welt 13–ix–1963.

Welt der Arbeit 4–ix–1964, p. 8.

Wiener Library, London.

WIERNIK, Y. (1945) *A year in Treblinka*. New York: Gen. Jewish Workers Union of Poland.

WIESENTHAL, S. (1967) *The murderers among us*. London: Heinemann; New York: McGraw Hill.

WOLF, S. (1960) *Grosses Wörterbuch der Zigeunersprache*. Mannheim: Bibliografisches Institut.

WÖLFFLING, S. (1965) 'Zur Verfolgung u. Vernichtung der mitteldeutschen Zigeuner unter dem Nationalsozialismus'. *Wiss. Zeitschr. der Martin Luther Univ.*, no. 7, pp. 501–8.

WÖLFFLING and MODE (1968) *Zigeuner*. Leipzig: Koehler & Amelang.

WIRTZ, E. (1954) 'Gypsies in Bavaria'. *JGLS* (3) xxxiii, pp. 165–8.

Yad vaShem. Jerusalem.

YATES, D. (1949) 'Hitler and the Gypsies'. *Commentary*, viii.

YIVO. New York. Document section Occ. E–3–61.

BIBLIOGRAPHY

YOORS, J. (1967) *The Gypsies.* New York: Simon & Schuster; London: Allen & Unwin.

(Die) Zeit. 9–v–1946.

Zigenaren. Stockholm.

Zirickli. Helsinki.

INDEX

INDEX

INDEX

INDEX

INDEX